THE BOOK ON
VA LOANS

An Essential Guide to Maximizing Your Home Loan Benefits

Veterans United.
Home Loans

CHRIS BIRK

The Book on VA Loans:
An Essential Guide to Maximizing Your Home Loan Benefits

By Chris Birk

2018 ©
ISBN: 9781791382759

DEDICATION

This work is dedicated to the more than 100,000 service members and veterans who have put their trust in us. To serve those who have served is a duty—and a privilege—we will never take for granted.

VETERANS UNITED HOME LOANS

Veterans United Home Loans is currently the nation's largest VA lender. We are a private company (NMLS #1907) and not a government agency.

We are passionate about serving our nation's veterans, service members and military families. We're a full-service lender that specializes in VA loans, and that dedication and focus has allowed us to streamline the homebuying and refinance process.

Leading the way is a team of more than 2,000 people dedicated to serving those who have served our nation.

Great communication and our expertise as VA loan specialists were cited as the top two reasons people chose Veterans United Home Loans, according to a recent survey of more than 10,000 borrowers.

The book you're holding is just one more way we're working to communicate with veterans, real estate agents and the community at large.

Our mission is to help veterans and military members take full advantage of the benefits earned by their service.

RESOURCES

Our VA mortgage specialists and service team are available to answer your questions and keep the process rolling. Please don't hesitate to contact us with your questions or concerns.

We're committed to enhancing lives every day.
Let us know what we can do to help.

CONTACT VETERANS UNITED HOME LOANS

Call us anytime at 800-884-5428

Start the loan process now at VeteransUnited.com

Interact with us at Facebook.com/vuhomeloans

Keep up with company news on Twitter @veteransunited

Reach author Chris Birk at chris@vu.com
or Facebook.com/VALoansInsider

Ready for more VA loan and homebuying education? Visit our in-depth homebuying course focused on helping veterans, service members and military families get the most from their budget and their home loan benefits. **VeteransUnited.com/education**

EXPLORE

✔ Watch video overviews and go deeper into The Book on VA Loans. **VeteransUnited.com/VALoanBook**

✔ Are you waiting to buy a home? Or are you dealing with some financial obstacles? The Veterans United Lighthouse Program is a complimentary service that prepares veterans and active military to prequalify for a VA Home Loan. **Talk to a Veterans United loan specialist at 800-884-5428.**

✔ Get a sense of your purchasing power and what you can afford. **VALoanCalculator.com**

✔ Learn more about the VA Funding Fee and whether you're exempt at **VAFundingFee.com**

✔ We're not the VA nor are we affiliated with any government agencies. You can visit the VA's online home loans hub at **Homeloans.VA.gov**

FOREWORD

A young soldier once asked me how he could become Sergeant Major of the Army.

I told him to start by being a good soldier and to listen to your noncommissioned officers to learn everything you can about the Army and your career field. I told this soldier the lessons he would learn by being a good soldier and becoming an expert in his profession would set him up for success as a junior noncommissioned officer. To become a great noncommissioned officer you have to teach everything you learned as a young soldier to your soldiers, your little piece of the Army, and make them good soldiers and experts in their profession.

I told this soldier and the group of leaders standing with him to apply these same thoughts to each level of responsibility as you get promoted and move up through the ranks. Develop and teach your subordinates and leaders in each piece of the Army you're responsible for throughout your career. Finally, I told him that taking care of soldiers, developing them as good soldiers and experts in their profession, is more important and carries more responsibility than any job he will ever have in any career.

After more than 35 years in the military, including seven as the most senior enlisted member of the U.S. Army, I have seen the tremendous work and sacrifice our service members and military families make every day. We have thousands of service men and women forward deployed to more than 80 countries around the world, performing vital missions and facing new challenges in an effort to protect America.

Quality of life for all our service men and women and their families is an inseparable element of our readiness posture. To improve that quality of life I've made it my mission to implement initiatives and improve resources in areas that are most important to those most affected by change.

As Sergeant Major of the Army, I was part of a leadership team that created our Warrior Transition Units to support wounded, ill or injured soldiers, with a singular focus on warrior healing and support for Army families.

This Army leadership team also boosted family programs at installations where we committed more than $1.5 billion to enhance quality of life programs. They standardized family programs, upgraded troop and family housing, further developed youth and child care facilities and supported single soldiers by offering additional recreation and travel through the Better Opportunities for Single Soldiers program.

This team had the opportunity to hire more than a thousand new Family Readiness Support Assistants to provide additional support to Family Readiness Groups in deployable units.

Following my retirement from the Army, I had the honor to serve as president of Homes for Our Troops, a national nonprofit organization that helps build specially adapted homes for severely injured veterans. It's through my work with Homes for Our Troops that I came to know Veterans United Home Loans. The company and its incredible employee-driven foundation, Veterans United Foundation, teamed with us to help build 100 homes for veterans nationwide. More than 90 percent of Veterans United employees donate at least 1 percent of their paycheck to their own foundation, which has raised more than $20 million since it was created in 2011.

For those who seek it, homeownership remains one of those critical foundations of American life, especially for those who serve. Our military members sacrifice so much to safeguard our nation's security and prosperity. They deserve a fair and equitable path to the American dream, one that honors their service and acknowledges the debt we owe them.

Seven decades ago, our nation set out to do just that. Congress passed the sweeping GI Bill of Rights in 1944, a major provision of which established a home loan guaranty program. The government pledged to stand behind these mortgages, a promise that opened the doors of homeownership to a generation of returning veterans.

In fact, more than 2.4 million veterans sought out and secured VA-backed loans from 1944 to 1952.

Flash forward to today. A fledgling program created to help the Greatest Generation has now guarantied more than 21 million loans. Veterans and active military members are turning to the safety, security and buying power of the VA home loan program in huge numbers.

That spirit of giving back, of serving all of those who have so proudly served our great nation, is stronger than ever.

I tell you all of this because it takes a team effort to make a real and lasting difference. I've come to trust Veterans United Home Loans as a genuine partner that's passionate about enhancing the lives of our nation's military members.

They understand how difficult it can be for military families to routinely move from installation to installation, both here in the U.S. and overseas, and how these frequent moves pose unique financial and emotional challenges. They realize that a stable home can provide service members and their families a much-needed sanctuary, especially when those warriors are deployed.

It's our duty as veterans to take care of our own, but we should never take for granted those who wish to help us in our endeavors to improve our quality of life. There will always be challenges in and out of service, but I know that Veterans United Home Loans will continue to take care of our military family.

Our benefit is this incredible company's mission.

Kenneth O. Preston
13th Sgt. Major of the Army (Ret.)
Veterans United Military Advisor

TABLE OF CONTENTS

INTRODUCTION

With the Second World War still raging in Europe and the Pacific, U.S. officials started planning to address the inevitable struggles American soldiers would face upon returning to civilian life.

The government created its concept of a home loan guaranty in 1944, part of a more widespread movement to shift from a wartime economy to a peacetime one. The idea was to provide those who proudly served our country with a simple and streamlined path to homeownership in the wake of the war.

Service abroad made it difficult for some soldiers and service members to build a solid financial profile. A home loan guaranty program would mitigate that concern and help level the playing field for those who spent months and even years fighting for American freedom.

Instead of providing loans, the Department of Veterans Affairs would guaranty a portion of every loan made to a qualified borrower. That layer of protection would spur lenders to issue loans to veterans and service members who might otherwise struggle to obtain financing.

Seventy years later, the Department of Veterans Affairs and its VA Home Loan Guaranty Program have helped millions of veterans and service members achieve the dream of homeownership.

Today, the financial flexibility and purchasing power behind the VA loan is more important than ever. Mortgage lenders have ratcheted up requirements in the wake of the subprime mortgage meltdown. Industry experts and government officials are working to redefine the concept of sustainable homeownership in America. For some borrowers, that means securing a home loan is becoming more difficult than ever before.

But the VA loan program has helped ensure service members are in a prime position to succeed. VA loans feature flexible requirements and significant financial benefits, chiefly the ability to purchase a home with no money down. In an era of tight credit and cautious lending, that kind of opportunity seems anachronistic. But it's a cornerstone of the program.

So is reliability.

VA loans have weathered the subprime collapse and proved incredibly resilient in the face of foreclosure. In fact, given the fiscal tumult of the last few years, VA loans have emerged as "a model of stability," as Thomas J. Pamperin, a VA deputy undersecretary, told a Congressional subcommittee.

To the average service member, VA loans often represent the clearest and most cost-effective path to homeownership. They come with an array of benefits that no other lending program can match. They are, in many ways, a financial lifeline for scores of service members and military families.

CHAPTER 1:
VA LOANS IN TODAY'S MARKET

Despite the recent economic free fall and sputtering recovery, homeownership remains a cornerstone of American society. About 65 percent of citizens own a home, which most see as a path toward wealth creation and financial stability. Rates for homeownership among veterans are even higher, right around 82 percent, according to the Department of Veterans Affairs.

The last few years have proved a mixed bag for homebuyers and existing homeowners. Purchasing a home today looks a bit different than it did a decade ago. For many people it's increasingly difficult. Borrowers who qualify have reaped the benefits of government-sponsored tax credit programs and historically low average interest rates. At the same time, the subprime mortgage meltdown and ensuing financial crisis created a restrictive credit environment and made it significantly tougher for some prospective borrowers to purchase homes or to refinance existing mortgages.

That relatively grim storyline isn't exactly the same for military members.

VA loans are consistently easier to qualify for than other loan products. Veterans and service members don't need to hit tough credit or income guidelines to participate in the program. In fact, credit history plays less of a role in determining homeownership for veterans than it does for non-VA borrowers.

These loans also come with significant financial benefits. Veterans routinely point to the program's signature benefit as its most powerful: Qualified borrowers can purchase a home with no money down.

Given the lending environment we now inhabit, it's almost difficult to believe anyone can buy a house today without putting money down. But it's true, it's incredibly powerful and it's a benefit that helps make homeownership possible for scores of borrowers who might otherwise struggle.

"Most people don't realize, especially younger people and first-time homebuyers, what a benefit it is," said Scott Dow, of Charleston, S.C., a former Coast Guard officer and Reservist who has purchased two homes using his VA benefit. "I would not have been able to purchase a home without a VA loan."

Neither would most military buyers.

Falling home prices and a watertight credit market have brought new attention to the long-cherished VA home loan program. VA loan volume has soared since 2007, as military borrowers have flocked to the agency's more flexible and often less costly alternative.

Here's a look at the last 12 years' worth of VA loan totals to give you a sense of the program's trajectory and its growing importance:

FY18: 610,513 loans
FY17: 740,389 loans
FY16: 705,474 loans
FY15: 631,142 loans
FY14: 438,394 loans
FY13: 629,312 loans
FY12: 539,884 loans
FY11: 357,592 loans
FY10: 314,011 loans
FY09: 325,690 loans
FY08: 179,670 loans
FY07: 133,313 loans

To put those numbers into perspective, the VA loan program has backed more loans in the last five years than it did in the previous dozen combined.

The VA loan program's credit and financial flexibility continues to make a tremendous difference for veterans, service members and military families. The one-two punch of lower credit standards and no down payment helps open the doors of homeownership to scores of people who might otherwise struggle to obtain home financing.

Foreclosure Avoidance

The incredible safety of VA loans is one of the most under-reported stories of the housing recovery. These have been the most foreclosure-resistant loans on the market since the housing crash, despite the fact that about 8 in 10 buyers purchase with no down payment.

A recent Urban Institute study highlighted the VA's foreclosure track record, but it's a mostly under-the-radar success. To be sure, there's certainly a benefit to and a place for down payments in the mortgage industry. But there's a pervasive misconception that the $0 down benefit makes this an unsafe loan program.

The reality is the VA loan program is becoming a model that other mortgage industry stakeholders are beginning to look to in terms of foreclosure avoidance.

The VA has invested in technology and personnel to help veterans keep their homes. Loan program staff members receive monthly updates on the more than 2 million active VA loans. The goal is to keep close tabs on every active VA loan in the country. The VA's foreclosure avoidance team reaches out to homeowners who get more than 60 days behind on their mortgage. They work as advocates on behalf of troubled homeowners and encourage lenders and servicers to offer alternatives to foreclosure, such as a repayment plan or a loan modification.

"We can reach out to them right at the beginning, rather than six months down the road, when it's much harder to address the difficulties," said Michael J. Frueh, former director of the VA Loan Guaranty Program. "With that, we've been able to make strides head and shoulders above everyone else to keep veterans in their homes."

The VA's efforts have helped more than 500,000 homeowners avoid foreclosure in the last six years alone.

"It's really nice to be part of a federal program that's actually been in front of the private sector," Frueh said. "As the Treasury Department created different programs to help all borrowers around the country through the mortgage crisis, a lot of it looked like what we do. I've had a lot of talk with other federal agencies about what we do, and they say, 'That's an outstanding model. We'd like to adopt it.'"

The VA's sound appraisal process and common-sense requirement for discretionary income (known as residual income) are two key additional factors that contribute to this loan product's remarkable safety. We'll look at each of these critical lending requirements later in the book.

The last big reason for this program's success in the face of foreclosure: VA homeowners themselves. Order, structure and obligation are deeply ingrained tenets for most service members. That conditioning tends to follow them throughout their lives, including when the time comes to follow through on structured loan payments.

Spreading the Word

This historic loan program is certainly enjoying some well-deserved time in the sun. Market share is at an all-time high, and veterans and service members are flocking to this loan option like never before.

Still, millions of veterans are missing out.

Surveys and studies have shown that about 1 in 3 homebuying veterans don't know this benefit program exists. Even among those who do, many wind up getting bad or inaccurate information about what these loans offer.

To be sure, VA loans make more sense for some buyers than for others. That's something we'll address throughout these chapters. But it's important that those who have served are at least aware of the benefits and programs out there. That also helps ensure veterans, military members and their families make the most informed decision possible when it comes to one of the biggest financial transactions of their lives.

VA loans aren't the right fit for every veteran. If you have excellent credit and solid assets, you'd absolutely want to compare rates, terms and costs between VA and conventional financing. But that financial picture isn't the norm for many service members, veterans and military families.

Please make sure the veterans, service members and military spouses in your life are fully aware of the VA's vast array of benefits, covering everything from medical and mental health assistance to job training and home lending.

Is a VA Loan Right For Me?

It's an important question and one that we'll evaluate as fully as possible within these pages. But there's an underlying question here that's probably more fundamental as a first order of business: Are you ready for homeownership?

Wanting to buy a home and being able to responsibly afford one are entirely different. As a homeowner, you're on the hook for repairs, maintenance, taxes, insurance and all the other hidden or often forgotten costs that come with owning a home.

There's something to be said for the freedom and relative autonomy of renting. At the same time, it isn't exactly a vehicle for building equity and net worth. Prospective homebuyers need to consider their unique economic and life situation.

Jumping from $600-per-month rent to a mortgage payment might be tough if your budget is already stretched drum-skin thin. Conversely, maybe you've got a great deal and are able to sock away a decent chunk of change each month.

Either way, you need to determine a baseline, an amount that you're able to afford each month for a mortgage payment and associated costs. At the outset, your best bet is to run some numbers using a legitimate online mortgage calculator (we maintain one at www.veteransunited.com/education/tools/mortgage-calculator/). There are also calculators devoted to helping consumers determine whether it's better to rent or buy (both Ginnie Mae and The New York Times have helpful ones).

Homeownership is an investment. But it's probably not wise to think of it purely in those terms. A $250,000 mortgage is going to wind up costing significantly more after 30 years of taxes, insurance and maintenance costs. And there's no guarantee the equity will be there down the road. Just ask the thousands of American homeowners who saw housing values plummet in recent years.

But that's more exception than rule when we look at the long road of the American housing industry. Home equity continues to represent a larger share of household wealth than retirement savings or any other financial asset, according to the Federal Reserve.

There's also the undeniable, irreplaceable feeling of living in a space that's truly yours. This will be your home, your refuge. You can paint the walls or rip off the wainscoting without asking for permission. You'll also spend a chunk of your monthly income building equity for yourself instead of for your landlord.

Homeownership isn't the right financial fit for everyone. But if it's a goal of yours, the best thing you can do is to prepare for the journey ahead. Take a cold, hard look at your credit and finances. Learn as much as you can about all of your home loan options. In other words, embrace the idea of a little homebuying boot camp.

Education and realistic expectations are the keys to making sure you get the most from your budget and your benefits.

C H A P T E R   2 :
GETTING READY FOR HOMEBUYING

Veterans and the military community share in a rich history of homeownership.

Generation after generation has embraced a deep-rooted desire to secure a piece of the American Dream they fought to protect. Owning a home can provide an unbeatable sense of security, comfort and financial stability. But no one can tell you that you're ready to start this journey. This is one of the biggest financial transactions you'll ever make. The right time to begin is when you're financially and emotionally prepared.

That means getting a clear handle on your finances, your credit profile and on the upfront costs of homebuying. That means making time to learn about this strange and sometimes intimidating world of mortgages and homebuying. It means making sure you understand that owning a home can come with both benefits and costs.

So let's start there.

Benefits & Challenges of Homeownership

Part of the preparation for homebuying is recognizing that owning a home can come with both benefits and challenges.

Here's a look at five big benefits of homeownership:

1) You have payment stability

Homeowners no longer have to worry about a landlord hiking the rent next year or the year after. With a fixed-rate mortgage, your principal and interest payment won't change during the term of your loan. For many buyers, that's 30 years of stability.

2) Your property can build equity

You own a little more of your home with every mortgage payment you make. That ownership stake is known as equity. Over time, you can look to leverage that equity, either by borrowing against it or by hopefully realizing a solid return when it comes time to sell. Homeownership can be a great financial investment depending on your specific goals and situation.

3) You're free to change décor and landscaping

Is your daughter in desperate need of bubblegum-pink walls? Want to start a backyard garden? Homeowners have the freedom to alter a space without a landlord's approval. That personal touch can help make a house a home.

4) Your credit can improve with homeownership

Owning a home can also unlock future credit opportunities. Banks and credit card issuers can favor those who own a home, which is why it's common to see "Do you rent or own a home?" on credit and loan applications. Securing a home loan is no small feat. Making your payments on time can help boost your credit score and show other creditors out there that you're a good bet.

5) You can accrue tax advantages through homeownership

You may be able to receive a tax deduction for your property taxes, mortgage insurance expenses and other costs associated with homeownership. It's always best to consult with a tax professional.

Now, let's talk about some of the challenges of homeownership. The VA loan program does a tremendous job helping ensure veterans can truly afford the homes they purchase.

In fact, as we mentioned in Chapter 1, this no-down payment program has an exceptionally low foreclosure rate.

Still, there are no guarantees. Job loss, family changes and scores of other things can affect your financial health. The mortgage still needs to be paid.

Take a careful look at some of the potential challenges of buying a home before jumping into the process:

1) New monthly expenses

Your monthly mortgage payment will typically cover your principal and interest on the loan, along with a portion of your annual property tax and homeowners insurance bills. You'll often see it expressed as PITI (principal, interest, taxes, insurance). The principal and interest portions won't change on a fixed-rate mortgage. But property taxes and homeowners insurance premiums can change annually. In addition, you might encounter an array of new expenses you didn't have as a renter, from water and trash bills to unexpected repairs.

2) You are responsible for maintenance

As a homeowner, you won't have to haggle with a landlord over repairs or improvements. But that also means you're responsible for paying for them. If the washing machine breaks or the septic system backs up, you're on the hook for repairs. There's also regular maintenance and upkeep to prevent those unexpected problems. Homeowners often budget about 1 percent of their home's value each year for maintenance and repair costs. That's $2,000 on a $200,000 home.

3) Relocation may be more difficult as a homeowner

Renters can wait for a lease to end, and active duty military members can actually break them without penalty in certain situations. But veterans and military homeowners on the move aren't allowed to walk away from a mortgage, at least without facing some steep credit and financial consequences. Most homeowners must sell or rent out their homes. You should also keep in mind that there are costs associated with selling your home.

4) Default does happen

No one expects to lose a job, go through a divorce or face a medical problem. For whatever the reason, failing to stay current on your mortgage payments can take a significant toll on your credit. Late payments, loan modifications and foreclosure can crush your financial profile.

When it comes to buying a home, just be honest with yourself about the potential risks given your own personal and financial circumstances. If the future is a bit cloudy, now may not be the right time to pursue a home purchase.

The goal is sustainable, responsible homeownership. Few things are more rewarding.

Upfront Costs of Homeownership

Buying a home is going to come with some upfront costs. But how much cash you'll need on hand can vary widely depending on the type of mortgage, the size of the loan and more. Some homebuyers will face steeper upfront costs than others.

Here's a look at five major expenses homebuyers may have to contend with:

1) Down Payment

VA and USDA loans don't require a down payment, which is a tremendous benefit. Conventional loans typically require a down payment of at least 5 percent, although some lenders may go as low as 3 percent. For FHA loans, the minimum is 3.5 percent. On a $200,000 mortgage, that's $10,000 for the traditional conventional down payment and $7,000 for an FHA down payment. Needless to say, it can take prospective buyers years to save that kind of cash. Buyers may be able to use gift funds or down payment assistance programs to help secure home financing, but policies vary depending on the loan type, the lender and more.

2) Earnest Money

Borrowers will often need to include a "good faith" deposit when they make a purchase offer on a home. This deposit, known as earnest money, signifies you're a serious buyer. There's no hard-and-fast rule for how much you need. Some buyers might put down $200, while others will write a check for $2,000. Buyers can typically get this money back if the deal falters; otherwise it's often applied to a down payment or closing costs. VA buyers often put this money toward closing costs or get it back in full because of the program's $0 down benefit.

3) Appraisal

Appraisals are a key part of the VA homebuying journey. This is a two-part process that assesses both the fair market value and the broad health and safety conditions of the property. We'll talk about the VA appraisal process in greater detail later. For now, it's important to understand that you'll be required to pay for an appraisal upfront. Costs can vary by state, but the fee is typically about $425 for a single-family home. VA borrowers can look to recoup this cost from the seller at closing as part of their closing cost negotiations.

4) Home Inspection

Appraisals and home inspections are not the same thing. They look at different parts of a home in very different ways. Buyers aren't required to get a home inspection, but it's strongly recommended, as they're much more detailed and granular than an appraisal. A home inspection can find defects that appraisals won't uncover, and borrowers can use the findings of a home inspection to renegotiate or even walk away from a contract. Costs will vary, but a good range is $300 to $500.

5) Closing Costs

There are costs and fees associated with originating and closing on your home loan. Closing costs can vary widely depending on the type of loan, where in the country you're purchasing and what you're able to negotiate with a seller. You'll get an estimate of your closing costs fairly early in the home loan process. From there, you'll want to talk with your real estate agent about how to proceed. You can negotiate the payment of these costs with the home seller. The VA allows sellers to pay all of buyer's mortgage-related closing costs and up to 4 percent in concessions, which can cover things like prepaid taxes and insurance and even paying off a buyer's collections or judgments at closing. It's not uncommon for VA borrowers to have a seller pay most or all of their closing costs. But that's not always feasible. Communicate with your lending team early and often about how much money, if any, you'll need for closing costs.

Financial Preparations for Homeownership

No one else can tell you that you're ready to be a homeowner. This is one of the largest purchases many consumers will ever make. It's something most of us do just a handful of times in our lives.

For many people, the right time is when they feel financially and emotionally ready for the responsibility. That's not always easy to discern, especially for first-time homebuyers. It's essential that prospective homebuyers take steps to prepare for the financial responsibilities of homeownership.

Let's take a look at a few key things you can do to better prepare yourself.

1) Build a Budget

A budget will help you create and save for financial goals and determine if a mortgage is manageable. It's important to get a clear picture of how much money is coming in and going out each month. Look for patterns and potential ways to save money. It's tough to know what kind of mortgage payment you can afford if you don't have a budget in place.

There are countless strategies, tools and best practices when it comes to budgeting. The goal is to figure out what works best for you while still giving you a clear, realistic picture of your finances.

Some consumers stick with the tried-and-true spreadsheet method, tracking all of their monthly expenditures in an editable document. Others prefer online tools and apps to track expenses and budget. Mint.com and "You Need a Budget" are among the most popular, but there's a host of options out there. You can log expenses as they happen, and some products will even link all of your financial accounts into a single profile. This form of real-time budgeting has become increasingly powerful for many would-be homebuyers.

Whatever your method, what's vital is knowing where your money goes each month. Log all of your expenses over the last month or more—and be sure to include all of them, like ATM fees and other easy-to-miss costs.

You can start by lumping them under broad headings or categories, along the lines of:
- Housing
- Installment loans (student loans, car payments, etc.)
- Credit cards
- Food
- Transportation
- Clothing
- Entertainment
- Utilities
- Infrequent expenses (auto insurance, holidays, vacations

and so on)

- Unexpected expenses (car repairs, medical bills and so on)

You may have different categories, or more, or fewer. You want your budget to accurately reflect your specific financial situation and your savings goals. There's no other way to get a handle on how to trim expenses and maximize savings.

Once you see all of your monthly expenses in black and white, you can start to set new spending goals. Let's say you want to trim your overall spending by 10 percent, build an emergency fund and start saving for a home purchase. Run through your expense categories and look for simple ways to cut costs and start saving.

Some ways you might be able to curb spending include:

- Buy groceries in bulk and plan meals ahead of time rather than eat out
- Try to negotiate better deals for current services, such as cable TV or Internet; or downgrade your current plans; or drop them entirely and get a library card
- Carpool or use public transportation
- Evaluate memberships and subscriptions
- Repair clothes or hit a thrift shop rather than buy new
- Look for free entertainment events in your community

Some consumers will earmark every dollar that comes in each month for a specific category or need, whether it's paying the cable bill, covering the month's groceries or putting money in a "new house fund." Automatic withdrawals and bill pay can help make it easier to dedicate those dollars every month. Other people use an envelope system to pay for some of their monthly expenses in cash. Once the "groceries" envelope is empty, for example, that's it until the next paycheck.

No matter your approach, it's important to be realistic and committed yet flexible.

Put a little money in a "Fun stuff" category every month.

Giving yourself some room to breathe will help you fight the urge to abandon what might feel like an overly restrictive new lifestyle. Common-sense budgeting is really meant to help you gain more financial freedom, not less.

It's also a critical step before you begin the homebuying journey.

2) Get Debt Under Control

You don't need to be debt-free to land a home loan. But lenders will calculate a debt-to-income (DTI) ratio based on your gross monthly income and major debts, including your new projected mortgage payment. For example, if your gross monthly income is $4,000 and your major monthly debts are $1,800, that's a 45 percent DTI ratio (1,800/4,000). Broadly, the VA likes to see a DTI ratio of 41 percent or less. You can have a higher ratio and still get a loan, but you'll often need to meet additional financial requirements. Different lenders can have different caps for DTI ratio, but the higher your ratio, the tougher it can be to secure financing. We'll talk more about DTI ratio later in the book.

In addition, some types of debt can be more troublesome than others. Lenders may have an in-house cap on how much "derogatory credit" borrowers can have. This catchall term can include things like collections, charge offs, judgments and liens. Whether it's $5,000 or $15,000 or more, these derogatory credit caps can vary by lender. And some of these issues, like judgments and liens, need to be satisfactorily addressed before a loan can close. That often means either paying the sum in full or establishing a repayment plan and a history of on-time payments.

The bottom line: Your major monthly debts will play a big role when lenders look at what you can afford and how much home you can buy. As with budgeting, there are multiple approaches and strategies out there for how best to pay down debt.

Here's a look at a few common approaches:

- Target the debt with the highest interest rate (it's often a credit card). Work on paying that down first before moving on to the account with the next-highest rate.
- Transfer high-interest balances to a lower-rate credit line. Be mindful of transfer fees.
- Pay more than the minimum on your accounts. This can speed your repayment plan considerably and cut down on how much interest you pay. By paying only the minimum, all you're doing is drawing out the repayment period.
- Start by paying off the accounts with the smallest balances and work your way up to the largest. Use the "little victories" method to build momentum.
- Stop taking on any new debt. Stick to your budget and live within your monthly means. Build an emergency fund to avoid racking up credit card debt if there's an unexpected expense.
- Have a garage sale or unload little-used household items online. Put the money toward debt repayment.
- Avoid short-term lending options like payday loans. These tend to have exorbitant interest rates that can lead to a debt spiral. Don't co-sign on loans for people, either.

Establishing a realistic budget is a key early step before you decide how best to tackle your debts. Set monthly savings goals that include funds earmarked for debt repayment. Finding the right strategy is important, but you also need the available cash to make those payments every month. You can't do that effectively without a good budget in place.

Then you can settle on a debt repayment approach that best fits your specific situation.

3) Practice Your Mortgage Payment

A mortgage "test run" can help you understand how much of a mortgage payment you can handle. You can use our VA home loan calculator to determine your estimated monthly payment. Let's say you're paying $800 a month in rent, and the kind of home you'd like to buy will have a mortgage payment of roughly $1,200. That's a $400 difference. Over the course of the next few months, pay your rent, and then take an additional $400 and put it in a separate account.

See what it's like to live without that $400 you'd normally have on hand. If you can manage just fine without it, you may be ready for a mortgage payment. Otherwise, you might want to revisit your budget or set your sights a little lower in terms of how much house you should buy.

What if you don't have housing expenses right now? If you're living with a family member or friend rent-free, lenders may be concerned about "payment shock" with a new mortgage. Ideally, prospective buyers who haven't been burdened with a rent payment should have been able to build a nice nest egg. Those who haven't socked away money thanks to their rent-free arrangement may come under closer scrutiny regarding their assets. Lenders may wonder: If you haven't saved a bunch of money while living rent-free, how will you able to afford your new $1,000 a month mortgage payment?

This is where assets and reserve funds can play a key role in showing mortgage lenders you're ready for the financial responsibility of a home loan.

4) Build Reserves

We've already talked about some of the upfront costs associated with home loans. There's no set amount of assets you'll need in the bank to begin this journey, but lenders will want to make sure getting a loan doesn't leave you penniless.

Before buying a home, consider stockpiling at least three

months' worth of living expenses in a separate account. This emergency housing fund is also known as "reserves," and it needs to be readily accessible in case of joblessness, illness or injury. An added bonus is that those reserves will make you look really strong in the eyes of lenders.

With the right financial preparation, mortgage payments will slip comfortably into your monthly routine. You'll have the diligence, experience and funds necessary to make that payment without a second thought. As prepared as you might be, a lender still has to decide if you're ready to handle a mortgage. A big part of the evaluation hinges on your credit profile.

Credit Scores & Your Home Purchase

A credit score is a tool. At its heart, it reflects your willingness and ability to repay debt.

Whether it's a mortgage lender, a car dealer or even a department store, anyone who's thinking about extending credit to you is taking a risk. They're giving you the opportunity to purchase something today and pay for it tomorrow.

Creditors and lenders want to do whatever they can to hedge that risk and make sure you're a safe bet—that you're someone who's likely to fulfill their obligations and repay that money on time every month.

A credit score allows lenders to make an instant judgment about your ability to repay debt. The higher your score, the more likely you are to pay back that money on time every month. Or that's at least how lenders and creditors tend to look at it.

People with higher scores have shown over time that they can handle credit responsibly. And that's really important, because your credit score comes into play with so many financial needs, such as home loans, car loans, student loans, business loans and more. Even landlords in some parts of the country run a credit check with your rental application.

But it's not just about showing lenders you're a safe bet. Your credit score can also play a big role in determining what it costs to borrow that money. Generally speaking, with home loans, people with higher credit scores can tap into lower interest rates. That can save you thousands of dollars over 15 or 30 years.

So how do you get a credit score?

There are three major credit reporting agencies: Equifax, Experian and TransUnion. You'll sometimes hear them called the Big Three. Many of the lenders that offer you credit will turn around and report how you use it to one, two or all three of these credit reporting companies. And it's at the Big Three where your credit history and your credit score take shape.

Generally, things like your payment history, your amounts owed, your length of credit history and more can all affect your score, for both good and bad. Paying your bills on time every month and keeping a healthy balance of debt in relation to available credit can boost your credit profile. Negative events like late payments, bankruptcies, foreclosures and collections can hurt your score and even force you to put your homebuying plans on hold.

Because not all creditors report to all three credit bureaus, you may have a different credit profile at each. What can be even more confusing for consumers is you don't have just one credit score. In fact, there are dozens and dozens of credit scores out there.

But when we talk about VA home loans and the mortgage industry as a whole, we're usually talking about one type of credit scoring model in particular. That's called the FICO score, which falls on a range from 300 to 850.

The FICO score relies on your credit information from each of the three credit bureaus. FICO uses sophisticated modeling and software to create scores for specific forms of borrowing, including car loans, credit cards and mortgages. Each of the three credit bureaus can use a slightly different FICO scoring formula to create your score.

That's a big reason why lenders will pull your mortgage-focused credit scores from all three credit bureaus and use the middle, or median, score as your credit score. It's also why consumers often see different credit scores than what lenders see.

When you purchase or otherwise get a look at your credit scores from FICO or other agencies, you're typically seeing a broad-based "educational" score. That's a more basic credit score, and it's often different from the industry-specific scores mortgage lenders will see.

Most VA lenders will have a minimum credit score requirement. These benchmarks can vary depending on the lender and other factors. We'll talk in more detail later about where you need to fall on that range for VA loans and other types of home financing.

For would-be VA buyers, the good news is that it's usually a lower score than what you would need for a conventional loan—and considerably lower than what you'd need to have a shot at the best rates and terms on conventional loans.

But even a lower credit score benchmark can be tough for some veterans and active military. That's why it's so important to get a good handle on your credit before you start this journey.

Credit Reports

Credit reports can look overwhelming. They're often loaded with all kinds of information, from dollar amounts and company names to strange abbreviations and unfamiliar terms. That's why it's important to spend a little time learning about how they work and what they include, along with what they don't.

These reports describe your history as a borrower and include details such as payment history, current balances and unpaid debts.

It's important to recognize that only certain types of accounts are monitored by credit reporting agencies, including credit cards; installment loans repaid at a fixed amount over a predetermined period of time, such as auto loans, student loans or mortgages; and retail accounts such as store credit cards.

Each credit bureau presents the information differently, but any report should contain the following data:

- Identifying information: Your name, address, Social Security number, date of birth and employment information.
- Credit accounts: This section will list each of your open accounts, the date the account was opened, the account balance, your payment history and your loan or credit limit.
- Credit inquiries: Credit reporting agencies record instances when potential creditors have accessed your report within the past two years.
- Public record and collection items: Your report will also list any judgments, bankruptcies, foreclosures and liens filed against you. This section also notes any overdue debt or items sent to collection agencies.

Late Payments

From credit cards and mortgages to student loans and more, many creditors report your monthly payment history to one or more of the big three credit bureaus. Getting more than 30 days behind on these major monthly payments can drag down your credit scores.

There are different categories of late payments based on how recent they are, how severe they are and how often they occur. Creditors typically report late payments once a balance is 30 days late. Paying your mortgage or a credit card bill outside of a standard "grace period" might incur penalties and fees, but it isn't typically truly "late" until the 30-day mark. Understand, though, that what's common isn't always universal. Some lenders and creditors may not give you that grace period, meaning it's possible to get hit with a 30-day late payment even if you're just a week or two late.

There are additional late categories for 60, 90, 120 and 150 days, each of which tends to inflict a higher degree of damage to your scores. Once you get beyond 180 days, creditors may "charge off" the debt or send it to a collection agency or both. Those can also hurt your score and in some cases even keep you from landing a home loan.

Collections, Charge Offs & Public Records

Items and issues that may be hurting your score are often grouped together in credit reports. Collections and public records are two common trouble spots. Once you become seriously delinquent on an account, a creditor may decide to involve a debt collection agency. Having credit accounts in collections can harm your score. In addition, mortgage lenders may have a cap on how much "derogatory credit" you can have, and amounts owed in collections will often count toward that limit.

Creditors can also "charge off" your bad debt if they determine repayment is unlikely. Writing off the debt as a loss is an accounting move for the creditor. But it doesn't mean you're suddenly in the clear. In fact, creditors will often sell the charged-off debt to a collections agency. Charged-off accounts can also appear on your credit report and hurt your score. Mortgage lenders can take differing approaches to charge-offs. Some lenders may count charge offs toward their cap on derogatory credit, while others ignore them all together in some cases.

The public records section of your credit report lists information gleaned from court records and other public documents, including bankruptcies, foreclosures, judgments and liens. Each of these can wreak havoc on your credit score. They can also each keep prospective buyers from being able to close on a home loan.

Depending on the specifics, prospective buyers who've experienced a bankruptcy or foreclosure may need to wait a certain number of years before being able to obtain a home loan. We'll talk more about bankruptcy, foreclosure and VA loans a little later.

Court judgments will typically need to be satisfied before you can close on a home loan. The same may be true with liens, although in some cases having a solid history of on-time payments as part of a repayment plan can satisfy lenders.

Credit Monitoring

Keep a careful eye on your credit report. Errors and faulty information can find their way onto anyone's credit report, and those mistakes could knock you out of contention for a VA loan. The best way to monitor your credit is with a periodic review of your credit report.

There's a host of credit monitoring tools and websites that offer a look at your credit score. But many of them require you to purchase credit monitoring or hand over other personal information. You can avoid that hassle and obtain truly free copies of your reports from a credit clearinghouse created by federal legislation. Under the Fair Credit Reporting Act, every U.S. citizen has the right to obtain a free credit report from each of the three major credit reporting bureaus (Equifax, Experian and TransUnion) once a year. To obtain a free copy of your credit report, visit www.annualcreditreport.com. There are a couple different approaches to consider.

You can order your reports from each of the three nationwide credit reporting companies at the same time, or you can order your report from each of the companies one at a time. The law allows you to order one free copy of your report from each of the nationwide credit reporting companies every 12 months.

That's why some consumers prefer to space out their requests and order a free report from one credit bureau every four months, which provides a window into your credit throughout the calendar year.

If you pay for most things in cash, you may be one of FICO's estimated 53 million Americans without a credit profile. Certain companies do not report regular activity to credit reporting agencies. It's possible for you to have a variety of accounts in your name but not have a credit report or a credit score. That's going to be a problem for mortgage lenders.

Accounts that typically don't show up on your credit report include cable, telephone and utility bills. Note that while these companies don't report "regular activity" to credit reporting agencies, they could report an unpaid bill or a payment that is late by 30 days or more.

One important piece of information you won't find on your free credit report is your credit score. Most companies require you to either pay a set fee or sign up for a monthly credit-monitoring service in exchange for a peek at your basic consumer score.

Credit Score Factors

The FICO credit score condenses your entire history as a borrower into a tidy three-digit number. That number ranges from 300 to 850 and is tabulated separately by each of the three credit reporting agencies.

FICO doesn't reveal exactly how it formulates a credit score. But the company does provide a more broad-based look at how it all comes together.

So, let's take a look at the five big factors that make up your FICO score:

- **Payment history (35% of your score):** Your payment history accounts for the single largest portion of your score. Your track record as a borrower tells a potential lender a lot about the way you handle credit. The payment history portion considers the number of timely payments, late payments and number of adverse credit items, including bankruptcy, judgments, liens, past due accounts and items in collection.

- **Amounts owed (30% of your score):** Having some debt isn't necessarily a bad thing. But having too much in relation to your available credit can drag down your score. There are different rules of thumb, but generally try to keep your amounts owed to about 30 percent or less of your total available credit. Think of it as a balance-to-limit ratio on your credit cards.

- **Length of credit history (15% of your score):** The next largest slice of your score is devoted to the length of your credit history. This can be a painful lesson for some first-time buyers. Sometimes borrowers have a slightly lower score just because they aren't old enough to have built an established credit history. This is also why it's important to keep old credit cards open whenever you've paid the balance. FICO scores consider the age of your oldest and new credit accounts, the average age of your accounts and how frequently some accounts are used.

- **Types of credit used (10% of your score):** The FICO score looks at the different types of credit you use, from credit cards and retail accounts to installment loans and mortgages. Opening new credit accounts for the sake of diversity isn't likely to help your score. FICO says your credit mix isn't usually a key factor, but it can become important if you don't have much in the way of a credit history.

- **New credit (10% of your score):** The FICO score looks at your number of new accounts and the type, as well as the frequency with which they were opened. A flurry of new loans or credit inquiries could signal a desperate grab for credit, so be cautious when opening new accounts. Applying for new credit may not hurt your score, and if it does, it's typically a small impact. FICO also allows for rate shopping within a 45-day window, meaning your credit score won't plummet if you're seeking loan preapproval from multiple mortgage lenders. The credit bureaus will treat all credit pulls within that time frame as just one big inquiry.

Remember: Not all creditors report data to the credit bureaus. Those who do may not report to all three agencies. That means you might have three different FICO scores, one from Equifax, one from Experian and one from TransUnion. Mortgage lenders will request your mortgage-focused credit score from each of them. If the scores are different, and they very often are, lenders will typically use the median, or middle, score as your official credit score.

For example, if Equifax shows a 640, Experian shows a 659 and TransUnion shows a 685, a lender will use 659 as your credit score for qualifying purposes.

There also isn't just one type of FICO score. There are dozens and dozens of different scoring formulas depending on the type of financing you're seeking. A mortgage lender, a car dealer and a credit card company could pull your credit and come up with three different versions of your credit score.

Credit Score Requirements

Credit score requirements are a fact of life in the mortgage industry. Regardless of the type of loan you're seeking, you'll typically need to meet a lender's minimum credit score in order to secure home financing. These cutoffs can vary depending on the lender, the type of loan you're seeking and your specific financial situation.

The good news is VA loans feature more flexible and forgiving credit guidelines than other loan types. In fact, the VA doesn't enforce a credit score minimum in order for veterans to utilize the program. Instead, it requires borrowers to be a "satisfactory credit risk."

But the VA doesn't actually make home loans. Instead, the VA loan program basically insures a portion of each loan issued by a mortgage lender. The lender takes on the bulk of the risk with each loan. Because of that, lenders are allowed to tack on requirements and standards that go beyond what the VA wants to see.

You'll often hear these additional requirements called "overlays." A credit score requirement is among the most common.

Different lenders can have different credit score cutoffs. But a 620 FICO score is a pretty good barometer for many VA lenders. For a conventional loan, it's often more like a 660 minimum score, although to get the best rates and terms you may need at least a 740 FICO score. We'll take a closer look at basic requirements for the different loan types later in this chapter.

It's important to know that everyone on the loan will need to meet the lender's credit score requirement. We'll talk more about co-borrowers and who can be on a VA mortgage with you in Chapter 4.

First, let's try to put that 620 score minimum into perspective. There's a common misconception that you need great or even perfect credit for a VA loan.

Check out where a 620 score typically falls in the grand scheme of credit scoring, according to Credit.org:

300-549: Poor credit

550-619: Subprime

620-679: Fair credit

680-740: Good credit

740-850: Excellent credit

You don't need anything near excellent credit to land a VA loan. The reality is you don't even need what's often considered "good" credit, although working hard to boost your score is definitely in your best interest. Consumers with higher scores are often in a better position to land a lower interest rate, which can save you thousands of dollars over the life of a loan.

Stronger credit can also encourage a lender to overlook other shortcomings or potential issues with your loan file. Lenders can consider a strong credit profile as a "compensating factor" that can help a borrower overcome things like a higher debt-to-income ratio.

Credit scores are a vital part of VA loan eligibility, but many other factors will also be considered. Lenders will take a careful look at your income, employment history, debt-to-income ratio and more before you can be approved for financing.

Bankruptcy & Foreclosure

Negative financial events like a bankruptcy, foreclosure or short sale can also have an impact on your ability to qualify for a VA home loan. Each of these things can hurt your credit score. Beyond that, lenders will usually have a "seasoning period" for borrowers who have experienced a bankruptcy or foreclosure. This is basically how much time you have to wait before being able to close on a mortgage. The seasoning period can vary depending on a host of factors.

Bankruptcy and foreclosure can be harrowing experiences. But they don't have to ruin your financial future or your dream of buying a home. Qualifying for a VA loan after bankruptcy or foreclosure is definitely possible, even if the foreclosure or short sale was on a previous VA loan.

In fact, VA loans offer so-called "boomerang buyers" more flexibility and speed compared to conventional loans. Still, make no mistake: It's not always a quick or easy road. Bankruptcy and foreclosure can absolutely devastate your credit. How much of a hit will depend in part on what kind of credit you have.

Bankruptcy

There are entire books dedicated to filing for bankruptcy and changes to the process in recent years. The two major types of personal bankruptcy protection—Chapter 7 and Chapter 13—come with their own hurdles, perils and benefits.

A Chapter 7 bankruptcy is known as a "liquidation" bankruptcy and forces an individual to sell certain assets in order to repay creditors. A Chapter 13 bankruptcy is known as a "reorganization bankruptcy" and creates a court-supervised plan for debt repayment.

In either case, bankruptcy has the potential to crush your credit. A bankruptcy can cause your score to drop anywhere from 130 to 240 points, according to credit score firm FICO.

In addition, you'll typically need to wait at least two years from the date of a Chapter 7 discharge to qualify for VA loan approval. You may be eligible for a VA loan once you're 12 months removed from filing for Chapter 13 bankruptcy protection.

To compare, conventional loans typically require a four-year wait following a Chapter 7 discharge and a two-year wait after a Chapter 13 discharge.

It's also important to note that it's not as if that prior bankruptcy just disappears after two years. A Chapter 13 bankruptcy can stay on your credit report for up to seven years, while a Chapter 7 discharge may linger for a decade. An underwriter will most certainly consider that prior bankruptcy as a negative compensating factor if there are any other risk factors present.

For example, say you slip and have a couple of late payments at some point after your bankruptcy filing. Even if they're relatively small credit accounts, an underwriter is almost always going to deny the loan application unless there's a really good explanation for those delinquent payments.

Here's the bottom line: A bankruptcy adds risk. That's why it's so important for military borrowers to be diligent when it comes to rebuilding and maintaining their credit.

Foreclosure

Foreclosure and its counterparts (a short sale or a deed-in-lieu of foreclosure) can prove more problematic for military buyers.

Foreclosure is when the bank takes back your house through formal proceedings because you can't make the payments. A short sale is when the lender allows an underwater homeowner to sell the home for less than what is owed in order to recover at least some of the cost. And a deed-in-lieu allows a homeowner to basically return the house to the lender without formal foreclosure proceedings. None are particularly beneficial outcomes for borrowers.

In terms of a credit crunch, foreclosure, a deed-in-lieu of foreclosure or a short sale might cause your score to drop somewhere from 85 to 160 points. Regarding foreclosures and deeds-in-lieu of foreclosure, you're typically looking at a minimum two-year wait before being able to obtain a VA loan.

Short sales can be a different story. Every buyer's situation is different, but Veterans United has no seasoning period in many cases following a short sale. Things can be more difficult for prospective borrowers who've lost a government-backed FHA loan to foreclosure. Default or delinquency on federal loans can be a problem for VA lenders. Homebuyers who default on FHA loans may need to wait three years in order to pursue a VA home loan.

Again, to compare, you may need to wait as many as seven years after a foreclosure in order to secure conventional financing. It's often a four-year wait after a short sale or a deed-in-lieu.

Borrowers who've lost a VA loan to foreclosure will have reduced VA loan entitlement, which will limit how much they can borrow without making a down payment. But that previous foreclosure doesn't automatically preclude them from using this hard-earned benefit again. We'll take a closer look at VA loan entitlement in Chapter 3.

Foreclosure After a Bankruptcy

One of the most consistently confusing situations for prospective homebuyers and lenders alike involves the thorny issues surrounding bankruptcy, foreclosure and the status of your mortgage.

Distressed homeowners may file for bankruptcy protection. Some want to keep their houses, while others seek to have their mortgage debt discharged in the bankruptcy. Sometimes months or even years later the house is foreclosed upon. That's a lot of serious financial consideration swirling around, and each puzzle piece can have a significant impact on your ability to secure a VA home loan.

A mortgage is a secured debt, which means it's backed by collateral, in this case your house. A Chapter 7 bankruptcy can eliminate your personal financial liability for the mortgage. It basically wipes away what you owe on the home. But a bankruptcy discharge doesn't eliminate the lien on the property. That gives the lender the ability to foreclose on the property and seek to recoup at least some of their investment.

As we just covered, VA borrowers will typically need to wait two years from the date of their Chapter 7 bankruptcy discharge to pursue a VA home loan. That date marks when the consumer is no longer legally responsible for the mortgage debt—and that, it turns out, is a significant distinction.

The reason is because it's not uncommon for a home to be foreclosed on after a bankruptcy. As we've explained, foreclosure comes with its own "seasoning period," typically at least two years for VA loans, during which you likely won't be able to secure home financing.

It can take banks years to foreclose on a property. The fear is that a veteran may be just a few months from the end of their bankruptcy seasoning period only to have their old property get foreclosed upon, kicking off a new two-year wait.

Different lenders can take different approaches to this. Our focus at Veterans United is when you were no longer legally responsible for the debt. If your responsibility ends with the Chapter 7 bankruptcy discharge, then a subsequent foreclosure doesn't typically "double hit" the veteran with a new two-year waiting period. You're not going to get penalized twice.

One of the big caveats is if the foreclosure occurs on an FHA loan. Even if you're no longer responsible for the debt by the time of foreclosure, the fact that it's a federal debt is an important distinction. In this case, the borrower will likely need to wait three years from when the federal government files a foreclosure claim.

Some homeowners seek to hold onto their homes during the Chapter 7 bankruptcy process. This is known as a "reaffirmation," and it means you're still on the hook for the mortgage debt and regular monthly payments. This won't be wiped as a part of the discharge. There are arguments for and against doing this. Definitely talk with a bankruptcy attorney in your area if you're considering reaffirming your mortgage.

If you don't reaffirm the mortgage, then your legal responsibility for the property ends with the bankruptcy discharge. Continuing to live in the home after that point can raise concerns unless you're still making payments or you have permission from the bank to live there rent-free. Some lenders may look at your recent rental or homeownership history to verify you've made on-time housing payments for at least 12 consecutive months.

It's important to note that homeowners can't fully discharge mortgage debt in a Chapter 13 bankruptcy. That means you're still legally responsible for payments. Following a Chapter 13 filing, lenders may want to see that you've made on-time mortgage payments for at least the last 12 months. Would-be buyers who walk away from their homes or otherwise stop making mortgage payments may be in a tough spot. Lenders will typically initiate foreclosure proceedings in cases like these, which means you'd need to wait at least two years from the foreclosure sale date to be eligible for another VA loan.

When it comes to pursuing a home purchase after a bankruptcy or foreclosure, understand that lenders can have different requirements. A lot can depend on the type of loan you're seeking and your unique situation. To be sure, these events can have devastating consequences for your credit profile. But as painful as they are, neither bankruptcy nor foreclosure will necessarily mean you can't land a VA loan.

How to Boost Your Credit Score

What's encouraging is that your credit score isn't set in stone. There are steps you can take to help improve your score, from changing the way you use credit to paying old debts and even fixing errors on your credit report. The challenge for a lot of people is knowing where and how to begin.

Here are some key tips for building and boosting your credit score:

Use Credit Responsibly

Each bill is your opportunity to tell a future lender what kind of borrower you are. Make the most of each of those opportunities. Pay your bills on time, and don't take on more debt than you can handle.

Be careful with excessive credit inquiries. Shopping around for credit cards or other types of loans is important, but hard inquiries can ding your credit score and be an indicator of risk, especially if you don't have a strong credit profile. There's a difference between comparison shopping and trying to rack up a bunch of new credit, and credit-scoring formulas (and lenders) can't always tell the difference. FICO does allow for mortgage rate shopping within a 45-day window, meaning you can seek preapproval from multiple lenders without having each credit inquiry count against you.

Another tip for responsible credit use: Don't co-sign on a loan with a friend or relative. Co-signing on a loan puts your financial future on the line. If your co-signee makes a late payment or goes into default, your credit score takes a hit. Keep your credit in your control. Don't share your credit with anyone.

Keep Credit Card Balances Low

You want to keep the balances on your credit cards relatively low, preferably 30 percent or less of your card's limit. You also want to keep your cumulative spending below 30 percent of your entire credit limit. So that's either no more than $300 on a $1,000 credit limit or a $3,000 on a total credit limit of $10,000 spread across multiple cards. Keeping big balances on your cards can drag down your score. For consumers who don't use credit cards, getting one or two may actually help improve their credit score, provided they use it wisely.

Don't Close Old Accounts

The length of your credit history plays an important role in your overall score. A more seasoned track record can help bolster your credit score. Even if you're no longer using older credit card accounts, don't close them out. Instead, keep them open and allow them to age.

Settle and Pay Outstanding Debts

Judgments, tax liens and federal debts may have to be paid in full before you can close on a mortgage. You may be able to move forward on a loan after establishing a repayment plan in some cases. But you'll typically need to show lenders at least a 12-month history of satisfactory payments on that plan. Items in collection are more of a gray area, but it's best to get these paid off as well.

Fix Errors

About 1 in 4 credit reports contain errors serious enough to result in denial of credit like a home loan, according to data from the U.S. Public Interest Research Group. Comb through your credit report carefully and watch for the following potential errors:

- Accounts that do not belong to you. Your report could contain information that belongs to someone else with the same name.
- Collection accounts. As the name suggests, collections are items that have been turned over to collection agencies. Review this section carefully for any inaccuracies, such as a collection that's been paid. Collection items can seriously tarnish your credit score.
- Accounts past due and late payments. Carefully check any items that are reported as "past due." It's certainly possible for a creditor to miss your payment or mistakenly report an item as delinquent.

Scour your credit reports line by line. Look for any credit cards, installment loans or anything else that shouldn't be there. If you're 30 years old and there's a 17-year-old credit card account on your profile, it's probably safe to say it isn't yours. It's not uncommon to find a foreign account on your report, especially if you have a common name. That can spell serious trouble for your credit score if someone else's account is delinquent, littered with late payments or swollen with a huge balance.

You're ultimately responsible for your credit report. That includes any errors that your report may contain. Dispute errors with the credit bureau. Obtain your credit report from all three credit bureaus. Send a letter to any bureau that is reporting the error. That could be either one or all three of the credit reporting bureaus (Equifax, Experian or TransUnion).

You'll also want to contact the appropriate creditor. This could be the credit card company, retailer or lien holder who is reporting the error to the credit bureau. You can typically send the same letter and documentation to both the credit bureau and the specific creditor.

Be prepared to back up your claims with documentation. Disputing items online is a simple, click-happy process. But if you're disputing late payments or other major inaccuracies, you're probably going to need canceled checks, bank statements or other verifiable documents that support your contention. It's not just a matter of submit and forget.

Credit bureaus are required to investigate errors within a short period of time, usually 30 days. Creditors can take a bit longer to respond, but generally reply within 30 to 90 days. If you fail to get a response, check back in writing and follow up with a phone call.

We also recommend that military buyers lean on their loan officers when the time comes to dispute credit report inaccuracies. The credit agencies actually service the lending industry, which means loan officers can usually get things done a lot faster and with considerably less headache. It's a competitive space, and credit companies that respond quickly and work seamlessly with loan officers tend to get their contracts renewed.

If for some reason you're not satisfied with the results of the investigation, you have the right to ask the credit agencies to include in your report a statement addressing the dispute. You can also ask the agencies to give that statement to anyone who got a copy of your credit report in recent months. But the hard truth is that these statements of explanation don't mean much to mortgage lenders. They're looking at the bottom line, which in this case is your score.

What to Avoid

Here's one thing we suggest you avoid: Paying a company or an individual for credit repair. The big reason why is that you can do everything they can. All they're likely to do is charge you to take the same basic steps you could have taken on your own.

We don't recommend credit-counseling services, either. There are some reputable agencies out there that will work with your creditors to arrange more manageable payments. But there aren't a lot of guarantees with these kinds of firms, and veterans can wind up doing more harm than good.

After a rash of scams in recent years, the Federal Trade Commission started issuing warnings to consumers on how to spot what officials call "credit clinics."

Some of the warning signs include:

- An organization that guarantees to remove late payments, bankruptcies or similar information from a credit report
- An organization that charges a lot of money to repair credit
- A company that asks the consumer to write to the credit reporting company and repeatedly seek verification of the same credit account information in the file, month after month, even though the information has been determined to be correct
- An organization that is reluctant to give out its address or one that pushes you to make a decision immediately

There are plenty of great free resources online that offer tips and other concrete ways to boost your score. There's no magic or secret to any of this.

It also doesn't cost anything when it comes to changing the way you use credit. That's just creating new and better habits.

Another thing you can do is learn more about the Lighthouse Program at Veterans United. Lighthouse consultants educate veterans, military members and their families about their credit reports and give them the information and tools they need to take action on their scores.

The Lighthouse Program

Military service can cause unique financial strains. Service members are hopping across the country and sometimes the globe, either on short-term assignments, permanent changes of station or overseas deployments. Bills and payments can easily get lost in the shuffle.

Spouses wholly unfamiliar with household finances sometimes find themselves faced with juggling a host of new responsibilities and financial obligations. Military marriages can even dissolve under the strain, which adds a whole new layer of financial difficulty.

Veterans can face an array of financial challenges post-service. Some prospective borrowers might have a bankruptcy or foreclosure in their past. Others may have fallen behind on credit card or mortgage payments. None of this automatically precludes you from obtaining a mortgage. But each of those can inflict major damage on your credit score and make the road to loan approval more difficult.

VA loans have more flexible and forgiving credit score requirements than other loans types. But even the 620 score benchmark that's common among VA lenders can be difficult to hit for some veterans, service members and military families.

Some lenders may simply send you packing if you fail to meet their credit score requirement.

Veterans United takes a different approach.

We created an entire department dedicated to helping service members, veterans and military families repair their credit and get on the path to loan prequalification. If you're unable to get prequalified for a VA home loan, our loan officers will connect you to the credit experts in our Lighthouse Program.

You'll work one-on-one with a Lighthouse home loan consultant, who'll create a personalized plan to help you:

- Identify and correct errors on your credit report
- Take concrete steps to strengthen your overall credit profile

- Develop goals and tactics to reduce debt

This is a free service open only to veterans, service members and military families. Lighthouse credit consultants work with veterans and service members for weeks, months and even years— the goal is getting you in position to get prequalified for the home loan you deserve, no matter how long it takes.

For Leroy Garcia, the post-bankruptcy journey back to qualifying credit took just four months thanks to Lighthouse.

Leroy left the Air Force after years of proud service and settled in Nevada. Stability didn't last long. His marriage collapsed and he found himself buried beneath a stack of bills after the divorce.

A two-income household was suddenly down to one, and Leroy found it difficult to keep his head above water. After weeks of fighting the current, he finally relented and filed for bankruptcy protection later that year. He lost the house and his credit score plummeted from 750 to about 590.

But he was bent on getting back into a house. He spent the next two years renting apartments and rooms and trying to regain his financial footing. He came to us shortly after his bankruptcy passed the two-year mark. Leroy connected with a home loan consultant in our Lighthouse Program. His Lighthouse consultant helped him develop a personalized plan to boost his score, and Leroy went to work.

"I had some stuff on my credit report that I didn't know about," Leroy said. "I still had banks showing I had a balance when that was all wiped out with the bankruptcy. They helped me get my credit score back up and guided me through the whole process."

Four months later, Leroy's Lighthouse consultant pulled his credit again and found his score had rebounded enough to qualify for a VA loan. Leroy made an offer on a house the same day he started looking. He moved in two months later.

The Lighthouse Program has helped more than 30,000 veterans

and service members overcome their credit challenges and go on to close on a home loan. Talk with a loan officer at Veterans United to learn more about how Lighthouse can help you.

When You Have Little to No Credit

Nobody's born with a credit history. It's something you earn and develop over time. But not everyone is an early adopter. Service members who join right out of a high school might not have a chance to open a credit card account or seek a loan until after their discharge.

Others simply choose to pay for things with cash or don't want the responsibility—and, at times, the temptation—that comes with purchasing on credit. The lack of a credit history doesn't mean you're unable to participate in the VA Loan Guaranty program. But it can certainly make things more challenging.

Policies and requirements can vary by lender. You'll typically need at least one FICO score in order for lenders to move forward. Lenders often want to see at least three active credit accounts, or tradelines, as they're known. But if your credit history is thin, lenders may be able to look at more nontraditional tradelines to get a feel for your creditworthiness.

Potential alternative tradelines can include things like:

- Renter's or car insurance
- Cellphone or cable bills
- Online streaming or DVD services
- Allotments appearing on your Leave & Earnings Statement (LES)
- P.O. Box payments

Some tradelines carry more weight than others. The size and frequency of payment are also important, and you may need to verify at least 12 months' worth of on-time payments. We've closed loans with as few as one traditional line of credit, provided we could verify those other payments (typically things like rent or utilities). These are always a case-by-case basis.

That's why building a credit history is so important, and it all starts with that first line of credit. No doubt it can seem daunting at first. Some would-be buyers start with retailers and gas stations. You can also consider starting with a secured credit card, which requires a deposit to open. Unlike prepaid credit cards, these actually report to the credit bureaus.

If your credit profile feels a little light, you might also check with our Lighthouse Program. Lighthouse consultants also help prospective buyers craft personal strategies for credit-building success.

Home Loan Basics

Homebuying comes with its own language and acronyms, from adjustable-rate and title insurance to APR (annual percentage rate), PMI (private mortgage insurance) and many more. Even the words "mortgage" and "loan" can get confusing. These often get used interchangeably, but they're actually two different things.

The lender makes a loan that allows you to purchase a property. You sign a promissory note pledging to repay that money (known as the principal) with interest over a certain period, typically 15 or 30 years.

A mortgage is a legal document you sign and give to a lender. The mortgage provides security for the loan, meaning the lender can take back the home if you stop paying on the loan. In some states, the legal instrument is called a "deed of trust" rather than a mortgage.

Once you pay off the loan, the lender releases the mortgage and has no further claim to the property.

Fixed- & Adjustable-Rate Mortgages

Homebuyers can also elect to have a fixed interest rate for the life of their loan or opt for an adjustable-rate mortgage (ARM).

A fixed-rate mortgage (FRM), true to its name, locks your interest rate for the length of the loan. You won't need to worry about your rate changing with the economy. That means your principal and interest payments won't change, either.

An adjustable-rate loan has a variable rate that can go up or down at different times during the life of the loan. There's a host of different types of ARMs, each of which carry their own potential risk and reward.

An adjustable-rate mortgage will typically begin with a lower interest rate than what you'll find on fixed-rate loans. That lower rate means you'll have more money in your pocket, which can even help you qualify for a bigger loan. The rate on an ARM is subject to change depending on a host of outside economic factors. If rates are steady or falling, that can help keep your adjustable rate under control.

The risk of ARMs is rooted in their uncertainty. A traditional 1-year ARM comes with a low interest rate that's subject to adjustment on an annual basis. That adjustment is tied to an economic index, often the one-, three- or five-year Treasury securities. In addition, lenders will tack on one or more percentage points, known as the "margin." So your rate is the sum of the index rate and the lender's margin.

But there are also ARMs that adjust monthly or biannually. In addition, there's an entire class of "hybrid ARMs" that have a fixed interest rate for a certain period before becoming eligible for annual adjustments.

For example, a 5/1 hybrid ARM features a fixed interest rate for five years before adjusting annually. That period of fixed interest gives borrowers an initial degree of certainty regarding their payment.

Adjustable-rate mortgages with government-backed programs provide homebuyers additional protection. A VA ARM features a government-mandated 1/1/5 cap.

Here's what this means:

- The highest your rate can increase on the first adjustment is 1 percentage point
- Each subsequent annual adjustment is limited to a 1 percentage point increase
- The rate cannot increase more than 5 percentage points over the life of the loan

Choosing between a fixed-rate and an adjustable-rate mortgage can be difficult. A lot of homebuyers who opt for an ARM want or need the upfront savings and look to refinance once the loan becomes eligible for annual adjustments. Others don't plan to live in the property for a long time and want to tap into the lower interest rates.

But refinancing or selling your home isn't always easy or cheap. It's impossible to know exactly what the future holds. Do your best to plot out the hypotheticals before choosing your rate option, and make sure to get your lender's assistance in crunching the numbers.

Mortgage Terms

The mortgage term determines how long you're scheduled to make payments before the loan is paid. The term length also affects how much you pay each month toward the loan's principal balance and interest.

The most common mortgage terms are 30 years and 15 years, although there are other options available. Loans with 15-year terms tend to come with lower interest rates than those with 30-years terms. The chief benefit of a shorter loan term is that you pay less in interest over the life of the loan. The downside is a bigger monthly payment because of that accelerated timeline.

Let's look at a fixed-rate $200,000 loan as an example:

- With a 30-year term and a 5 percent interest rate, your

monthly principal and interest payment is about $1,075 and you pay $186,500 in interest over the life of the loan.

- With a 15-year loan term and a 4.5 percent interest rate, the monthly principal and interest payment jumps to about $1,530, but you pay only $74,000 in interest over the life of the loan.

That's a significant savings because of the shorter loan term. But your monthly principal and interest payment jumps by nearly 50 percent.

Consider how long you plan to live in the home, how much of a housing payment you can afford and other factors when thinking about your mortgage term.

In addition, many home loans today don't have any kind of prepayment penalty, which means you can pay off the loan early without taking a financial hit. Tacking on additional money every month or year toward your principal balance can help you build equity faster and pay off your loan sooner, even with a 30-year mortgage term.

A Quick Look at Loan Products

Not all home loans are created equal. Some mortgage types will be a better fit for you than others.

Home loans are broadly divided into two categories: government-backed loans (including VA, FHA and USDA loans) and conventional loans (those that aren't guaranteed or insured by the government). They each come with benefits and drawbacks, all of which impact consumers in different ways.

Credit scores: Credit score minimums will vary based on the lender, the loan type and other factors. FHA loans technically allow for credit scores in the 500s, but you're more likely to see lenders requiring a 620 or a 640 FICO score for any government-backed loan, be it FHA, USDA or VA. The credit score benchmark for conventional loans is usually higher, often around a 660. But you'll typically need excellent credit—more like a 740 FICO score—to have a shot at the best rates and terms. Conventional loans also tend to be less flexible and forgiving when it comes to things like previous bankruptcies, foreclosures and other derogatory credit.

Down payments: Down payment requirements also vary by loan type. FHA loans typically require a 3.5 percent down payment. On a $200,000 purchase, that comes out to $7,000. Both USDA and VA loans allow qualified buyers to purchase with zero down, which is a huge benefit. It can take veterans and military families years to save enough for an FHA down payment, let alone the 5 percent most conventional lenders want to see. On a $200,000 loan, that's $10,000 in cash for a typical conventional down payment.

Upfront funding fees: Unlike the government-backed options, one thing conventional loans don't have is any kind of upfront funding fee or mortgage insurance premium. Those fees are usually tacked onto your loan balance. The upfront mortgage insurance premium for FHA borrowers is currently 1.75 percent of the loan amount, and it's 1 percent for USDA borrowers. Most first-time VA buyers pay a funding fee of 2.15 percent. VA buyers who receive compensation for a service-connected disability are exempt from the VA Funding Fee. We'll talk more about the VA Funding Fee in Chapter 5.

Mortgage insurance: FHA and USDA loans have annual mortgage insurance premiums that can add $80 to $100 or more to your payment every month. Conventional borrowers usually need to pay for private mortgage insurance unless they can put down 20 percent of the purchase price. PMI fees can vary depending on your credit, your loan-to-value ratio and other factors. It's typically anywhere from 0.2 to 1.5 percent of the loan balance. VA loans have no mortgage insurance.

Interest rates: This surprises a lot of people, but government-backed loans tend to have lower average interest rates than conventional loans. The rate you get quoted will depend on a host of factors, including your credit profile and the lender you're talking with. But qualified buyers may be able to tap into lower interest rates utilizing their VA loan benefits.

Closing costs: Your closing costs will also vary depending on a range of factors, including the type of loan, the lender and your loan-to-value ratio. This ratio reflects the percentage of the property that's being financed in relation to its value. Conventional borrowers with a loan-to-value ratio greater than 90 percent can ask a seller to contribute 3 percent of the purchase price. You can ask for up to 6 percent if your loan-to-value-ratio is 75 to 90 percent. FHA loans allow sellers to contribute up to 6 percent toward a buyer's closing costs. VA buyers can ask a seller to pay all of their mortgage-related closing costs and up to 4 percent in concessions, which can cover things like prepaid taxes and insurance, paying off judgments and liens and more. We'll cover closing costs in Chapter 5.

For so many veterans and service members, the VA loan program represents the most powerful mortgage product on the market. VA loans come with no down payment, no mortgage insurance, more flexible requirements and other big-time benefits.

But a home loan isn't a one-size fits all product. Everyone's homebuying journey is different. When you're talking with lenders, the focus should be on finding the right loan for you—the one that makes the most sense given your credit, your finances and your homebuying goals.

So what's the best loan for you? Like so many things in life, the answer is: It depends. A good loan officer can help you weigh the pros and cons of all your options.

Generally, FHA loans might be a good fit for buyers with low credit and little cash to put down. USDA loans could be a good fit for buyers looking in more rural areas. VA loans can be a great fit for qualified buyers who don't have great credit or a 20 percent down payment. And conventional loans can offer a lot to buyers with excellent credit and solid down payments.

Sometimes it helps to look at the four major loan options using hard, real-world numbers. For this example, let's say you're looking at a $200,000 mortgage with an interest rate of 4.75 percent. We'll estimate your property taxes and homeowners insurance costs at $260 per month.

Loan type	Minimum Down Payment	Funding Fee	Principal & Interest	Taxes & Insurance	Mortgage Insurance	Monthly Payment
FHA	$7,000	$3,378	$1,025	$260	$139	$1,424
USDA	$0	$2,000	$1,054	$260	$59	$1,373
Conventional	$10,000	$0	$991	$260	$114	$1,365
VA	$0	$4,300	$1,066	$260	$0	$1,326

At a glance, VA homebuyers have the lowest monthly mortgage payment given these parameters. But there are advantages and disadvantages to every loan option.

VA loans: Being able to purchase without a down payment is a tremendous advantage. The flip side is you won't have equity in the property to start. The VA Funding Fee varies based on the nature of your service, down payment and whether you've used the VA program before. In this example, we used the 2.15 percent most first-time buyers pay. A buyer reusing their VA loan benefits would pay a higher fee (3.3 percent), which would bump the monthly payment to $1,338. As with the other government-backed options, the fee in this example is financed into the loan.

Conventional loans: This loan requires the highest down payment, but you begin with the most equity. Borrowers who can't put down 20 percent (which in this example would be $40,000) will pay private mortgage insurance. For this example, we used a real-world PMI rate of 0.72 percent.

USDA loans: This is the only other no-down payment mortgage program. Mortgage insurance on USDA loans is less expensive than other types, but borrowers pay it for the life of the loan. These are also the most restrictive loans of the group. Homebuyers are required to purchase in a "qualified rural area" and have an adjusted annual income at or below 115 percent of the area median income.

FHA loans: These loans have more lax credit requirements and a lower minimum down payment than conventional loans, but they also feature the most expensive mortgage insurance, which borrowers now pay for the life of the loan.

Determining which loan product is the best fit for you is a conversation that should include a loan officer you trust. They can help you run the numbers and give you a clear sense of what makes the best financial sense.

For veterans and service members, just knowing VA loans are out there is critical. Being able to compare rates, costs and terms across different loan types helps buyers get the most from their dollar.

A VA loan isn't going to be the right fit for every military buyer. Veterans with great credit and enough cash to put down 20 percent would want to take a long, hard look at conventional loans. But that kind of financial picture isn't the norm for many veterans and military families. That's a big reason why the historic VA loan program is more important today than ever.

Borrower spotlight:
Todd and Karen Fontenot
Family of 11 Finds Their Dream Home With a VA Loan

Smyrna, Georgia—After nine years of proud service, Staff Sgt. Todd Fontenot was ready to leave the Air Force and return to civilian life.

The biggest draw was greater stability for his growing family, which can sometimes be hard to come by for service members. Todd began his military career as a single 18-year-old at Tyndall Air Force Base in Florida. He left his final assignment a married father of four.

Todd and his wife, Karen, returned to their hometown of Smyrna and started renting. Todd floated between jobs but landed steady side work doing lawn care for a local firm. He soon found himself in high demand and decided to open his own lawn-care business. A sole proprietor, Todd eventually picked up a second, part-time job to secure health benefits.

All the while, business wasn't the only thing growing. A few years later, Todd and Karen were anxiously awaiting the birth of their ninth child. The family had all but outgrown their 2,000-square-foot rental. Todd and Karen started looking for a home of their own.

They worked with a local conventional mortgage broker and put offers on a couple homes, but problems with the properties ultimately turned them off. The real estate market was still booming, and the Fontenots struggled to find a home that could fit their space needs and price range. Their real estate agent dropped them as clients. They eventually found a sprawling rental through a friend from church.

Five years passed, and the family grew into the home. One day the owners of the rental contacted the Fontenots with some surprising news: They planned to hike the rent to $1,200 per month from $750 per month.

Todd and Karen were stunned and began to rethink a home purchase. Karen went online to search for homes and found an advertisement for VA loans and Veterans United Home Loans. She thought about Todd's military service and decided to fill out a simple form on the Veterans United website.

A Veterans United loan officer called her within minutes.

"She couldn't believe how fast he responded," Todd said.

The family then began to learn about the benefits of VA loans and the loan approval process.

The VA Loan Guaranty program currently allows qualified service members to purchase a home worth up to $453,100 (and more in high-cost parts of the country) without a down payment. VA loans typically feature lower average rates and more buyer-friendly terms than conventional financing.

Brandon also connected the family to a local real estate agent through Veterans United's unique partnership with Veterans United Realty, a network of more than 5,000 real estate agents nationwide who specialize in helping veterans and military members purchase homes.

Still, both Karen and Todd were anxious first-time buyers. They would sometimes call their loan officer two or three times a day with questions or concerns.

"Just talking with him made the whole process easier," Todd said. "I was wound up tighter than a jackrabbit on caffeine, and he was always cool and calm."

Their loan officer preapproved the couple for a $140,000 loan but told them he would need tax returns and other information to fully verify Todd's self-employment and part-time income. While their lending team worked to gather Todd's financial documentation, the couple fell in love with a massive two-story on four acres.

There was just one problem. The home was priced at $160,000, which was well above their prequalification amount. Todd and Karen put in an offer at their maximum. The seller countered at $150,000.

All that separated the Fontenots from their dream home was $10,000. Karen called their loan officer in tears, afraid they would lose their only shot. He told the couple to rush them Todd's tax information so he could get it reviewed by the company's underwriters. An underwriter took a look at the file and said based on Todd's verifiable income the preapproval amount could be increased to $150,000.

The Fontenots were suddenly able to meet the seller's counteroffer.

Todd and Karen got under contract and closed soon after. Their monthly mortgage payment is less than the $1,200 they would have been paying in rent.

"During these economic times, you guys were why we were able to buy a house," Todd said. "It's nice to know I won't get a phone call and someone's going to tell me I have to pay more in rent. It's nice to know that we're in control."

CHAPTER 3:
ELIGIBILITY AND ENTITLEMENT

The heart of the VA loan is a promise.

As a way to honor and thank those who served, the government pledges to stand behind VA borrowers. That promise comes in the form of a financial guaranty, a commitment to repay a portion of a borrower's loan to the lender in the event of default.

The VA guaranty is reflected in a dollar amount known as "entitlement." Your amount of entitlement helps determine how much you might be able to borrow before having to factor in a down payment. We'll explain this concept in more detail later in this chapter and look at what it means for service members and their families.

Before we get there, let's first talk about who may be eligible to tap into this historic home loan program. The VA guaranty is like a type of insurance, and it's only available to those who meet specific time-in-service requirements or related guidelines.

Millions of veterans and military members are eligible for a VA home loan. It's ultimately up to the VA to determine a loan applicant's eligibility status. And, of course, prospective buyers need to meet both program and lender requirements for things like credit score, debt-to-income ratio and other benchmarks.

Veterans and service members should look at these eligibility guidelines closely. But remember the final decision rests with the VA to determine an applicant's status. A veteran who isn't deemed eligible by the VA cannot receive a VA-backed loan under any circumstances.

To be sure, being eligible for a VA loan and ultimately being able to get one are two different things. But you can't be in position to take advantage of big-time benefits like $0 down payment and no mortgage insurance if you don't meet VA eligibility requirements.

Eligibility: Regular Military

The VA has separate requirements for those who served during wartime and during peacetime. The agency defines the two as:

Wartime	Peacetime
World War II 9/16/1940 – 7/25/1947	Post-World War II period 7/26/1947 – 6/26/1950
Korean conflict 6/27/1950 – 1/31/1955	Post-Korean period 2/1/1955 – 8/4/1964
Vietnam Era 8/5/1964 – 7/1975 (The Vietnam Era begins 2/28/1961 for those individuals who served in the Republic of Vietnam	Post-Vietnam period 5/8/1975 – 8/1/1990
Persian Gulf War 8/2/1990 – date to be determined	

Veterans are eligible if they served on active duty in the Army, Navy, Air Force, Marine Corps or Coast Guard after Sept. 15, 1940, and were discharged under conditions other than dishonorable after either:

- 90 consecutive days or more during wartime, or
- 181 consecutive days or more during peacetime

Veterans whose service began after Sept. 7, 1980, or who entered service as an officer after Oct. 16, 1981, must have completed:
- 24 consecutive months of active duty, or
- The full period they were called or ordered to active duty, as long as it's not less than 90 days during wartime or 181 days during peacetime

Eligibility: Reserves or National Guard

Current and veteran members of the Reserves and National Guard from the Gulf War era may be eligible if they've served at least 90 consecutive days on active duty. Otherwise, Guard and Reserve veterans may have VA loan eligibility if they have six years of service.

Prospective borrowers must have received an honorable discharge, unless they were placed on the retired list, were transferred to the Standby Reserve or continued to serve in the Selected Reserve.

Eligibility: Surviving Spouses

An unmarried spouse whose veteran died on active duty or because of a disability connected to his or her service is eligible for VA home loan benefits. In some cases, eligibility also extends to surviving spouses of certain totally disabled veterans whose disability may not have been the cause of death. Surviving spouses who got a VA loan with the veteran before his or her death can also obtain a VA Interest Rate Reduction Refinance Loan (see Chapter 7 for more on refinancing).

There are also provisions for surviving spouses who remarried. Those who remarried upon or after turning age 57 and on or after December 16, 2003, may be eligible for a VA home loan. Surviving spouses who remarried before that date are no longer eligible to participate.

The spouse of an active duty member who is listed as missing in action (MIA) or a prisoner of war (POW) for at least 90 days is eligible for one-time use of the VA home loan benefit. Surviving spouses are exempt from paying the VA Funding Fee.

Eligibility: Others

There's a whole class of people who may be eligible for the VA Loan Guaranty. This broad category often includes:

- Public Health Service officials
- Military service academy cadets
- Some merchant seamen
- National Oceanic and Atmospheric Administration officials
- Certain citizens who served in armed forces of a U.S. ally during World War II

For folks who might be on the fringes, it's best to inquire with a trusted VA lender or your VA Regional Loan Center.

Exceptions

The VA will usually look further into applications from prospective borrowers whose discharges were under conditions other than honorable. It's also important to note that there are a host of exceptions to the length of service requirements for both Armed Forces members and Guardsmen and Reservists. For example, a service-connected disability can shorten the required service time to just a single day. Because of the sheer number of exceptions, it's always in the veteran's best interest to talk with a VA loan specialist.

The Certificate of Eligibility (COE)

Even if you're positive you meet the eligibility requirements, there's only one way to be sure: the Certificate of Eligibility. This is where the VA will separate belief from reality.

The Certificate of Eligibility is an official document that details your VA loan entitlement and basically attests to your right to participate in the program. But you don't actually need your COE in hand to start the VA loan process. In fact, you don't even need to know if you're eligible for a VA loan.

To be sure, you're more than welcome to get your Certificate of Eligibility on your own. Many borrowers can get it online through the VA's eBenefits portal. You can even fill out a Request for a Certificate of Eligibility, which in military parlance is known as Form 26-1880, and send away for it in the mail. But eligibility is something many lenders will help you assess at the outset. They'll also look to obtain your COE on your behalf during the loan preapproval process.

Veterans who have found a trusted VA lender can ask their loan officer to request their Certificate of Eligibility electronically. The veteran simply provides the lender with his or her proof of service. The lender then uses the VA's online COE portal, better known as the Automated Certificate of Eligibility, or ACE.

The creation of the ACE system in 2002 was more than a form processing upgrade. In many ways, it's a symbol of how far the VA has come in the last three decades. For years, real estate agents, mortgage brokers and borrowers steered clear of the agency because of its reputation as a bloated, bureaucratic mess.

Paperwork was done by hand and through the mail. The appraisal process (which we'll cover in Chapter 6) gave people nightmares. Loans could take months to close, leaving both buyers and sellers in the lurch. Some of those vestiges still linger, but the VA loan process of today is a much more user-friendly and efficient experience compared to years past. The ACE system is an important cog in that more streamlined machine.

Today, nearly 90 percent of all requests for a Certificate of Eligibility from veterans and lenders are fulfilled in seconds. The only wrinkle is that applicants must have proof of their military service. For those who served in the Armed Forces, that's a DD Form 214, also known as a Certificate of Release or Discharge From Active Duty. Specifically, it's the "Member 4" copy.

Those still serving on active duty have to submit a current statement of service signed by a commanding officer. There isn't a standard form for a statement of service, so talk with your loan officer about what information to include.

Generally, these statements will often feature:

- Official military letterhead
- Veteran's full name, date of birth and Social Security number
- Rank and active duty entry date
- Unit of assignment and current duty station
- Duration of time lost, if any
- Current date of separation and whether you're eligible to re-enlist

Veterans should know there are a handful of cases where ACE cannot make a determination about eligibility. Some of those cases include:

- Reservists and National Guard members
- Veterans who had a previous VA loan go into foreclosure
- Those who didn't serve the minimum required length of service and were not discharged for an authorized exception
- Veterans discharged under conditions other than honorable
- Veterans wanting to restore a previously used entitlement
- Unmarried surviving spouses

Reservists and National Guard members don't have a single discharge certificate like the DD-214. Instead, they should submit their latest annual retirement points summary along with evidence of their honorable service.

Army or Air National Guard members can submit NGB Form 22, a Report of Separation and Record of Service, or a points statement.

Like their Armed Forces counterparts, active members of the Reserves or National Guard must provide a signed statement of service that shows their key personal information. The statement also needs to clearly state that the applicant is an active Reservist or Guard member.

There's no need to panic if you're unable to find your proof of service. Documents get lost to time.

Veterans discharged from regular active duty can go ahead and submit their Request for a Certificate of Eligibility without the proof of service. It's important to keep the process moving, plus the VA can often issue a decision regarding your request based on its own internal records about your service.

But the VA doesn't have internal records on Reservists or National Guard members. In those cases, applicants need to submit a Request Pertaining to Military Records (Form SF-180) in order to obtain the necessary documents.

It's also important to note that veterans can't transfer an ACE-generated Certificate of Eligibility from one lender to another. That means you'll have to get a new COE if you decide to hop to a different lender at some point during the homebuying process.

Otherwise, there's rarely a need for eligible veterans to update their COE before closing on their VA loan. The only time that's typically an issue is if a service member is discharged or released between when they start the loan process and their loan closing. At that point, the lender is going to request a new determination of the veteran's eligibility.

The VA tells mortgage lenders flat out: The COE is the only reliable way to prove a veteran is eligible for a loan. But, again, getting the certificate doesn't have to be your first step. We can and often do issue loan preapproval without a Certificate of Eligibility.

But obtaining eligibility determination is important early in the process. Any delays or questions about the veteran's status down the road could delay closing or even upend the entire process.

Eligibility Isn't a Guarantee

It's also important to remember that being eligible for a VA loan and actually getting one are two very different concepts.

To be eligible means the VA has determined you meet the time-in-service requirements and have earned some degree of home loan entitlement. But your Certificate of Eligibility isn't a coupon you can just redeem for a VA loan or refinance of your choice.

It just doesn't work that way. And, for that matter, it couldn't work that way. The reason is that veterans aren't getting a loan directly from the VA. Instead, the agency basically insures a portion of a loan that's being issued by a lending institution. And mortgage lenders aren't in the business of doling out housing loans to folks who merely meet some basic requirements, even if those requirements are rooted in service to our country. Lenders simply have too much to lose.

That's why the process can't just stop once a veteran obtains the COE. If anything, that's the point of acceleration. It's also, to borrow a tired cliché, where the rubber begins to meet the road. The reality is that not every veteran and service member who qualifies for a VA loan will ultimately receive one.

A housing loan, even one backed with a VA guaranty, represents a major vote of confidence on behalf of a lender. And what they've become confident in is your ability to repay the hundreds of thousands of dollars they're loaning you. With interest, of course.

Veterans and service members with a shaky financial profile can find themselves on the outside looking in. The VA doesn't have strict, chiseled-in-stone criteria when it comes to obtaining a loan. There are some broad requirements—we've already discussed a few—that are generally much more forgiving than consumers typically find with conventional loans.

But satisfying the VA is only part of the battle. You also have to convince the lender that you're worth the investment. And, as we talked about earlier, because lenders take on most of the risk, they may have requirements and standards that go beyond what the VA wants to see.

VA Loan Entitlement

The idea of VA loan entitlement can be one of the most confusing aspects of this incredible benefit program. In fact, we've come to find there are a lot of people in the mortgage industry who don't have a good grasp on entitlement. That's a big reason why working with lenders that truly know this loan program can make a difference. We've helped countless veterans after another company—one that didn't understand how entitlement works—led them to believe a VA loan wasn't in their future.

So let's take a closer look at VA loan entitlement. Warning: There's some math involved.

The government provides a financial guaranty on every VA loan. The guaranty is a promise to repay the lender a portion of the loan—typically 25 percent—in the event a VA borrower defaults.

The guaranty is essentially a type of insurance that mitigates risk for VA lenders. It also gives them the confidence and ability to extend $0 down financing along with some other great benefits. Your amount of entitlement in part determines how much you could potentially borrow before having to factor in a down payment. And your Certificate of Eligibility helps detail your entitlement picture.

There are two layers of entitlement, a basic and a bonus, or secondary, level. The basic entitlement is $36,000. For borrowers in most parts of the country, there's an additional, second tier of entitlement currently valued at $77,275. Add those together and you get $113,275. That's the maximum entitlement for VA buyers in all but the country's most expensive housing markets.

Here's the math so far: $36,000 + $77,275 = $113,275

In most cases, when you purchase a home using a VA loan, you're using a quarter of your entitlement to do so. That's because the VA typically backs a quarter of the loan. That also means qualified buyers with their full entitlement can borrow up to $453,100 in most parts of the country before having to factor in a down payment.

Here's the math for this: $113,275 x 4 = $453,100

That figure ($453,100) currently represents what's known as the conforming loan limit for most counties in the United States. Veterans purchasing in what the VA deems high-cost counties can have a higher loan limit, allowing them to tap into even more entitlement. That allows qualified borrowers to purchase well above $453,100 without having to make a down payment. We'll take a closer look at VA loan limits shortly.

But it's worth noting now that VA loan limits don't represent a cap on how much you can borrow. Veterans who can afford larger loans can seek what's known as "jumbo" financing. These limits just represent how high you can go before the need for a down payment, which must be at least 25 percent of the difference between your entitlement cap and the purchase price.

Here's a better look at how VA loan entitlement works on the individual level.

Let's say you purchase a home for $200,000 with no money down in a county with the standard VA loan limit of $453,100. Given the VA's guaranty, you've utilized one-quarter of your entitlement for this property, which comes out to $50,000 ($200,000 x 25 percent). In most places, that leaves you with $63,275 in remaining entitlement ($113,275 – 50,000).

That remaining entitlement is how qualified borrowers can look to have two or more VA loans at the same time. It's also how VA buyers who lost a home to foreclosure can purchase again using the program.

Continuing our example, let's say you get PCS orders a couple years after buying the $200,000 home. Rather than sell the home, you decide to hold onto the property as a rental and buy again at your new duty station in a non-high-cost county (you'd have even more entitlement available if you were buying in a high-cost county). With your remaining entitlement of $63,275, you could look at buying up to $253,100 ($63,275 x 4) before needing to factor in a down payment. Again, you could look to buy more house than that. But buying above that $253,100 cap would require a down payment of 25 percent of the difference. For example, if you wanted to buy a $280,000 home, you'd be on the hook for an $8,250 down payment.

Here's the math for that:

$280,000 - 253,100 = $26,900

$26,900 x 25 percent = $6,725

That could still wind up being a great deal compared to conventional and FHA financing, which typically require minimum 5 percent and 3.5 percent down payments, respectively. The $8,250 down payment in our example represents 2.4 percent of the purchase price. And, unlike FHA and conventional buyers, VA buyers wouldn't pay mortgage insurance fees on top of that.

One important thing to know is your Certificate of Eligibility will not clearly reflect your secondary layer of entitlement. That means you may be able to obtain another VA home loan even if your COE indicates $0 entitlement. A VA lender that truly understands entitlement can help walk you through it.

We'll take a more in-depth look at reusing your VA loan benefit in Chapter 7.

VA Loan Limits

Much like entitlement, the VA's loan limits can be confusing not just for military homebuyers but even for people in and around the mortgage industry. You're likely to find a lot of misconceptions and bad information out there online.

One of the most common misunderstandings is that the VA loan limits represent the absolute maximum amount of money you can borrow using this long-cherished home loan benefit. The fact is there's no maximum loan amount on a VA loan. You can get whatever a lender is willing to extend.

What these loan limits represent is how much a qualified military borrower can obtain without having to factor in a down payment.

As we mentioned in the previous section, the VA loan limit for most counties in the country is currently $453,100. That's a pretty sizable loan amount for no money down. But in some of the country's more expensive real estate markets, even that size of a loan may still leave VA buyers at a disadvantage. To counter that, the VA institutes higher loan limits in costlier counties, basically increasing the amount qualified borrowers can get without having to put money down.

In other words, qualified VA buyers have more entitlement available when they're buying in a high-cost county. That can be a huge benefit if you already have a VA-backed loan or if you've lost one to foreclosure.

For example, let's say you're looking to buy in a county where the loan limit is $625,500. Instead of the typical $113,275 in full entitlement ($453,100 x 25 percent), a qualified veteran buying in this high-cost county would have $156,375 in entitlement available ($625,500 x 25 percent).

Now, let's use the same scenario from the previous section—you bought at $200,000 in a regular cost county (using $50,000 of your entitlement), then later received PCS orders. But this time you're PCSing to a high-cost county and want to retain the first home and buy another.

Here's where that additional entitlement becomes so powerful:

$156,375 – 50,000 = $106,375

$106,375 x 4 = $425,500

That $425,500 figure in this example represents your $0 down ceiling. As you can see, buying in a high-cost county can make a huge difference for buyers who want to have multiple active VA loans or those who've lost a VA loan to foreclosure.

The VA's loan limits can change annually. Check the VA Loan Guaranty program's website for the latest figures.

Remember, too, that these limits aren't a cap on borrowing. Qualified borrowers who want to blow past those limits certainly can. Homebuyers considering a purchase above the county loan limit (or even below it in high-cost counties, depending on the amount) are entering "jumbo" financing territory. VA jumbo loans can be a bit tougher to land than a traditional VA loan in terms of credit and asset requirements. Jumbo borrowers may also need to put some money down. But these loans also offer a lot of big-time benefits for veterans looking for a large mortgage.

Regardless of the VA's county limit, anytime a veteran wants a loan greater than $453,100, they're likely looking at jumbo financing. Borrowers will usually encounter tougher credit and underwriting requirements for VA jumbo loans. Jumbo guidelines will vary depending on the lender, the size of the loan and other factors. But they're often considerably more lenient than what veterans and military buyers will need for conventional jumbo loans.

Whether you need a down payment will depend on a couple things, chiefly the county loan limit and how much VA loan entitlement you have. A veteran with full entitlement wanting to purchase a $500,000 home in a county where the loan limit is $525,000 doesn't have to worry about a down payment. The loan size is definitely in jumbo territory, but it's also below the VA county loan limit.

Now, let's say that same veteran decides to purchase a $600,000 home. Because that's above the $525,000 county loan limit, the borrower in this case would need to make a down payment. As we've covered, the down payment in situations like this needs to be at least 25 percent of the difference between the loan limit and the loan amount.

$600,000-525,000 = $75,000

$75,000 x 25 percent = $18,750

The veteran in this example would need a down payment of $18,750 in order to move forward. That's about 3 percent of the loan amount. For a conventional jumbo loan, it's not uncommon for buyers to need 10 or 20 percent down, which would be anywhere from $60,000 to $120,000. Pretty big difference.

Keep in mind the required down payment can increase significantly if you've already used some of your loan entitlement and it can't be restored, either because you currently have a VA loan or your lost one to default. But between the more relaxed guidelines and down payment setup, VA jumbo financing can offer a tremendous purchasing opportunity for qualified borrowers.

Acceptable VA Loan Uses

The VA loan program was created to help open the doors of homeownership to more veterans, military members and their families. The vast majority of military buyers use their VA loan to purchase or refinance an existing single-family home. But veterans interested in buying a condo or even building a home from the ground up may be able to use a VA loan.

Here's a quick look at the VA loan's primary eligible purposes:

- **Buying a single-family home.** The single-family home is the bread-and-butter of the VA loan program. Single-family homes are a great option for a multitude of buyers, and they're the most commonly purchased property of VA loan recipients.

- **Buying a condominium unit in a VA-approved development.** Condo developments need to be approved by the VA. Your lender and a VA-savvy real estate agent can help you identify suitable properties if you're searching for condos. With help from your lender, you can ask the VA to approve a development that isn't on the list. But understand that process can take months to complete.
- **New construction.** The VA also allows for a $0 down loan to build a new home. But it's difficult to find VA lenders willing to offer a true no-down payment construction loan in today's economic environment. A more common approach is to obtain a construction loan from a builder or local lender and then refinance the short-term loan into the VA program upon the home's completion.
- **Buying a manufactured home.** The VA does allow for manufactured homes, but it's difficult to find VA lenders willing to finance these properties. Manufactured homes generally decrease in value over time, making them a risky investment for lenders. You'll typically need to work with a community lender or a mobile home manufacturer. Like many VA lenders, Veterans United does not currently lend on manufactured housing.
- **Buying a modular home.** You can also use a VA loan to purchase a modular home. These are not the same as a manufactured, or mobile, home. Mobile homes are built to national HUD standards and have a HUD identification tag. Modular homes are typically built on site using prefabricated pieces. Purchasing a new modular home may require the use of a construction loan. Buying an existing modular home is treated the same as any other stick-built home.
- **Buying a multiunit property.** Military buyers can purchase up to four one-family residential units in a multiunit property. Duplexes are among the most common. You would need to

occupy one of the units as your primary residence.

- **Refinancing a current VA loan** in order to get a lower interest rate or get out of an adjustable-rate mortgage
- **Refinancing a non-VA loan** into a VA loan to tap into lower rates and/or extract cash from equity. We'll cover VA refinance options in Chapter 7.

Now, let's take a closer look at few of these acceptable uses in more detail. Putting some into practice can be more challenging than others.

VA Loans & Condos

Borrowers can use their VA home loan benefits to purchase a condominium. But there are some additional requirements that differ from purchasing a single-family residence or a multiunit property.

A condo complex must be approved by the VA in order for a borrower to purchase a unit. Hundreds upon hundreds of condo developments across the country are already on the approved list. You can check the VA's condo database online to see if the unit you want to purchase is in an approved development: https://vip.vba.va.gov/portal/VBAH/VBAHome/condopudsearch

What happens if the condo you hope to purchase isn't in a VA-approved development?

Borrowers can ask their lender to seek approval from the VA for the condo development they want. The lender will need to make a written request for approval and include a copy of the condo's organizational documents. These can include:

- Declaration of covenants, conditions and restrictions
- Homeowner association bylaws and budget
- Plat, map or air lot survey
- Special assessments and litigation statement
- Minutes of the last two homeowner association meetings

Condo developments are under no obligation to provide this documentation.

The VA will want to ensure the condo development doesn't put any undue burden or restrictions on veterans or lenders. One example is if the development has rules in place that prevent foreclosure or resale of a property without approval from the homeowners association. Deed restrictions like that will typically be a problem.

Communities with age restrictions can also be challenging. With something like an "Over 55" development, for example, lenders and the VA will need to take a closer look at the community's organization documents. Lenders want to ensure these communities are compliant with fair housing and lending laws and don't impact the future marketability of the property.

Vacancy rates can also come under scrutiny. When a development is first under consideration for approval, lenders may require that a certain percentage of the condo units are either sold or under contract. The same can hold true for developments that have already been approved by other government agencies.

VA officials will review the request and paperwork and either approve or deny the development or alert the lender regarding missing documents or other issues that can be addressed and resubmitted.

It's important to know going in that this process can take months. Lenders won't be able to order an appraisal on the property until approval is granted. Don't expect to rush through the condo approval process if you're in need of a quick closing.

VA Loans & New Construction

Building your dream home is a possibility with a VA home loan. But it isn't always an easy road.

This no-down payment program allows qualified borrowers to use their VA entitlement to obtain a mortgage for new construction.

But it can be challenging for VA borrowers to locate a lender willing to issue a $0 down construction loan.

There's a level of risk in new construction that many are shying away from in the wake of the housing market collapse. What's increasingly common is that veterans need to secure a construction loan from a builder or a local lending institution. As the homebuilding process wraps up, qualified borrowers can then refinance that short-term construction loan into a permanent VA mortgage.

This approach can present hurdles like a down payment, which may be required to secure a construction loan. You can and should talk with as many builders and local banks as possible. Look for the best possible terms out there in terms of down payment, interest rate and more.

Some builders may have programs or deals especially for veterans and military families. Be sure to do your homework on the company and ensure it's a legitimate builder with a track record of success and satisfied homeowners.

You can also check with lenders to see if they'll actually do a true, $0 down VA construction loan, where the lender pays draws to the builder as the project progresses. But know going in that you might struggle to locate one. Like so many other lenders, Veterans United does not make construction loans to build new homes.

You'll have considerably better luck locating VA lenders willing to turn that short-term construction loan into a long-term VA loan. This is something Veterans United can help you with.

Prospective borrowers will need to meet the same credit, debt-to-income, residual income and other requirements as a veteran purchasing an existing home. VA lenders require builders to provide a one-year warranty.

The home will need to have a VA appraisal. Builders need to obtain a VA Builder ID, which isn't difficult or time consuming. It's also possible to self-build, with the veteran basically serving as the general contractor. It's important to talk with a VA lender at the beginning of your new construction journey. Lining up a construction loan is obviously the critical first step, but you'll need to be able to turn that short-term loan into a long-term mortgage once the home is built. That's not something you want to wait to explore.

VA Loans & Multiunit Properties

Veterans and service members who want to purchase multiunit properties often see it as an investment opportunity. There's certainly something appealing about the idea of having tenants help pay some or even all of the mortgage.

But it's important to understand that you may not be able to factor that rental income into the equation when it comes to qualifying for the loan. Policies and requirements can vary by lender.

Here at Veterans United, we couldn't consider rental income from the new property unless you have tax returns documenting at least a two-year history as a landlord. There is an exception to the two-year requirement, although it isn't a common occurrence: We can consider 75 percent of the projected rent as effective income if you contract with a property management company who will guarantee payment even if the unit is vacant.

You also can't use the projected rental income to offset a portion of the mortgage payment. You would need to have the income to qualify for the full amount.

Borrowers who qualify to use projected rental income will also need six months' worth of reserves in the bank—that's six months' of full mortgage payments, including taxes, insurance and any homeowners association dues.

VA Energy Efficient Mortgages (EEMs)

Qualified VA borrowers can also borrow additional money to make qualified energy efficiency improvements to their home using an

Energy Efficient Mortgage, or EEM. This is a specialized mortgage that allows veterans to make improvements to a home they're purchasing or refinancing. An EEM can be a solid investment for veterans and their families, especially those planning to stay in the home for a while. Spending money at the outset on energy improvements can ultimately lower heating, cooling and other related energy costs for years to come. That monthly savings can be funneled into additional payments to the mortgage principal or dozens of other household necessities.

Veterans can't use an EEM to install an energy-efficient swimming pool or make cosmetic upgrades to the property. But there are more than a dozen acceptable improvements, including:

- Thermal windows and doors
- Insulation for walls, ceilings, attics, floors and water heaters
- Solar heating and cooling systems
- Furnace modifications (but not an entirely new furnace)
- Heat pumps
- Vapor barriers

EEMs allow the borrower to tack on $3,000 to the loan amount as long as the veteran can verify the cost of improvements through bids, contracts and other documents. For veterans who want to spend from $3,000 to $6,000 on improvements, the lender has to make sure the energy improvements generate enough savings to offset the new, higher monthly mortgage payment. In other words, it makes no sense to boost your monthly payment by $150 if the energy improvements only save you $15 in utility costs.

Improvements that cost more than $6,000 require special consideration by the lender and the VA. This is a relatively rare occurrence.

You may need to get a Home Energy Rating System (HERS) report or an energy audit from a local utility company in order to move forward. Veterans can check with their local utility companies to see if there are free or reduced-cost energy audits available. Private firms may also offer discounts for military members, veterans and their families. As with any in-home service like this, make sure you hire a legitimate company with a proven track record.

VA borrowers typically have to complete the improvements within six months of closing. Small fixes can be taken care of before closing. Otherwise, the lender may decide to open an escrow account for the improvement funding. EEMs aren't exceptionally common with VA loans.

Ineligible Uses

Despite the program's flexibility, there are some things a VA loan cannot be used for at the present time. Part of that stems from the VA loan program's focus on helping veterans purchase primary residences. Like the other government-backed loan options, VA loans come with occupancy requirements. We'll take a closer look at occupancy in Chapter 5.

For now, here's a look at some of the common ineligible uses for VA home loans:

- **Purchasing a home as an investment property.** Veterans can't use VA financing to purchase a home solely as an investment property. VA loans are designed to fund primary residences for service members. You can look to turn an owner-occupied home into a rental down the road, but you would need to intend to occupy any home you're buying with a VA loan.
- **Using as a business loan.** VA loans can't be used to purchase a storefront, office space or any other nonresidential properties.
- **Buying unimproved land.** Veterans can't use VA loans to purchase bare land or farm ground that does not contain the borrower's primary home. You also can't buy land with the intent of someday putting a house on it.

- **Buying abroad:** VA loans can only be used for properties in the United States and its territories, which include American Samoa, Guam, the Northern Mariana Islands, Puerto Rico and the U.S. Virgin Islands.

It's important to know that lenders are free to add their own property restrictions to this list. For example, many VA lenders won't offer financing for manufactured homes. Others will decline to lend on properties like a working farm or a geodesic dome. We'll take a closer look some of these potential property issues in Chapter 5. Know that acceptance or denial from one lender does not necessarily translate into acceptance or denial from all lenders.

Eligibility & Approval

Not to belabor this point, but it's critically important and worth another mention: Being eligible for a VA loan doesn't mean you'll be able to get one. To be sure, it's important to get a look at the broad eligibility requirements and a sense of this loan product's acceptable uses.

But you'll need to meet credit, financial and property requirements set by both the VA and by mortgage lenders. For most homebuyers in today's housing market, this journey really begins with pursuing loan prequalification and preapproval.

That's what we'll cover next.

Borrower spotlight: Mario Batiste

Hospital Corpsman-turned-Naval Instructor Uses VA Benefits to Become a First-Time Homebuyer

Grayslake, Illinois—Mario Batiste joined the Navy for one reason: College tuition.

Bent on becoming a radio disc jockey, the Chicago native expected to serve four years and then use his GI Bill benefits to study broadcasting. But that plan began to fade when Mario was sent to Naval Hospital Corps School after boot camp.

He was immediately enthralled with medical training and the life of a hospital corpsman. Mario spent the next decade at Naval hospitals and clinics in Washington, Hawaii and California.

He left the Navy at age 30 and decided to pursue that dream of a college education — only this time to earn a degree in biological science. But college life proved more humdrum than he expected, and Mario began to miss his old life. About a year after his separation he joined the Naval Reserves.

His second attempt at college stalled when he deployed to Kuwait with an expeditionary medical force. After a year in the Mideast, he was sent back to Washington state to help beef up the Navy's depleted stateside medical staff.

A few years later, Mario left Washington for good. He married his long-time girlfriend, Sherri, and returned to southern Illinois to take one more crack at college.

It didn't last long this time, either.

Soon after arriving Mario spotted a job opening he couldn't pass up: Health technician at Naval Station Great Lakes, which is the Navy's largest training station. It's also on the north side of Chicago, about an hour from where Mario grew up.

The Navy offered him the job. Mario accepted immediately and is still teaching future generations of hospital corpsmen.

"Learning how to treat people, that compassion for the sick and injured, that's what I loved being close to," he said. "To teach these younger kids how to do that, it's amazing."

Lifelong renters, Mario and Sherri decided their move to Chicago marked the perfect time to become homeowners. Mario had heard military friends talk about VA loans but knew next to nothing about the program.

Mario connected with a Veterans United loan officer after visiting our website. He got prequalified in a few minutes, and his loan officer also connected Mario with a real estate agent from Veterans United Realty, a national network of more than 5,000 agents who work routinely with military borrowers and understand the power of VA loans.

Mario and Sherri looked at properties for months before finding one they truly felt could be home, a 50-year-old, four-bedroom one-story with a lake on the property. The couple made an offer, received a favorable counteroffer and came to an agreement with the seller. They were ecstatic when the home appraised for more than the purchase price, another signal that they got a great deal. The sellers even agreed to cover all closing costs.

Mario became a first-time homeowner without spending a dime upfront on a down payment, closing costs or any kind of mortgage insurance.

"To military friends, I always stress the VA loan now," Mario said. "I was very much a novice. I knew nothing of how the process worked, and I didn't even think I would qualify for anything. So everything your team did was awesome!"

CHAPTER 4:
LOAN PREQUALIFICATION AND PREAPPROVAL

We've given you a rather quick, high-level snapshot of the basic eligibility and usage requirements for a VA loan. These loans are an incredibly dynamic tool that offers significant flexibility and savings to those who have served. But they're not for everybody.

For example, a veteran interested in acquiring a rental property will have to look elsewhere. There are other circumstances and economic situations that might also make a VA loan untenable for some military borrowers.

Maybe you've been thinking about purchasing a home for months or years, like the Fontenot family or Mario Batiste. Or perhaps you're just now considering the possibility and trying to decide if homeownership represents a good fit. Everyone comes to the process with a different perspective and singular desires and needs.

Here's a little secret that might relieve some pressure: You don't need to know right away. Some prospective borrowers start the process without a clue as to whether they can actually afford a home. Others come to the table unable to tell the difference between PMI and the PTA. And there are some buyers who steamroll from start to finish, certain of their ability to qualify for, obtain and pay off that mortgage.

Once a veteran decides to move forward, the first question is usually: Where do I start?

The answer often depends on whether you're asking a real estate agent or someone on the mortgage side of the equation. Some military borrowers prefer to start by finding a real estate agent to work on their behalf. Others may decide to hunt for a qualified mortgage company that can give them an idea of how much they can actually afford to spend.

Granted, we're a bit biased on the subject. But if you begin by finding a real estate agent, one of their first questions will be: Have you been preapproved for a loan? So, you're going to circle back to a mortgage lender sooner rather than later. We figure you might as well start there. Movement will be glacial at best until you've been preapproved for a loan.

If you start with the real estate agent, they'll quickly point you to a mortgage company. If you start with the mortgage company, they'll look to connect you with real estate agents they've worked with in the past. That's the way it works in general, no matter the type of home loan you're pursuing.

We tend to believe VA loans represent a unique wrinkle that tilts the balance.

The fact is VA loans aren't run-of-the-mill for a vast majority of real estate agents and mortgage companies. It's important for borrowers to understand that a lot of mortgage lenders and real estate agents are unfamiliar with VA loans or rarely work with military borrowers.

There are also some longstanding misconceptions and institutional stereotypes about VA loans and the process at large. Some of those are grounded in a bit of truth. But the process today is much more streamlined and efficient than in decades past. Despite updates and changes, VA loans can still conjure a negative image or a bad taste for some agents and mortgage brokers. The mistaken impression can wind up pushing veterans away from a program designed explicitly to help them become homeowners with relative ease.

Veterans should find someone they're comfortable with and trust. It doesn't have to be us, but we know this program better than just about anyone out there. We've become one of the country's five biggest VA lenders over the last 15 years, and we made available more than $6 billion in financing in 2015 alone. We also have a national network of real estate agents who have worked extensively with military families. But enough of the commercial.

There are certainly other qualified mortgage companies out there. Finding folks who truly understand this unique home loan program and work with it routinely is paramount.

Prequalification v. Preapproval

No matter which route you've chosen, you're going to wind up in search of loan preapproval.

It's important for veterans and military buyers, especially first-timers, to recognize that getting preapproved for a loan is different from getting prequalified for one. A ham sandwich can get prequalified. OK, maybe it's not that easy, but loan prequalification involves a cursory, barebones look at a borrower's finances. You can call a lender, dish out some basic financial information and typically get prequalified for a loan in minutes. Heck, you don't even have to call anymore. Lenders will issue prequalification online.

You will get a broad, ballpark estimate of your loan amount generated without a look at your holistic financial profile or your ability to afford a home purchase. You will get a tool, albeit a rather dull and blunted one.

Prequalification can help veterans get a feel for some of the general questions and issues they might need to address. Does your credit score fall a bit short? Is your income likely to be a problem? Prequalification is the time to isolate and start addressing these issues. But just know that the word "prequalified" does little to light the eyes of real estate agents and prospective sellers.

Preapproved is another story.

By comparison, getting preapproved for a loan is a much more arduous and involved process. It also carries much more weight with sellers and means you're really ready to shop for a home under realistic conditions and budgetary constraints.

In most cases, veterans and other military borrowers need to get preapproved for a VA loan before they go house hunting in earnest.

Your loan officer understands all of this perfectly. So why is he or she talking to you about getting prequalified for a loan? Mainly because you have to start somewhere.

VA Loan Prequalification

Prequalification is a process of conversation and faith, at least of the financial sort. The process does three basic things:

- Helps lenders assess a borrower's credit and service eligibility
- Gives the prospective borrower a broad estimate of purchasing power
- Lays a foundation for the underwriting process to begin once a contract is in place

Let's say you're tooling around online for VA home loan information and you come across our company. You fill out a form with some basic, best-guess information, such as an estimate of your credit rating, the prospective loan amount, when and where you plan to purchase and a couple others. Veterans who call us or any other lender will give the same basic information over the phone.

You don't need exact figures and precise data, at least at this stage. The loan officer is taking you at your word in regard to your job status, income and other pertinent information.

But there's one part of the equation that requires more than just a good faith guess: the borrower's credit score. And that's because bad credit can kill your chances of getting a VA loan right out of the starting gate.

At the present time, prospective borrowers with a credit score below 620 may have trouble securing a VA loan. The cutoff varies among lenders, but that's a pretty representative baseline.

You can ballpark your annual income. Heck, you can pretty much fudge most of the information you provide, although it really doesn't do you much good. But the loan officer is going to ask for permission to conduct a hard credit inquiry and pull your mortgage credit scores.

That you can't fake or fudge. At our company, prospective borrowers with a score below 620 have the chance to work with our Lighthouse Program, which we talked about earlier. Any co-borrowers on the loan would also need to meet the lender's credit score requirement. If you're purchasing in one of the nation's nine community property states, lenders can consider your spouse's credit and debts even if he or she won't be on the loan. We'll look closer at co-borrowers later in this chapter.

A hard credit inquiry can ding your credit score, although it's typically only a few points, if any. When you're shopping for a mortgage, the credit bureaus won't count every hard inquiry against you. Instead, they'll typically consider all lender inquiries within a 45-day period as one single check, which minimizes any harm to your credit and allows you to comparison shop.

Along with checking your credit, lenders will also seek to learn more about your employment, your income and your overall financial and homebuying goals. Different lenders may take different approaches to the prequalification conversation. But it's common for loan originators to ask you about:

- Your desired loan amount
- Your current and previous employment
- Your gross (pre-tax) monthly income
- Your assets, like bank accounts and retirement funds
- Your monthly liabilities, like day-care costs, child support or alimony

- Any previous bankruptcies, foreclosures or judgments
- Any delinquencies or default on federal debts, like student loans
- Whether you've recently owned a home

Lenders will also get a good look at your major monthly debts from your credit reports. They'll use those and the income information you provide to calculate an initial debt-to-income (DTI) ratio. For VA loans, this key mortgage industry metric looks at your monthly debts in relation to your overall monthly income.

They'll calculate this figure based in part on the loan amount you're seeking. And that means flexibility can be important for prospective borrowers whose DTI ratio is on the edge. Depending on the lender's requirements and your unique situation, you may need to seek a lower loan amount to get a workable debt-to-income ratio.

The VA typically wants to see a DTI ratio of 41 percent or less. But it's possible to go above that and still secure financing. Lenders will usually have their own maximum allowable DTI ratio. Low credit and high DTI ratio are two of the most common reasons why some prospective buyers are unable to get prequalified. We'll dig deeper into DTI ratio later in this chapter.

The prequalification process holds key benefits for prospective borrowers. It's a non-binding step you can take with multiple lenders, which will help you compare rates and terms. It's typically a 10- to 20-minute conversation or purely online exercise.

Fudging the Facts

Now, a word here about honesty: There's absolutely no point in inflating your income level, your monthly debts or any other financial figures when you first start talking to mortgage folks. The bold, bare facts are going to become plainly evident if you continue down the path to purchasing. So gross exaggerations or patently false information only serves to waste time and resources, both on the lender's end and on the borrower's.

It's also illegal to falsify loan documents.

Lenders and loan officers have heard it all before. They've worked with multimillionaires and folks struggling paycheck to paycheck. The fastest way to make your homebuying process a tough and miserable one is to start with dishonesty. Don't ever be afraid to utter the phrase "I don't know." That's perfectly acceptable. But outright falsehood is something entirely different.

If there are no immediate, wildly apparent hurdles, the loan officer will take your credit score and unverified financial information and feed it into a what's called an AUS, or Automated Underwriting System. This is a high-tech computer program that instantly analyzes an applicant's key financial information and spits out a loan approval or a loan rejection.

At this stage, running the numbers and cranking out an estimated loan amount is mostly academic. Loan prequalification is free and completely nonbinding for the veteran. It allows the lender to get a borrower profile and some basic information set up in the AUS. It allows the veteran to get a broad measuring stick weighed down with caveats and conditions.

It's worth noting that not every application is suitable for an AUS evaluation. There are a few adverse situations—almost always involving the veteran's credit history—when the loan will require a manual underwrite. We'll cover that shortly.

Getting prequalified is where this journey begins. It can also start the flow of paperwork. Every lender is different, but once you're prequalified you'll typically move on to the more in-depth step of loan preapproval. That often involves filling out and returning paperwork and documents, either online, via the mail or both.

Preapproval Paperwork

Mortgage preapproval is incredibly important in today's homebuying environment. Getting preapproved shows sellers and real estate agents you're a serious and strong homebuying candidate. Some listing agents won't accept a purchase offer from buyers without a copy of their preapproval letter.

Preapproval also gives buyers a clear sense of their purchasing power and what it'll take to get to closing day. To be sure, loan preapproval isn't any kind of guarantee of financing. Loan preapproval and loan approval are two very different things. But with loan preapproval you'll know what you can afford under realistic financial conditions and be able to make a strong offer without stretching yourself too thin.

During the preapproval process, lenders want to verify information. You'll typically need to provide financial documents like pay stubs and bank statements and to sign non-binding forms and paperwork. Lenders also want to make sure you've got stable, reliable income that's likely to continue. They'll be looking at cold, hard numbers and creating the most realistic picture possible of your purchasing power.

This is one area where you have a lot of control—the faster you return paperwork, the faster your loan process moves.

Here's a look at some of the documents you may need to provide or give a lender permission to obtain:

- Copy of government-issued photo ID, typically a driver's license
- Copy of DD-214 member 4 copy for veterans; some National Guard and Reserve veterans may need to provide points statements or similar paperwork
- Statement of service letter signed by commanding officer and Leave and Earnings Statement (LES) for active military members. There isn't a standard form for a statement of service, so talk with your loan officer about what information to include.

- Copy of recent pay stubs and last two years' worth of W-2 statements
- Federal tax returns for the last two years
- Copy of most recent bank statements
- VA awards letter documenting VA disability percentage and monthly income amount
- Social Security awards letter documenting monthly income amount
- Copy of most recent retirement account statement
- Copy of divorce decree or court papers specifying alimony or child support obligations
- Child care statement explaining why you don't have monthly child care expenses or detailing the monthly cost

Many lenders will also have their own in-house forms in addition to the standard, government-required documents. Your loan officer may fill in some of the blanks ahead of time, meaning some documents require nothing more than a signature. Here's a look at some of the paperwork you may encounter during the loan preapproval stage.

Uniform Residential Loan Application

The first significant document is the loan application itself, the Uniform Residential Loan Application.

This is the epitome of the standardized form, littered with boxes and requests for personal and financial information. There's no escaping it, either. If you're hoping to buy a home, you're filling out this form. It's the standard for all residential loans, no matter whether it's VA, FHA or conventional. You might hear it called a 10-oh-3, as it's formally known as Fannie Mae Form 1003 (it's also Freddie Mac Form 65). Whatever you want to call it, it's a time suck that's absolutely crucial.

We're going to go over each of the form's 10 sections one at a time. You can also download the application directly from the Fannie Mae website at www.fanniemae.com.

The reality is your loan officer will likely handle a lot of this. Borrowers will obviously provide key information, but lenders have a duty to explain to consumers how to complete these forms accurately. Reproducing them here is meant to help give prospective borrowers a sense of what lies ahead.

Section I: Mortgage Type and Terms

Uniform Residential Loan Application

This application is designed to be completed by the applicant(s) with the Lender's assistance. Applicants should complete this form as "Borrower" or "Co-Borrower," as applicable. Co-Borrower information must also be provided (and the appropriate box checked) when the income or assets of a person other than the Borrower (including the Borrower's spouse) will be used as a basis for loan qualification or the income or assets of the Borrower's spouse or other person who has community property rights pursuant to state law will not be used as a basis for loan qualification, but his or her liabilities must be considered because the spouse or other person has community property rights pursuant to applicable law and Borrower resides in a community property state, the security property is located in a community property state, or the Borrower is relying on other property located in a community property state as a basis for repayment of the loan.

If this is an application for joint credit, Borrower and Co-Borrower each agree that we intend to apply for joint credit (sign below):

Borrower			Co-Borrower			
I. TYPE OF MORTGAGE AND TERMS OF LOAN						
Mortgage Applied for:	☐ VA ☐ FHA	☐ Conventional ☐ USDA/Rural Housing Service	☐ Other (explain):		Agency Case Number	Lender Case Number
Amount $	Interest Rate %	No. of Months	Amortization Type:	☐ Fixed Rate ☐ GPM	☐ Other (explain) ☐ ARM (type)	

You're applying for a VA loan. That's probably self-explanatory. You can always go back and change your selection if the VA for some reason finds you ineligible or if you decide another loan program makes better sense.

That's true for any other part of the loan application. You can make changes as the process moves forward, so don't worry about being locked into early choices.

Your loan officer will fill in the agency and lender case numbers. There are also spaces for the loan amount you're seeking, the length of your requested loan term (30 years is the most common) and the amortization type.

Section II: Property and Purpose

There usually isn't a property address at this stage. A legal description will come down the road once you have a property in mind.

The purpose and property lines are important. We'll talk about refinancing with a VA loan in Chapter 7. We've already discussed how lenders frown upon, to put it mildly, VA construction loans. So the odds are you're either checking the Purchase or Refinance boxes here.

We've also already talked about how veterans can't use a VA loan to buy investment or rental properties. And make no mistake: Trying to beat the system is a bad idea. Lenders in general aren't apt to take a borrower at his or her word.

In fact, they will automatically review the property, examining things like the distance from work, drop in cost from current residence and other signs that this property isn't intended as a primary residence. In short, lenders will check thoroughly to satisfy this requirement.

Now, as we touched on earlier, there are times when a qualified borrower can have two VA loans in play at the same time. But whether you're looking to refinance or purchase, you're likely checking the "primary residence" box here.

The areas for title and estate holding sound confusing but are relatively simple to navigate. Your loan officer can help answer specific questions, but in general the title will be in your name or in conjunction with your spouse's name. To hold the estate in "fee simple" means that you own both the residence and the property it rests upon, while "leasehold" means you own the home but lease the land.

Veterans and service members will usually check the "fee simple" box here. A leasehold arrangement requires a closer look and approval from the VA loan program.

Section III: Borrower Information

This one probably looks painfully familiar. It's a request for the basic personal information you've given out dozens of times. The "Yrs. School" box is a vestige of decades past, when the loan approval process included a type of calculation to ballpark how much money you might make in future years. Since it's against the law to lie on a loan application, it's probably a good idea to play it straight here. Your loan application won't wind up in limbo or get rejected because you didn't finish high school or college.

Section IV: Employment Information

Borrower			IV. EMPLOYMENT INFORMATION (cont'd)		Co-Borrower	
Name & Address of Employer	☐ Self Employed	Dates (from – to)	Name & Address of Employer	☐ Self Employed	Dates (from – to)	
		Monthly Income $			Monthly Income $	
Position/Title/Type of Business	Business Phone (incl. area code)		Position/Title/Type of Business	Business Phone (incl. area code)		
Name & Address of Employer	☐ Self Employed	Dates (from – to)	Name & Address of Employer	☐ Self Employed	Dates (from – to)	
		Monthly Income $			Monthly Income $	
Position/Title/Type of Business	Business Phone (incl. area code)		Position/Title/Type of Business	Business Phone (incl. area code)		

Lenders like stability and predictability.

Someone who's been in the same job and the same line of work for two years or more usually files an application that screams "stable." That isn't to say that layoffs and career changes don't occur, but every loan is a gamble, at least to a degree. Mortgage lenders lose money by betting on the wrong horse.

Having a track record of job stability certainly helps. Moving from job to job isn't necessarily a bad thing, especially if that movement comes with corresponding pay hikes. But applicants who have been in their current job or line of work for less than two years might be looked at a bit differently.

For now, focus on filling out these fields as accurately as possible. Lenders will follow up with your employers to verify information, especially as it relates to your experience and income. If you've been out of work during the previous two years, make sure to note the time frame and list the reasons for it. We'll look at employment and income shortly.

Section V: Monthly Income and Combined Housing Expense Information

V. MONTHLY INCOME AND COMBINED HOUSING EXPENSE INFORMATION						
Gross Monthly Income	Borrower	Co-Borrower	Total	Combined Monthly Housing Expense	Present	Proposed
Base Empl. Income*	$	$	$	Rent	$	
Overtime				First Mortgage (P&I)		$
Bonuses				Other Financing (P&I)		
Commissions				Hazard Insurance		
Dividends/Interest				Real Estate Taxes		
Net Rental Income				Mortgage Insurance		
Other (before completing, see the notice in "describe other income" below)				Homeowner Assn. Dues		
				Other:		
Total	$	$	$	Total	$	$

* Self Employed Borrower(s) may be required to provide additional documentation such as tax returns and financial statements.

Describe Other Income	*Notice:* Alimony, child support, or separate maintenance income need not be revealed if the Borrower (B) or Co-Borrower (C) does not choose to have it considered for repaying this loan.	
		Monthly Amount
B/C		$

Accurate income information is critical to the loan approval process. So is determining what kind of monthly obligations and debts a prospective borrower might have. Later in this process, the lender will determine your debt-to-income ratio.

For now, this section focuses on income and expenses related only to housing and shelter. Under the "Other" income heading, veterans don't need to include sources like alimony or child support if they don't want that considered.

The housing expense side is especially breezy for renters. Current homeowners should be sure to include information on all mortgages along with their tax and insurance information.

Section VI: Assets and Liabilities:

This Statement and any applicable supporting schedules may be completed jointly by both married and unmarried Co-Borrowers if their assets and liabilities are sufficiently joined so that the Statement can be meaningfully and fairly presented on a combined basis; otherwise, separate Statements and Schedules are required. If the Co-Borrower section was completed about a non-applicant spouse or other person, this Statement and supporting schedules must be completed about that spouse or other person also.

Completed □ Jointly □ Not Jointly

ASSETS	Cash or Market Value	Liabilities and Pledged Assets. List the creditor's name, address, and account number for all outstanding debts, including automobile loans, revolving charge accounts, real estate loans, alimony, child support, stock pledges, etc. Use continuation sheet, if necessary. Indicate by (*) those liabilities, which will be satisfied upon sale of real estate owned or upon refinancing of the subject property.		
Description Cash deposit toward purchase held by	$			
List checking and savings accounts below		LIABILITIES	Monthly Payment & Months Left to Pay	Unpaid Balance
Name and address of Bank, S&L, or Credit Union		Name and address of Company	$ Payment/Months	$
Acct. no.	$	Acct. no.		
Name and address of Bank, S&L, or Credit Union		Name and address of Company	$ Payment/Months	$
Acct. no.	$	Acct. no.		
Name and address of Bank, S&L, or Credit Union		Name and address of Company	$ Payment/Months	$
Acct. no.	$	Acct. no.		

Uniform Residential Loan Application
Freddie Mac Form 65   7/05 (rev. 6/09)

Page 2 of 5

Fannie Mae Form 1003   7/05 (rev. 6/09)

Name and address of Bank, S&L, or Credit Union		Name and address of Company	$ Payments/Months	$
Acct. no.	$	Acct. no.		
Stocks & Bonds (Company name/ number & description)	$	Name and address of Company	$ Payments/Months	$
		Acct. no.		
Life insurance net cash value	$	Name and address of Company	$ Payments/Months	$
Face amount: $				
Subtotal Liquid Assets	$			
Real estate owned (enter market value from schedule of real estate owned)	$			
Vested interest in retirement fund	$			
Net worth of business(es) owned (attach financial statement)	$			
Automobiles owned (make and year)	$	Acct. no. Alimony/Child Support/Separate Maintenance Payments Owed to:	$	
Other Assets (itemize)	$	Job-Related Expense (child care, union dues, etc.)	$	
		Total Monthly Payments	$	
Total Assets a.	$	Net Worth (a minus b) ►	$	Total Liabilities b. $

Schedule of Real Estate Owned (If additional properties are owned, use continuation sheet.)

Property Address (enter S if sold, PS if pending sale or R if rental being held for income)	Type of Property	Present Market Value	Amount of Mortgages & Liens	Gross Rental Income	Mortgage Payments	Insurance, Maintenance, Taxes & Misc.	Net Rental Income
	▼	$	$	$	$	$	$
Totals		$	$	$	$	$	$

List any additional names under which credit has previously been received and indicate appropriate creditor name(s) and account number(s):

Alternate Name	Creditor Name	Account Number

Just a quick glance at this one is enough to make the eyes glaze over. It isn't as bad as it might look. It's definitely a good idea to go over this part with your loan officer. And please—please—ask questions, not just about Assets & Liabilities, but also about any aspect of the loan process or the mortgage industry at large.

This is one of the biggest investments you'll ever make, and probably the largest single purchase. Asking questions makes for an informed consumer. You should always work with a lender that's genuinely concerned with your best interests, but that doesn't absolve you from being your own best advocate. Start asking questions if you don't understand something or feel out of the loop. And don't stop until you get a satisfactory answer that you truly understand.

A prospective borrower's standing as it relates to assets has become increasingly important to lenders. In some ways, assets are almost as important as a solid credit history. And like a negative credit profile, an unhealthy asset balance can kill a transaction.

Let's take a look at the form. The first space is for information on the earnest money you put forth. As we covered earlier, earnest money is basically a financial showing of seriousness and good faith. You'll put up an agreed-upon amount to show the seller you're interested in purchasing. You can also just think of it as a deposit. The amount you must put forward depends on where you live, the property in question and a few other key factors, but it's generally not more than a few thousand dollars.

Your earnest money goes into an escrow account that, if all goes as planned, will eventually be put toward a down payment or closing costs or that you'll simply get back at closing. Earnest money and the amount you have in reserve can also serve as a compensating factor to potentially offset lower credit scores. For example, having six months worth of mortgage payments in reserve might help convince a lender to work with your slightly dented credit.

The rest of the asset section is self-explanatory. You don't need to list every account you have, just the major ones that showcase your ability to handle the financial obligations that come with homeownership. There's also room for non-liquid assets, or more tangible things like real estate, business net worth and even your car. The "other" category can prove a bit nebulous with anything from art and automobile collections to antiques up for consideration. If you've got something along these lines, by all means include it, but leaving this space blank won't raise any eyebrows.

As for your liabilities, the lender is looking for the kind of big-ticket items that can help or harm your credit score. Credit cards, bank loans, student loans and liabilities in that vein need to be documented to the best of your ability. Borrowers won't usually complete this section. Instead, the lender will go directly from a credit report.

Section VII: Details of Transaction

VII. DETAILS OF TRANSACTION	
a.	Purchase price	$
b.	Alterations, improvements, repairs	
c.	Land (if acquired separately)	
d.	Refinance (incl. debts to be paid off)	
e.	Estimated prepaid items	
f.	Estimated closing costs	
g.	PMI, MIP, Funding Fee	
h.	Discount (if Borrower will pay)	
i.	Total costs (add items a through h)	

VII. DETAILS OF TRANSACTION	
j.	Subordinate financing	
k.	Borrower's closing costs paid by Seller	
l.	Other Credits (explain)	
m.	Loan amount (exclude PMI, MIP, Funding Fee financed)	
n.	PMI, MIP, Funding Fee financed	
o.	Loan amount (add m & n)	
p.	Cash from/to Borrower (subtract j, k, l & o from i)	

Veterans can usually just skip this section entirely. In the age of automation, most loan officers will use a mortgage program to crunch the numbers and spit out the results for this section.

Section VIII: Declarations

VIII. DECLARATIONS				
If you answer "Yes" to any questions a through i, please use continuation sheet for explanation.	**Borrower**		**Co-Borrower**	
	Yes	No	Yes	No
a. Are there any outstanding judgments against you?	☐	☐	☐	☐
b. Have you been declared bankrupt within the past 7 years?	☐	☐	☐	☐
c. Have you had property foreclosed upon or given title or deed in lieu thereof in the last 7 years?	☐	☐	☐	☐
d. Are you a party to a lawsuit?	☐	☐	☐	☐
e. Have you directly or indirectly been obligated on any loan which resulted in foreclosure, transfer of title in lieu of foreclosure, or judgment?	☐	☐	☐	☐
(This would include such loans as home mortgage loans, SBA loans, home improvement loans, educational loans, manufactured (mobile) home loans, any mortgage, financial obligation, bond, or loan guarantee. If "Yes," provide details, including date, name, and address of Lender, FHA or VA case number, if any, and reasons for the action.)				

VIII. DECLARATIONS				
If you answer "Yes" to any questions a through i, please use continuation sheet for explanation.	Borrower		Co-Borrower	
	Yes	No	Yes	No
f. Are you presently delinquent or in default on any Federal debt or any other loan, mortgage, financial obligation, bond, or loan guarantee?	☐	☐	☐	☐
g. Are you obligated to pay alimony, child support, or separate maintenance?	☐	☐	☐	☐
h. Is any part of the down payment borrowed?	☐	☐	☐	☐
i. Are you a co-maker or endorser on a note?	☐	☐	☐	☐
j. Are you a U.S. citizen?	☐	☐	☐	☐
k. Are you a permanent resident alien?	☐	☐	☐	☐
l. **Do you intend to occupy the property as your primary residence?**	☐	☐	☐	☐
If Yes," complete question m below.				
m. Have you had an ownership interest in a property in the last three years?	☐	☐	☐	☐
(1) What type of property did you own—principal residence (PR), second home (SH), or investment property (IP)?				
(2) How did you hold title to the home— by yourself (S), jointly with your spouse (SP), or jointly with another person (O)?				

There's no real magic or mystery to this section. It's a list of 13 questions that require a Yes or No answer.

Section IX: Acknowledgment and Agreement

Read and sign.

Section X: Information for Government Monitoring Purposes

Housing discrimination is illegal. Lenders cannot make decisions about an applicant or in any way discriminate on the basis of color, race or religion. There are also mandates on lenders to make sure they're providing opportunities to communities in need.

Submitting this personal information is optional. But it helps the government track patterns and more fully evaluate lenders from this perspective. If you don't voluntarily provide this information, the loan officer may have to make a guess as to your sex, ethnicity and race, strange as it may sound. So it's usually just easier and more accurate to fill in the information yourself.

Next document: Borrowers Certification and Authorization

Borrowers' Certification and Authorization

CERTIFICATION

The Undersigned certify the following:

1. I/We have applied for a mortgage loan through _____. In applying for the loan, I/We completed a loan application containing various information on the purpose of the loan, the amount and source of the down payment, employment and income information, and the assets and liabilities. I/We certify that all of the information is true and complete. I/We made no misrepresentations in the loan application or other documents, nor did I/We omit any pertinent information.

2. I/We understand and agree that _____ reserves the right to change the mortgage loan review processes to a full documentation program. This may include verifying the information provided on the application with the employer and/or the financial institution.

3. I/We fully understand that it is a Federal crime punishable by fine or imprisonment, or both, to knowingly make any false statements when applying for this mortgage, as applicable under the provisions of Title 18, United States Code, Section 1014.

AUTHORIZATION TO RELEASE INFORMATION

To Whom It May Concern:

1. I/We have applied for a mortgage loan through _____. As part of the application process, _____ and the mortgage guaranty insurer (if any), may verify information contained in my/our loan application and in other documents required in connection with the loan, either before the loan is closed or as part of its quality control program.

2. I/We authorize you to provide to _____ and to any investor to whom _____ may sell my mortgage, any and all information and documentation that they request. Such information includes, but is not limited to, employment history and income; bank, money market and similar account balances; credit history; and copies of income tax returns.

3. _____ or any investor that purchases the mortgage may address this authorization to any party named in the loan application.

4. A copy of this authorization may be accepted as an original.

Borrower Signature _____   Co-Borrower Signature _____

SSN: _____ Date: _____   SSN: _____ Date: _____

Calyx Form - borcers.frm (12/05)

This is a standard release form that gives the lender the right to verify and distribute personal and financial information. Getting a home loan from a mortgage lender means you're interacting in the primary mortgage market. But many lenders turn around and sell some or all of their loans and the right to service them to investors in what's known as the secondary mortgage market.

This is a marketplace where investors purchase mortgages, group them together and package them into mortgage-backed securities. These securities are then sold to other investors. The government-sponsored enterprises Fannie Mae and Freddie Mae are the country's two biggest investors on the secondary market.

The secondary market is one reason why underwriting requirements can vary among lenders. Lenders may need their loans to meet an investor's requirements, and some may be more stringent than others. This form basically says that you're OK with the lender and secondary investors checking out your key financials, such as credit history, income and tax returns.

Next document: Request for Transcript of Tax Returns

Form **4506-T**
(Rev. January 2010)
Department of the Treasury
Internal Revenue Service

Request for Transcript of Tax Return

➤ Request may be rejected if the form is incomplete or illegible.

OMB No. 1545-1872

TIP: Use Form 4506-T to order a transcript or other return information free of charge. See the product list below. You can also call 1-800-829-1040 to order a transcript. If you need a copy of your return, use Form 4506, Request for Copy of Tax Return. There is a fee to get a copy of your return.

1a Name shown on tax return. If a joint return, enter the name shown first.	1b First social security number on tax return or employer identification number (see instructions)

2a If a joint return, enter spouse's name shown on tax return.	2b Second social security number if joint tax return

3 Current name, address (including apt., room, or suite no.), city, state and ZIP code

4 Previous address shown on the last return filed if different from line 3

5 If the transcript or tax information is to be mailed to a third party (such as a mortgage company), enter the third party's name, address, and telephone number. The IRS has no control over what the third party does with the tax information.

CAUTION: If the transcript is being mailed to a third party, ensure that you have filled in line 6 and line 9 before signing. Sign and date the form once you have filled out these lines. Completing these steps helps to protect your privacy.

6 **Transcript requested.** Enter the tax form number here (1040, 1065, 1120, etc.) and check the appropriate box below. Enter only one tax form number per request. _____1040_____

a **Return Transcript,** which includes most of the line items of a tax return as filed with the IRS. A tax return transcript does not reflect changes made to the account after the return is processed. Transcripts are only available for the following returns: Form 1040 series, Form 1065, Form 1120, Form 1120A, Form 1120H, Form 1120L, and Form 1120S. Return transcripts are available for the current year and returns processed during the prior 3 processing years. Most requests will be processed within 10 business days. ☒

b **Account Transcript,** which contains information on the financial status of the account, such as payments made on the account, penalty assessments, and adjustments made by you or the IRS after the return was filed. Return information is limited to items such as tax liability and estimated tax payments. Account transcripts are available for most returns. Most requests will be processed within 30 calendar days ☐

c **Record of Account,** which is a combination of line item information and later adjustments to the account. Available for current year and 3 prior tax years. Most requests will be processed within 30 calendar days ☐

7 **Verification of Nonfiling,** which is proof from the IRS that you **did not** file a return for the year. Most requests will be processed within 10 business days. ☐

8 **Form W-2, Form 199 series, or Form 1098 series, or Form 5498 series transcript.** The IRS can provide a transcript that includes data from these information returns. State or local information is not included with the Form W-2 information. The IRS may be able to provide this transcript information for up to 10 years. Information for the current year is generally not available until the year after it is filed with the IRS. For example, W-2 information for 2007, filed in 2008, will not be available from the IRS until 2009. If you need W-2 information for retirement purposes, you should contact the Social Security Administration at 1-800-772-1213. Most request will be processed within 45 days. ☐

CAUTION: If you need a copy of Form W-2 or Form 1099, you should first contact the payer. To get a copy of the Form W-2 or Form 1099 filed with your return, you must use Form 4506 and request a copy of your return, which includes all attachments.

9 **Year or period requested.** Enter the ending date of the year or period, using the mm/dd/yyyy format. If you are requesting more than four years or periods, you must attach another Form 4506-T. For requests relating to quarterly tax returns, such as form 941, you must enter each quarter or tax period separately.

_12 / 31 / 2008_   _12 / 31 / 2009_

Signature of taxpayer(s). I declare that I am either the taxpayer whose name is shown on line 1a or 2a, or a person authorized to obtain the tax information requested. If the request applies to a joint return, either husband or wife must sign. If signed by a corporate officer, partner, guardian, tax matters partner, executor, receiver, administrator, trustee, or party other than the taxpayer, I certify that I have the authority to execute Form 4506-T on behalf of the taxpayer.

Telephone number of taxpayer on line 1a or 2a
614-949-6084

Sign Here

Signature (see instructions)   Date

Title (if line 1a above is a corporation, partnership, estate, or trust)

Spouse's signature   Date

For Privacy Act and Paperwork Reduction Act Notice, see page 2.   Cat. No. 37667N   Form **4506-T** (Rev. 1-2010)

Like most government forms, this one often goes by its formal number: 4506-T. It's a basic form that allows the lender to pull income tax transcripts for the previous two years. Those play a critical role in determining the veteran's debt-to-income ratio and employment status. It's crucial that prospective borrowers fill out these forms correctly. Double check names, spellings, date of birth, Social Security number and every other field to ensure accuracy. Any errors can cause big delays when it comes time to process and underwrite the loan.

Next document: Credit Score Information Disclosure

NOTICE TO THE HOME LOAN APPLICANT
CREDIT SCORE INFORMATION DISCLOSURE

APPLICANT(S) NAME AND ADDRESS	LENDER NAME AND ADDRESS (ORIGINATOR)

In connection with your application for a home loan, the lender must disclose to you the score that a consumer reporting agency distributed to users and the lender used in connection with your home loan, and the key factors affecting your credit scores.

The credit score is a computer-generated summary calculated at the time of the request and based on information a consumer reporting agency or lender has on file. The scores are based on data about your credit history and payment patterns. Credit scores are important because they are used to assist the lender in determining whether you will obtain a loan. They may also be used to determine what interest rate you may be offered on the mortgage. Credit scores can change over time, depending on your conduct, how your credit history and payment patterns change, and how credit-scoring technologies change.

Because the score is based on information in your credit history, it is very important that you review the credit related information that is being furnished to make sure it is accurate. Credit records may vary from one company to another.

If you have questions about your credit score or the credit information that is furnished to you, contact the consumer reporting agency at the address and telephone number provided with this notice, or contact the lender, if the lender developed or generated the credit score. The consumer reporting agency plays no part in the decision to take any action on the loan application and is unable to provide you with specific reasons for the decision on a loan application.

If you have questions concerning the terms of the loan, contact the lender.

The consumer reporting agencies listed below provided a credit score that was used in connection with your home loan application.

Consumer Reporting Agency	Borrower:		Co-Brw:	
Experian	Score:	Created:	Score:	Created:
P.O. Box 9701	Factors		Factors	
Allen, TX 75013				
(P)888-397-3742				
Model Used:				
Range of Possible Scores ___ to ___				

Calyx Form – csid1.frm (11/07)

At least government forms tend to sound straightforward, even if the devil eagerly waits in the details. This one pretty much delivers what it promises. Military borrowers will see their credit scores from all three credit reporting agencies along with the factors affecting each of those scores (even folks with scores in the 800s still have a few negative factors). The disclosure also tells you when your credit was pulled, which is typically part of the prequalification process. This is the first of a two-page document.

Department of Veterans Affairs — **VERIFICATION OF VA BENEFITS**

(VA FORM 26-8937, SEPT 2006)

This document is only for military borrowers who are, were or should be receiving VA disability benefits. It might look nondescript, but it's actually an incredibly important form. Veterans who receive compensation for a service-connected disability and surviving spouses of veterans who died on active duty or because of a service-connected disability are exempt from paying the VA Funding Fee.

Next document: Request for Certificate of Eligibility

OMB Control No. 2900-0086
Respondent Burden: 15 minutes

VA Department of Veterans Affairs **REQUEST FOR A CERTIFICATE OF ELIGIBILITY**	TO	Department of Veterans Affairs Eligibility Center P. O. Box 20729 Winston-Salem, NC 27120

NOTE: Please read information on reverse before completing this form. If additional space is required, attach a separate sheet.

1. FIRST-MIDDLE-LAST NAME OF VETERAN	2. DATE OF BIRTH	3. VETERAN'S DAYTIME TELEPHONE NO.

4A. ADDRESS OF VETERAN (No. street or rural route, city or P.O. State and ZIP Code)	5. MAIL CERTIFICATE OF ELIGIBILITY TO (Complete ONLY if the Certificate is to be mailed to an address different from the one listed in Item 4A)

4B. E-MAIL ADDRESS OF VETERAN (If applicable)

6. MILITARY SERVICE DATA (ATTACH PROOF OF SERVICE - SEE PARAGRAPH "D" ON REVERSE)

A. ITEM	B. PERIODS OF ACTIVE SERVICE DATE FROM	DATE TO	C. NAME (Show your name exactly as it appears on your separation papers or Statement of Service)	D. SOCIAL SECURITY NUMBER	E. SERVICE No. (If different from Social Security No.)	F. BRANCH OF SERVICE
1.						
2.						
3.						
4.						

7A. WERE YOU DISCHARGED, RETIRED OR SEPARATED FROM SERVICE BECAUSE OF DISABILITY OR DO YOU NOW HAVE ANY SERVICE-CONNECTED DISABILITIES? ☐ YES ☑ NO (If "Yes," complete Item 7B)	7B. VA CLAIM FILE NUMBER C-

8. PREVIOUS VA LOANS (Must answer N/A if no previous VA home loan. DO NOT LEAVE BLANK)

A. ITEM	B. TYPE (Home, Refinance, Manufactured Home or Direct)	C. ADDRESS OF PROPERTY	D. DATE OF LOAN	E. DO YOU OWN THE PROPERTY? (YES/NO)	F. DATE PROPERTY WAS SOLD (Submit a copy of HUD-1 Settlement Statement if available)	G. VA LOAN NUMBER (If known)
1.						
2.						
3.						
4.						
5.						
6.						

I CERTIFY THAT the statements herein are true to the best of my knowledge and belief.

9. SIGNATURE OF VETERAN (Do NOT print)	10. DATE SIGNED

FEDERAL STATUTES PROVIDE SEVERE PENALTIES FOR FRAUD, INTENTIONAL MISREPRESENTATION, CRIMINAL CONNIVANCE OR CONSPIRACY PURPOSED TO INFLUENCE THE ISSUANCE OF ANY GUARANTY OR INSURANCE BY THE SECRETARY OF VETERANS AFFAIRS.

FOR VA USE ONLY

11A. DATE CERTIFICATE ISSUED	11B. SIGNATURE OF VA AGENT

VA FORM APR 2008 **26-1880** EXISTING STOCKS OF VA FORM 26-1880, JAN 2006 WILL BE USED.

Lenders eligible to use the automated system will certainly do so, but they still need the veteran to supply a member 4 copy of their DD-214 and sign the request. Unmarried spouses of deceased eligible veterans don't have to fill out this form, but they are required to complete VA Form 26-1817, the Request for Determination of Loan Guaranty Eligibility—Unmarried Surviving Spouse (they can find the form at http://www.vba.va.gov/pubs/forms/VBA-26-1817-ARE.pdf).

Income & Employment

You don't need a job to secure VA loan preapproval—just ask military retirees. It's more an issue of whether you have stable, reliable income that's likely to continue. There's an array of income types, and some are more stable and reliable than others.

For most VA borrowers, their primary income source is a job, whether it's serving in the military or working in the civilian world. A solid employment history says a lot about your ability to repay a loan.

The gold standard of employment for many lenders is two years of reliable, full-time employment, ideally with the same employer. But real-world resumes aren't always this pristine.

That's why the VA and lenders allow flexibility when it comes to employment standards. There are no clear-cut "pass/fail" employment criteria. Rather, each applicant is considered on an individual basis, with a focus on three key measures:

- Is employment reliable?
- Is employment likely to continue?
- Is employment income sufficient in amount?

Let's take a look at a few employment and income scenarios. Understand, too, that requirements can vary among lenders when it comes to employment and income.

Full-time workers employed less than two years

It's certainly possible for applicants to earn VA loan approval if they have been employed for less than two years. If you have less than two years of full-time employment under your belt, a lender may take a careful look at these indicators:

- Your MOS and past employment record, including length of time at other jobs
- Your training, education and qualifications for your current job

- Your employer's confirmation that your job is likely to continue

Applicants with less than one year of employment will have a tougher time earning VA loan approval. But exceptions can be made, so talk to a lender about your specific situation. Continuity is often key in these cases.

For example, veterans who recently separated from military service obviously won't have two years on the job. But that may not matter if lenders are satisfied there's sufficient continuity between their MOS and their new employment.

John King and his wife, Becky, serve as a great example. John had recently completed his military service, and the couple was preparing to move from California to Oregon so John could start work with the Oregon State Police Department. They were hoping to land a loan based on John's anticipated income from the new job, before he received a single paycheck. Our underwriter gave the go-ahead to close the loan, provided John could produce a signed offer, an acceptance letter detailing his salary and a letter from the state police explaining why he was qualified for the job (in this case, his military experience).

Underwriters and lenders often wrestle with these and other significant questions regarding newly discharged service members. Underwriters who approve shaky loans that ultimately default don't stay in their jobs for long. At the same time, veterans seeking a fresh start in the civilian world deserve a thorough look and a genuine shot at homeownership.

With a short job history, you'll need to do all you can to impress a lender. Make sure you satisfy all other VA loan requirements. Provide a letter of explanation from your current employer showing that your job is stable and likely to continue.

Part-time employment

Part-time employees typically need a two-year history to count that income toward mortgage qualification. Guidelines and requirements can vary by lenders.

Some lenders won't care if that two-year history is with the same employer or spread among different companies, as long as there are no gaps in employment and the work is consistent. Policies about job gaps and changes in general can vary by lender. We'll take a closer look at job gaps and changes later in this chapter.

Borrowers without that two-year history of part-time income may be able to use the income to offset other debts.

Self-employment

Self-employment income can be less consistent than income from a salaried position. That inconsistency will trigger additional scrutiny from a lender. Self-employed applicants usually need two years of business tax returns to qualify for a home loan.

If you're self-employed, you'll need to show that your business is on solid financial ground. Lenders may closely examine the following records to assess your company's stability:

- Year-to-date profit and loss statements
- Current business balance sheets
- Individual income tax returns
- Federal business income tax returns for the previous two years (if the business is a corporation or partnership)
- A list of all stockholders or partners

Borrowers who work for a family member or family owned business need only to have worked at the business for a year for some lenders. But lenders will still typically require two years' worth of tax returns. In these situations, the borrower won't typically be considered self-employed unless they have at least a 25 percent ownership stake in the company, as verified by a third party.

If you're just starting your business, take your time, maintain good credit and consider a VA home loan once you've built that two-year track record. Also note that lenders can only count income on which you pay taxes, meaning write-offs, or unreimbursed business expenses, will be averaged and deducted from your total income.

Military employment

Active duty service members can provide a recent Leave and Earnings Statement (LES) as a record of employment. As long as your enlistment is expected to continue more than 12 months after your loan's closing date, you should be set.

If your military service will end within 12 months of your loan closing, you'll need to show a lender that you'll have stable, reliable income post-separation. These borrowers will need to provide either an offer of civilian employment, evidence of re-enlistment or other proof of their ability to afford the mortgage. Retirement income can absolutely suffice for borrowers retiring from work all together, although it will need to be documented prior to closing on your mortgage.

Retirement income

Veterans and service members planning to retire full time after their loan closing can look to qualify for a home loan using their retirement income. Lenders may take varying approaches to how this works in practice.

At Veterans United, we would typically need to have your official start date and exact retirement pay in writing. You would qualify based on the lesser of either your current full-time income or your retirement income.

In addition, you may need reserves available if you'll have a gap of more than 60 days between your last full-time paycheck and your first retirement payment. Talk with a loan officer in more detail.

Commission and overtime income

Commission-based workers generally need to document at least two years of income. Anything less typically can't be considered stable.

If you're paid on commission, you may need to provide a healthy amount of documentation to a lender, including:

- The actual amount of commissions paid year-to-date
- The basis for your commission (Are you paid a base salary plus commission, commission only, or periodic draws against commission?)
- Your commission schedule
- Your individual income tax returns for the previous two years

Having those two years spread among multiple employers may be fine, as long as the work is consistent. The same is generally true for counting overtime income. Lenders want to see that employers consistently extend overtime hours and that would-be buyers can handle the extra work. It's tough to do that without a two-year track record. Talk with lenders about their policies and potential exceptions.

Basic Allowance for Housing

Basic Allowance for Housing (BAH) is a monthly housing allowance provided to eligible service members. BAH rates vary based on geography, pay grade and dependency status. They're subject to change annually.

The goal of BAH is to help service members have equal access to housing based on costs and financial realities in the civilian housing market. BAH payments can be counted as effective income toward qualifying for a mortgage.

BAH rates are calculated using local rental data. The Defense Department looks at current market rent and the average costs of utilities and renters insurance. The rate is based on a service member's duty location, not residence location.

Service members stationed in more expensive parts of the country typically have higher BAH rates, allowing them to compete for civilian housing when government quarters aren't provided.

Service members can use some or all of their monthly housing allowance to pay for housing costs, be it rent or a mortgage payment. Depending on that monthly cost, they may have additional money left over to pay for things like utilities and other household expenses.

While rates are subject to change each year, the Defense Department has instituted rate protection that prevents housing allowance decreases. This protection remains in place unless the service member changes duty stations; experiences a pay grade reduction; or has a change in dependent status.

Basic Allowance for Housing can be a powerful tool. Mortgage lenders can count this income and use it to qualify you for a home loan. It's important to understand that BAH may not cover your entire mortgage payment. Remember, too, that changes to your service or family situation can affect your BAH rate. In turn, that can have an impact on your ability to pay the mortgage each month.

Other income sources

There are additional sources of income that lenders can count as "effective income" toward qualifying for a mortgage, including some types of non-taxable income.

Some of those additional income sources may include:

- Disability pay
- Social Security income
- Workers compensation
- Annuities
- Child Support
- Alimony

Not all of these income streams are automatically acceptable. Lenders may want to see a proven track record of you receiving it, or have some kind of guarantee that you'll continue earning it in the months and years ahead. Generally, you'll need to show that sources of income like these will continue for at least another three years.

A big no-go worth mentioning is GI Bill income. Veterans can receive housing assistance through their education benefit. But VA lenders cannot count this as effective income toward a home loan. In fact, it's difficult to find any lender or loan type that will.

Job Gaps & Changes

Having a gap in your employment history isn't uncommon. But lenders will want to take a closer look if you've had some time without a job in the lead up to pursuing a home loan. You may need to have been back to work for a certain number of months before lenders can move forward.

Policies and requirements can vary by lender. At Veterans United, our broad approach is based in part on the duration of your job gap:

- **0-2 month gap:** These situations can often move forward immediately as long as we have the most recent 30 days' worth of pay stubs from your old job. We will verify that you've started the new job, your exact pay and that you'll receive your first pay stub prior to your first mortgage payment.
- **3-6 month gap:** These can require anywhere from 30 days to six months back on the job depending on the reason for the gap, type of job, total work history, length of time in the field and more.
- **6-12 month gap:** These can require six to 12 months back on the job depending on most of the factors above.
- **12+ month gap:** These situations will typically require 12 months back on the job unless the circumstances were beyond the borrower's control.

Prospective borrowers with a job gap longer than 30 days will need to provide a letter of explanation describing the gap in employment. Remember, too, that these are broad baselines and not set-in-stone rules. Talk with a loan officer for more details.

Post-College Employment

Recent college graduates obviously haven't been able to build a two-year job history. But they can still qualify for a VA loan in some cases. To be sure, requirements will vary among lenders. Generally, you'll need to show continuity between your area of study and your post-graduation employment.

Lenders will often need copies of your school transcripts, and you may need 30 days of pay stubs from the new job, although there can be exceptions.

Temporary Leave from Work

Lenders may have additional requirements for prospective borrowers who are on a temporary leave from work during the loan process. Policies can vary among lenders. At Veterans United, we consider any leave shorter than six months to be temporary, as long as it's not a job change.

When we verify your employment situation, if your employer indicates you're on temporary leave, we'll look at your return date when evaluating your income:

- If you're coming back to work before your first mortgage payment is due, we can consider your regular income for loan qualification.
- If you're returning after that first payment is due, we will consider the lesser of your temporary leave income (if you're receiving it) and your regular income. We can also consider available assets, as long as they can keep your monthly income consistent for at least three years.

In addition, we would need written confirmation of your intent to return to work and your anticipated return date. Your employer would also need to confirm in writing that you can return to work at a comparable position and pay rate.

Job Changes

Changing jobs just before starting the homebuying journey, at anytime during your loan process or right after your closing can present challenges. Lenders want to make sure you'll continue to have stable, reliable income that's likely to continue. These situations are always evaluated on a case-by-case basis.

Lenders may slam on the brakes if you change jobs during the loan process. They'll often want to ensure there's continuity between the old job and the new one. If you're jumping to an entirely new career field, you may need to build a longer job history before moving forward. Even a promotion could be problematic if, say, some or all of your income switches to a commission basis.

If you're starting a new job after your loan closing, lenders will also need to take a deeper look. At Veterans United, we would typically need to approve you based on the lessor of the two incomes, although borrowers with sufficient assets may be able to count the higher future income. Also, there can't be any contingencies regarding your future job.

Lenders will confirm your employment situation on or just before your closing day. Talk with your loan officer about any pending changes to your employment as you move through the loan process.

VA Loans & Co-Borrowers

You may also be able to count another person's income to help you qualify for a larger loan amount.

Having a co-borrower on the loan with you can be a tremendous benefit. This person will be legally and financially obligated on the loan. They'll also need to occupy the home with you as their primary residence. Counting this person's income can help you buy more house. But there are some restrictions and requirements that co-borrowers will need to meet.

That means there's good and bad when it comes to co-borrowers. Just as a co-borrower's income can help, this person's credit and debt profile can also harm your loan approval chances. You may be separate people, but lenders will look at your loan application as a single entity.

The most common co-borrower on VA loans is a military spouse. Your spouse will also need to meet the lender's credit score requirement. In addition, lenders will include your spouse's monthly debts and income when calculating your DTI ratio. They'll also take into account any derogatory credit, collections, foreclosures, bankruptcies or liens.

Another veteran who has VA loan entitlement can be a co-borrower, as long as this person will live in the home with you as his or her primary residence. They'll face the same credit and financial scrutiny as a spouse. VA approval is required for this type of setup, unless the veteran happens to be your spouse. You can choose to use your entitlement solely in cases like this or opt for a "dual entitlement" scenario, with each eligible borrower utilizing a portion of their VA loan entitlement. It's usually best to talk with a VA lender in more detail about how to proceed in cases like this.

What if your co-borrower isn't a spouse or another veteran with VA loan entitlement?

These situations can present more of a financial challenge. These are known as "joint loans," and not all VA lenders make them. Veterans United currently does.

On a joint loan, the VA's guaranty applies only to the veteran's half of the mortgage. Remember, the VA typically guarantees 25 percent of the loan to a lender. With a non-spouse, non-veteran on the loan, the guaranty is cut in half, to just 12.5 percent.

That's a risk for lenders, which is why they'll typically require a 12.5 percent down payment for a joint loan.

VA Loans & Your Debts

Lenders are going to look at your major recurring debts as part of their assessment. They're considering housing payments, student loans, car payments, child support payments and other consistent expenses. They'll also look at things like collections, judgments and other forms of derogatory credit.

Generally, you don't need to be debt-free to qualify for a VA loan. Lenders are looking for a healthy balance between monthly debt and monthly income. But some types of debt are worse than others.

Having accounts in collection, judgments against you and liens can all hurt your ability to qualify for or close on a home loan. Lenders will often have a limit on how much derogatory credit a potential borrower can have. This cap on derogatory credit might be $5,000 or $10,000 or more. It can vary by lender, and there may be exceptions in certain cases.

For example, some lenders ignore collections on your credit report if you're actively working to pay the debt and can document on-time payments for the last 12 months. Some might also ignore charge-offs, which are essentially bad debts at least six months past due that creditors have written off.

Federal debts and delinquent accounts can be especially problematic. VA lenders will run your name against the Credit Alert Interactive Voice Response System (CAIVRS). This specialized database tracks current delinquencies and defaults within the last three years on things like federal student loans, FHA loans and other federal programs.

Federal agencies that report to the CAIVRS database include:
- Department of Education
- Department of Housing and Urban Development
- Department of Agriculture
- Department of Justice
- Small Business Administration

Problems with student loans and FHA loans are two of the most common reasons prospective borrowers wind up in this database. With student loans, for example, getting on a repayment plan can help speed the process if you're unable to repay the government in full. If you default on an FHA loan, you won't typically have a clear CAIVRS until you're three years removed from when the government pays the foreclosure claim. Whatever the reason, you won't be able to close on a VA loan until you have a "clear" CAIVRS.

CAIVRS doesn't track data from the Internal Revenue Service, but federal tax liens will usually appear on a borrower's credit reports. Tax liens can also make it tough to obtain home financing. Lenders will look to obtain your tax transcripts directly from the IRS in order to verify your income and financial information.

Let your loan officer know if you haven't filed taxes for either of the past two years, even if you have received an extension from the IRS. If you haven't filed tax returns because you receive non-taxable income, you may need to obtain a verification letter of non-filing from the IRS.

The IRS can place a lien on your property or your assets if you don't pay your federal income taxes. Having an active lien can make it more challenging to secure home financing. Ideally, you can pay the debt before starting the homebuying process. But that's not always possible.

Different lenders can have different policies when it comes to tax liens. But you may be able to move forward with a current tax lien if:

- You've entered into a repayment plan with the IRS and have at least a 12-month history of on-time payments
- You can meet the debt requirements for the lender and the loan type with that monthly repayment included
- You note the tax lien on Page 4 of the standard mortgage loan application

Still, there are no guarantees. In fact, would-be borrowers with active tax liens may also encounter tougher lending requirements. A tax lien often means lenders can't process your loan file through an Automated Underwriting System, which means your file would require "manual underwriting," as it's known. Manual underwrites typically come with tougher lending requirements. We'll take a closer look at manual underwriting later in this chapter.

Debt-to-Income Ratio

The VA doesn't set an income threshold for potential borrowers. You don't have to make a certain amount per hour, month or year to qualify for financing. Instead, one way the VA and lenders evaluate what you can afford is by comparing your major monthly debts to what you earn. This calculation is known as a debt-to-income (DTI) ratio.

Mortgage lending generally involves two types of ratios, a "front-end" ratio that compares only the new housing cost to your monthly income and a "back-end" ratio that looks at all of your major monthly expenses. VA loans focus solely on the back-end ratio.

Lenders will calculate your major monthly debt, including housing, loans and other significant expenses. That figure is divided by your total monthly gross (pre-tax) income. Only certain types of debts and income count toward your DTI ratio. VA lenders will focus on your major revolving and installment debts, mostly pulled directly from your credit reports. But they can also consider other obligations that don't make your credit report, like child-care costs, alimony and even commuting expenses.

Here's an example:

New mortgage payment:	$1,000
Auto loan:	$200

Student loan:	$100
Child support:	$100
Total monthly debt:	$1,400
Total monthly gross income:	$3,500
DTI ratio:	40 percent

If you have collections or charge-offs on your credit report, lenders won't typically factor those into your DTI ratio calculation unless you're making regular monthly payments on those debts. But lenders may have a cap on how much of this derogatory credit you can have.

The VA wants to see borrowers with a DTI ratio of 41 percent or less. It's definitely possible to be above that threshold and still obtain VA loan approval. But you'll need to meet a higher benchmark for residual income (we'll explain this unique financial standard next) and fall within a lender's cap for DTI ratio. Those can and will vary depending on the lender and other factors.

What happens if your DTI ratio is too high for lenders? There are a few possible solutions. One is to find more income, which is easier said than done. Two is to pay down debts or eliminate them completely, which can also be tough. Three is to seek a lower loan amount. A good chunk of your DTI ratio will be based on your projected monthly mortgage payment.

Residual Income

Despite the $0 down payment benefit, VA loans have been the safest mortgage on the market for much of the last decade. One of the big reasons why is the VA's unique financial requirement for discretionary income, which it calls "residual income."

VA borrowers must have a minimum amount of money left over each month after paying their major expenses. The amount varies based on your family size and where in the country you're buying.

The aim is to make sure borrowers have enough discretionary income to cover everyday needs like gasoline, groceries and medical bills.

To calculate your residual income, a lender will simply subtract your major monthly debts from your gross monthly income. You may be able to omit a spouse or dependent from the calculation if they're not on the loan and have verified income to support themselves. Also, lenders may be able to reduce the residual income requirement by 5 percent for active duty borrowers, because on-base goods tend to be cheaper.

Here's a look at the VA's current residual income guidelines:

9. How to Complete VA Form 26-6393, Loan Analysis,
Continued

e. Item 44, Balance Available for Family Support (continued)

Table of Residual Incomes by Region For loan amounts of $80,000 and above				
Family Size	Northeast	Midwest	South	West
1	$450	$441	$441	$491
2	$755	$738	$738	$823
3	$909	$889	$889	$990
4	$1,025	$1,003	$1,003	$1,117
5	$1062	$1,039	$1,039	$1,158
over 5	Add $80 for each additional member up to a family of seven			

Key to Geographic Regions Used in the Preceding Tables			
Northeast	Connecticut	New Hampshire	Pennsylvania
	Maine	New Jersey	Rhode Island
	Massachusetts	New York	Vermont
Midwest	Illinois	Michigan	North Dakota
	Indiana	Minnesota	Ohio
	Iowa	Missouri	South Dakota
	Kansas	Nebraska	Wisconsin
South	Alabama	Kentucky	Puerto Rico
	Arkansas	Louisiana	South Carolina
	Delaware	Maryland	Tennessee
	District of Columbia	Mississippi	Texas
	Florida	North Carolina	Virginia
	Georgia	Oklahoma	West Virginia
West	Alaska	Hawaii	New Mexico
	Arizona	Idaho	Oregon
	California	Montana	Utah
	Colorado	Nevada	Washington
			Wyoming

Continued on next page

Based on the chart, a family of four living in the Northeast would need at least $1,025 available each month after paying the mortgage and other significant expenses. Veterans and service members who fail to meet that residual income standard will have a hard time obtaining a loan.

Prospective borrowers with a DTI ratio above 41 percent must exceed their residual income requirement by 20 percent. To continue the example, that same Northeastern family of four would now need $1,230 in residual income to satisfy the requirement.

There's a fixation on debt-to-income ratio in the mortgage industry. But residual income may be a more powerful and realistic metric way to look at affordability and a borrower's ability to stay current on their mortgage if emergencies arise. It's also a big reason why VA loans have such a low foreclosure rate, despite the fact that 9 in 10 people purchase without a down payment.

When DTI ratio or residual income or both are toward the margins, lenders can turn to what are called compensating factors. These are strengths that help offset concerns and weaknesses in the buyer's loan application. There's a laundry list of things that can be considered, including:

- A sterling credit history
- Minimal debt
- Long-term employment
- Significant liquid assets
- Military benefits
- Conservative use of credit
- And many others

The VA explicitly notes that compensating factors have to go above and beyond what would be considered a normal program requirement. Many of our veterans and service members benefit from a combination of compensating factors.

Now, in terms of DTI ratio and residual income, there is another way to proceed. When a loan officer calculates your DTI ratio and residual income, he or she is doing so based on the estimated loan amount you're seeking. So, if you're looking at a 30-year fixed-rate mortgage at 5.25 percent and $250,000, the loan officer is crunching numbers based on a monthly mortgage payment (without taxes and insurance) of about $1,380.

Let's say she runs the numbers and determines your DTI ratio is 50 percent and your residual income is also less than stellar. Well, here's an easy way to curb those monthly debts: Try a lower loan amount. If a $250,000 loan looks to be too much for the veteran, the loan officer can essentially just play with the numbers until they become workable.

Instead of $250,000, maybe try $225,000 or $215,000. This kind of plug-and-play with loan amounts is standard fare for lenders nationwide. It's also one more reason why seeking loan preapproval before shopping for a home is critical. We'll get to that in the next chapter.

Sure, it's disappointing when veterans discover the $250,000 house they've been eyeing for months isn't really in their price range. But a $215,000 house may represent a better fit for their budget. And, of course, the other option is for prospective borrowers to tackle their credit and financial issues first and hold off on purchasing a home.

Manual Underwriting

One of the biggest benefits of the VA loan program is that veterans who've hit a rough financial patch can still qualify for a mortgage. But lenders may need to take a closer look to try and ensure you can handle the responsibility of a monthly mortgage payment.

In these cases, you may hear a loan officer say that your loan will need a "manual underwrite" or to be "manually underwritten." The first question in the minds of many prospective borrowers is: What exactly does that mean, and how does it differ from the standard underwriting process?

There are times when an AUS approval isn't possible for a prospective borrower. Almost always, the reason why relates to the veteran's credit history. Some issues that can knock an application from AUS consideration include:

- A lack of credit depth or history
- A bankruptcy in the last 24 months
- Default or delinquency on federal debt

- Late mortgage payments
- Foreclosure, short sale or deed-in-lieu of foreclosure

A file that gets bounced from the automated system may be eligible for a manual underwrite. All this basically means is that a human will have to crunch the numbers and evaluate the risk from Day One, rather than later in the process like normal. In addition, veterans facing a manual underwrite will likely need to meet tighter requirements when it comes to things like debt-to-income (DTI) ratio, residual income, derogatory credit, financial documentation and more.

Loan officers will try to determine whether you need a manual underwrite during the prequalification and preapproval process. Today, the vast majority of VA loans are processed through an AUS. Part of it is efficiency and ease. But it's also because lenders like to ensure they're not exposed to financial harm if their loans go bad.

The VA guaranty only extends to qualified lenders issuing loans that meet agency guidelines. If a lender goes beyond VA guidelines and issues a loan that ultimately defaults, the VA is under no obligation to cover its guaranty.

That means lenders will be extremely cautious—and routinely rigorous—when considering a manual underwrite. Most lenders have their own distinct guidelines for working with manual underwrites. For example, some lenders on an AUS file may be able to work with a DTI ratio up to 60 or 65 percent. But on a manual underwrite that threshold isn't likely to exceed 45 or 50 percent.

Others are more lenient. Each case is different, except for one common thread: A human underwriter will ask for documents upon documents when examining the application of a veteran closer to the edge.

On a manual underwrite you may also have to go an extra mile regarding your current living situation. Veterans who aren't currently homeowners will often need what's known as a

Verification of Rent (VOR) if they're planning to purchase a home. Lenders want to see that you've made on-time rent payments, which in part helps lessen any "payment shock" that can come with suddenly having a monthly mortgage payment.

There are all kinds of rent and living scenarios. Some borrowers rent from individuals and pay cash. Others live with a relative and essentially barter by helping out on some bills. You'll likely need bank records, cancelled checks and/or a letter of explanation to satisfy VA lenders.

Preapproval Letters

That's a snapshot of some of the major considerations of VA loan preapproval. The goal of this process is to obtain what's known as a preapproval letter. It's an increasingly important document in housing markets nationwide.

Loan preapproval is not a guarantee of financing. But it's a significant step that real estate agents and sellers love to see. It showcases a lender's confidence in your ability to handle a home loan. Sellers want to feel like you're a safe bet to make good on the deal and close on the loan.

The preapproval letter will typically list a series of conditions that need to be met in order for the loan to move forward. These conditions help protect both lenders and borrowers in case things don't go as planned or financial circumstances change.

Typically included with the preapproval letter is a list of conditions the borrower must meet in order to secure full loan approval. This gives the veteran a clear understanding of the documents and information that still need to be verified or obtained. For example, this sample preapproval letter lists seven outstanding areas, five of which are part of almost every preapproval:

- Acceptable appraisal to support the value on signed purchase agreement
- Acceptable title policy

- Acceptable flood certification
- Clear termite inspection
- Final underwriting approval

At minimum, these five issues will have to be addressed in order for VA borrowers to receive full loan approval. There certainly might be more paperwork and documentation necessary as the process rolls on. Most preapproval letters also make clear that changes to your credit, income or other important financial metrics can cause the document to expire. Again, loan preapproval is not the same thing as formal loan approval. It's also not a binding step. You can seek preapproval from multiple lenders.

Would-be buyers often ask: How long is my preapproval good for? Some lenders date their preapproval letters, while others don't. Credit, income and asset documentation may need to be reordered or resupplied after a few months. In some respects, the expiration doesn't matter a great deal, as preapproval isn't binding or a guarantee of financing. Lenders are going to verify your income, employment and credit information again once you're under contract on a home.

Some lenders may allow you to alter the date and the preapproval amount (up to your max) in order to craft a strong offer without tipping your hand. You might be preapproved for a $300,000 loan, but it's not usually in your best interest for home sellers to know how high you can go.

While this document isn't any kind of guarantee, a preapproval letter gives you a clear sense of what you can afford and what it will likely take to land a VA home loan. Loan preapproval also gives you the confidence and clarity to start seriously shopping for your home. Sellers and their agents will be looking for this.

Borrower Spotlight: Cameron Calhoon
Air Force Loadmaster Utilizes Basic Allowance for Housing (BAH)
to Nab His First Home

Destin, Florida—Military service was always in the cards for Staff Sgt. Cameron Calhoon.

Homeownership seemed a much less certain path.

Growing up in California, at the southern edges of Sequoia National Forest, Cameron heard stories of his great-grandfather, a Navy sailor, and his grandfather, an Air Force fireman. By the time he turned 21, Cameron was ready to continue the family tradition.

He enlisted in the Air Force and settled at Pope Air Force Base in North Carolina. But he quickly learned his stay at the sprawling base would be a limited engagement. Days after his arrival, Pope AFB landed on the Base Realignment and Closure (BRAC) list of installations to be shuttered.

Cameron had planned to pursue a home purchase in North Carolina, but word of the BRAC decision forced him to reconsider. He didn't see a lot of sense in moving forward, given that he could get reassigned at a moment's notice.

Instead, Cameron spent the first two years living on base before moving in with his sister, who lived in nearby Fayetteville. Three years passed before Cameron, a C-130 loadmaster, received his new orders. He would be moving in 12 months to Hurlburt Field, in the shadow of Elgin Air Force Base in northwestern Florida.

The shift would bring newfound certainty. The nature of Cameron's job meant that Elgin was the only base in the country where he could work. There was little doubt he would be there for years to come.

He started looking for homes online in February, but the process fizzled after just a couple months. Cameron had to leave in early spring for what was slated to be 60 days of specialized training. He planned to revisit his home search in earnest upon his return. But delays and other problems stretched his training to 120 days. He finished in August, with just four months remaining until his departure day.

This time, he decided to dive into the homebuying process full bore. He had heard of the VA home loan program but didn't know much about mortgages and buying a home. Most of what he found online only confused him. So, it was with some relief that his online search led him to Veterans United Home Loans. He decided to call and talk with a VA loan specialist.

With that, his confusion and questions came to rest. Cameron's loan officer walked him through the process of loan preapproval. Cameron learned within minutes that he was eligible for a VA loan with $0 down payment.

He would also be able to use his Basic Allowance for Housing to defray some or all of his mortgage expenses. BAH payments represent a verifiable and reliable income stream that can be used to calculate a prospective borrower's debt-to-income ratio, a key factor in loan underwriting.

Cameron also connected with a local real estate agent through Veterans United Realty. Cameron spent a week in Destin in the fall. He looked at more than two dozen houses in a two-day frenzy. One of the first houses he and his girlfriend looked at stuck in their minds during the visit. The original owners were an older couple who did a great job keeping the home up to date.

On his third day in Destin, Cameron decided to put down an offer on the home. He received and accepted a counteroffer that was a mere $600 off his asking price. The home passed a couple inspections, including one for wind mitigation, a necessity in hurricane-prone regions. Cameron closed on the home just a few weeks after inking the contract.

Cameron's BAH completely covers his $871 monthly mortgage payment, leaving enough to pay his electric bill. His flight pay covers the rest of the utilities. He has friends in nearby apartments who pay more per month in rent than his mortgage.

This story does not represent an endorsement of Veterans United Home Loans by the Department of Defense, the Department of the Army or any other governmental agency.

CHAPTER 5:
BUYING A HOME WITH A VA LOAN

Once you're preapproved, the next step is to find a house that meets your needs and your budget. Buying a home is one of the biggest and most personal investments a veteran will ever make. It's also a process that comes with its own language, complexities and pitfalls.

That's one of the main reasons we recommend veterans relinquish any ideas they have about navigating the process alone.

Use a real estate agent when purchasing a home. It's that simple.

Actually, it's almost that simple.

Use an agent who understands VA loans.

Finding a real estate agent who's worked with military buyers in the past and has familiarity with the VA home loan program can make a huge difference for borrowers. Before we start parsing among real estate agents, let's first look more closely at why they're important in general.

Why You Should Use a Real Estate Agent

So why bother? There's a litany of reasons, but we'll look at a few of the big ones:

- **Expertise**

Real estate agents help people purchase homes every day. This is their business, their profession. In contrast, buying a home is something you'll probably do a couple times in your life at most. It's true the Internet has taken much of the mystery out of the process. But we still think it's better to have a trained, professional advocate to navigate the process, order inspections, help craft an offer and finalize the contract. Agents have ready access to information on comparable home sales, school districts, zoning and land use regulations and all kinds of community-related data.

- **Hunting for Houses**

Real estate agents will have access to the Multiple Listing Service, or MLS, in your area. Agents can use the MLS's exhaustive categorizing to create custom searches for your dream home. They can get constant updates whenever a home that meets your parameters hits the listings. That doesn't mean you can't hunt for houses on your own. Just be sure to have your agent on speed dial.

- **You Have an Advocate**

In most cases, the person selling the home will be using a listing agent to showcase the property and find a buyer. His or her sole job is to get the best offer possible from a qualified buyer. It's a good idea to have an expert who can advocate for you and, if necessary, go toe-to-toe with the listing agent. Your buyer's agent is there as a surrogate, charged with acting in your best interests.

- **It Costs Zero Dollars**

It's not because real estate agents work for free. They don't. But throughout most of the country, the person buying the house pays nothing to use a real estate agent. Instead, the agent working on your behalf will split with the listing agent a commission from the home sale proceeds. Leveraging a real estate agent's expertise and access costs a borrower nothing. If you have any doubt on that, simply ask the agent. Look elsewhere if you don't get a straight answer.

About 90 percent of homebuyers use a real estate agent or broker, according to the National Association of Realtors. Does that mean you have to?

No.

You can certainly spend time scouring real estate sites and home listings online. The Internet has a wealth of information that has helped to demystify the homebuying process. Being an educated buyer is key to getting the best deal possible. But it doesn't replace the expertise and familiarity that comes with having a real estate agent.

If nothing else, consider the size and scope of this investment. You're getting ready to make a huge purchase—maybe it's $150,000, or $350,000, or even more. Why go it alone?

Now Dig a Bit Deeper

That said, all real estate agents aren't created equal. It might not matter too much if you're purchasing with a conventional, run-of-the-mill loan. But the VA loan is a unique tool that requires specialized knowledge.

The VA mandates that a home have proper maintenance and be in good repair. Condos require VA approval. Private wells, septic systems, termite inspections and shared maintenance of roadways all have specific VA guidelines. A good buyer's agent will know this.

But many do not.

So, it's not enough to find a real estate agent. We urge military borrowers to try and find an agent who understands their unique needs and truly knows VA loans. It's not always an easy task.

Sometimes, it's because veterans get pulled by forces closer to home—a cousin, a former coach or a friend from church happens to be a real estate agent. Those bonds are hard to break, and it's understandable if you sacrifice VA expertise for the sake of the social contract.

But, more often than not, it's difficult because real estate agents have varying degrees of exposure to military borrowers and the VA Loan Guaranty program. In military-dense parts of the country, finding a real estate agent who's recently closed VA loans shouldn't present much of a problem.

Veterans who live near military installations have a distinct advantage. Expertise with VA loans is a competitive advantage for agents in these areas, and military borrowers should have a much easier time finding a qualified agent. In these parts, good real estate agents won't be shy when it comes to advertising their VA loan expertise.

But what about everywhere else? Veterans make up fewer than 10 percent of the population in all but three states (Alaska, Maine and Montana), according to data from the Washington Post.

It can be much more of a struggle to find real estate agents who have experience closing VA loans in areas with minimal veteran populations. What's worse is that military borrowers in these communities often find flat-out resistance to VA loans from agents who don't really understand how the program works in today's marketplace.

It then becomes a matter of finding the right VA-savvy agent.

"Don't just open the phone book and say, 'I'm going to choose this person,'" said Ruben Moya, who with his wife, Kerry, an Air Force veteran, purchased their Nevada home with a VA loan. "Do your homework on this person. Make sure they're looking out for your best interests. It's one of the biggest investments in your life."

Spend time talking with a couple promising agents who clearly understand the incredible benefits of the VA loan.

Here's a look at six questions you can ask to help get the conversation flowing:

1) Do you have significant experience in this market?

Ask your agent how long they've lived and worked in the area. Learn more about how many homes they sold last year and for what average price. Make sure you're comfortable with their experience. Look for seasoned real estate agents who know your desired neighborhoods and have a track record of success.

2) Do you have VA loan experience?

VA loans aren't more onerous or complicated than other types of loans. They're just different. Make sure your agent understands that you'll be considering or using VA financing and why this program is so powerful for military borrowers.

3) How many clients are you working with, and are they mostly sellers or buyers?

You can't expect to be an agent's sole client, but you also don't want an agent who never has time for you. Working with a lot of clients can actually be a sign of efficiency and demand. Learn more about how the agent strikes the right balance.

4) Will I work with you from start to finish?

Ask if the agent will handle every part of the homebuying process. Some may have an assistant take care of more transactional or administrative tasks. That's not always a bad thing, but it's important to be able to talk directly with your agent regularly.

5) How will you keep me informed during the process?

Make sure your communication needs and expectations match. Some buyers want to connect via text message or email, while others prefer phone calls. Agents can also be more hands-off for buyers who would prefer to lead their own home search. Some agents may give you access to their property search database and allow you to take full control.

6) Can I have references?

Ask your agent to provide contact information for some recent clients. Steer clear of anyone who hesitates. These previous buyers can provide helpful insight if you're choosing among multiple potential agents.

Personalities clash, and some partnerships simply don't succeed. House hunters spend a lot of time with their agents, and that time should be productive and enjoyable. Keep in mind that your agent will be with you for all home tours, during negotiations and throughout the closing process.

Go with your gut in the end. Let comfort, rapport and trust be your guides.

Myths & Misconceptions Among Agents

For years, VA loans have been dogged by a reputation as bureaucratic, time-sucking black holes. A lot of it goes back to the VA of yesteryear, which certainly had some institutional problems.

Part of that was the nature of doing things by hand. Part of it, to be quite honest, was the nature of a giant governmental agency doing business. At the same time, some major pillars of the VA's loan program have long been misunderstood or mischaracterized.

The agency caps what a veteran can pay in closing costs and upfront fees, a significant benefit that helps extend housing opportunities to those who might not otherwise have the financial ability. It's another small way to thank those who have served.

But they're also costs that have to be covered. The lender can step in and take care of them, but it's usually the seller who winds up footing the bill for a decent chunk of those closing costs. In the past, that's been a big hurdle for some agents to scale. Many, understandably, were worried about losing commissions or getting tied up for weeks with a slow-moving bureaucracy.

The VA appraisal process is another big one. It's a fair but stringent process that puts a premium on a veteran's health and safety. A VA appraisal is more thorough than a typical appraisal and can mandate repairs to meet agency guidelines.

There are always exceptions, but most VA loans close within the same 30- to 45-day window as conventional loans. As we mentioned before, VA loans tend to have lower average interest rates than conventional loans. They've also had a better closing success rate than conventional loans in recent years.

But real estate agents who haven't closed a VA loan in years might be needlessly concerned about costs and delays. That's not only a shame but a huge disserve to military borrowers hoping to capitalize on the benefits earned by their service.

And now you can begin to see the hurdles possibly lurking.

Military borrowers in those low-density areas will find agents fluent in the language of conventional loans. You'll also find a good deal who speak FHA. But there might be a lot of silent shrugs when it comes to VA loans.

Or worse—the agent will try to talk you out of even considering your VA loan benefits.

Finding an Agent Who Speaks VA

If you can find local real estate agents who tout their experience with VA loans online or in traditional advertisements, consider starting there. Another good place is within your own community of military colleagues. Check with people at the local VFW or American Legion post. Ask every home-owning veteran you come across: Did you use a VA loan and, if so, who helped you with it?

If those paths fail to turn up anything meaningful, your best bet might be to focus on *who* a real estate agent knows instead of *what* an agent knows. In this case, look for agents who work with established lenders that possess a track record of helping military borrowers navigate the VA process.

Still, it's not the most ideal situation. Real estate agents are there on the ground, showing houses and shepherding veterans through the process in person. Those who work frequently with military borrowers can wind up making a huge difference on behalf of their clients. Agents who can maneuver through the agency's procedures and requirements can save borrowers from big-time hassles and headaches on things like appraisals and property requirements (we'll cover both of these later).

Army veteran Calvin Eley is a great example.

He and his fiancée, Lynnecia Johnson, came to us hoping to purchase a home in northern Maryland. The couple had done some cursory home shopping and figured a townhome would be their only real option. They opted to take advantage of Veterans United Realty, our national network of more than 5,000 real estate agents who work routinely with military buyers.

Calvin and Lynnecia's agent took them through dozens of homes, pointing out deficiencies and issues that would likely prove problematic for the VA appraisal. The agent ultimately found a single-family home that met the couple's needs and actually came in below their price point.

"The home we found, I believe we were the only ones who had a chance to walk through and see it," Lynnecia said. "It went on the market, [our agent] notified us the same day, we saw it and put in an offer. She was able to steer us in the right direction as far as finding a home that the VA would approve."

We want to underscore that any military borrower can utilize Veterans United Realty. It's not a service solely reserved for our customers, and it's completely free. Let this be another avenue to explore if your search for a local VA-savvy agent comes up dry.

Working Relationships

Before you decide to work with an agent, it's important to be familiar with buyer's agreements. Many real estate agents will expect you to sign a buyer-broker agreement before they agree to represent you.

A buyer's agreement creates a formal, legal relationship between you and your agent. It's practically mandatory for buyers and lays out the rules of your partnership.

Here are the three most common types of buyer's agreements:

1) **Exclusive Right to Represent:** This is the most common form of buyer agreement. By agreeing to an exclusive right to represent, a buyer cannot employ more than one agent to locate property.

2) **Non-Exclusive:** In a "non-exclusive" agreement, a buyer can work with more than one agent to locate property.

3) **Non-Exclusive, Right to Represent:** In a non-exclusive agreement with a "right to represent" clause, a buyer can purchase a home through another agent, provided the home is

not introduced to the buyer by the initial broker.

Always read a buyer's agreement carefully and ask about exit clauses. Some agents are willing to prematurely end a buyer's agreement if the relationship is no longer working, but some will not. When in doubt, start with a short contract (30 days is a good place to start). You can always choose to renew the contract at a later time.

Also, keep in mind that our needs, wants and lives can all change. So do business relationships. At some point after selecting an agent, you may need to reassess your working relationship.

Ask yourself these questions to help you decide if you should continue working with a particular agent:

- **Does your agent seem eager to help?**

If you feel like your agent is doing you a "favor" by helping you find a home, you probably need a new one. No matter how much you're spending on a home or how long it takes to find one, you should feel valued and respected.

- **Does your agent show up on time?**

Poor time management is often an indicator of other shortcomings. Your time is valuable. Don't put up with an agent who doesn't respect you or your schedule.

- **Does your agent seem prepared?**

Make sure your agent has done his or her homework before meeting with you. Your agent should be well informed on the homes you are considering and recent comparable sales.

- **Does your agent exhaust all options?**

Good real estate agents are experts on the local market. The best agents can help their buyers become experts by showing you a wide variety of homes and keeping you in tune with the market. Someone who is unwilling to take this extra step might not be your best advocate. But there's a careful balance here. You want to see a healthy selection of homes, but someone who continues to show you homes that aren't a good fit for your needs probably isn't a good fit for you, either.

Defining Needs v. Wants in a Home

What do you want in a home? It's a simple question. But it's not necessarily the right one to ask when you're preparing to start the house hunt. Add a few more words and you've got a better question: *What do you want in a home, and what do you really need?*

Carefully considering your wants and needs is a key early step. You're not likely to get everything you want in a home, unless you're building it from the ground up (with the budget to match). Your home search could be a frustrating experience unless you separate the things you truly need from the amenities and features you'd love to have but can live without.

Consider "needs" to be true essentials that aren't easy (or possible) to change. These are genuine must-haves that leave little room for compromise. Your "wants" are the kind of non-essential things readymade for a wish list.

In fact, making a list—a real, on-paper list—can be a helpful tool and something you can show a real estate agent and reference during the house-hunting experience. It's helpful to have a starting point.

One approach is to compile a list that can help you set initial priorities. Try thinking about four categories:

- Features and amenities you need
- Features and amenities you want
- Features and amenities you don't want
- Deal breakers

For first-time buyers, it can be tough to get started. Consider what you like and what you don't like about your current living situation. Think about the features and amenities you like in other people's homes. Think about your plans, your goals and your life trajectory in the coming years and how that might affect both your wants and needs.

Here's a look at some key areas to consider when drafting your list of wants and needs:

- **Location**

This one isn't exactly easy to change. Do you need to be in a certain school district or closer to work? Are you looking for a more urban setting or would you rather be nestled in the suburbs? Younger buyers without a family on the horizon might want to live closer to city centers. Property taxes and homeowners insurance costs can vary depending on the location, and those can have a real impact on your homebuying budget.

- **Size and Type**

Do you have a family or are you likely to start one while living in the home? Your current or future family size can impact your needs in terms of bedrooms, bathrooms and more. You might need or want a basement or rec room if you have older kids or teenagers. Are you set on a single-family home, or are you open to condos and townhouses? Maybe you're not interested in two-story homes or large lots, which then fall in the category of "deal breakers."

- **Lot Size**

Do you need a big yard for kids or pets? Some buyers want room for a garden or to have some privacy from neighbors. Others hate the idea of spending weekends on a lawnmower or with a rake in hand. The average new single-family home is built on about 14,000 square feet (about a third of an acre), according to the National Association of Home Builders. You may want more or less. Hiring someone to mow your yard could be pricey, and doing your own lawn maintenance requires tools and time.

- **Amenities**

This is usually where the "want" floodgates open. Many buyers want things like a master bedroom with adjoining bathroom; fireplaces; updated kitchen with granite countertops and stainless steel appliances; hardwood floors; updated bathrooms; walk-in closets; patio or deck; and so much more. And it's OK to want all of this and more. But try to prioritize all those amenities and features and determine if any are true needs. If you're passionate about woodworking or some other hobby, you might need a dedicated workspace in a basement or a garage. Maybe a media room or an eat-in kitchen is a true need for you. On the other hand, some buyers reject outright any property with a swimming pool because of the upkeep and costs.

The key is to be honest and open with yourself. You also have to be flexible. It's not uncommon for both needs and wants to change as you look at more homes. Amenities you thought were essential might become less so the more properties you see. On the other hand, something that started out as a "want" might move into the "need" category as the home tours roll on.

- **Time in Home**

The average homebuyer expects to live in their home for 12 years, according to the National Association of Realtors. But everyone's situation is different. If you're likely to PCS a few years after purchasing, your wants and needs might be a lot different than someone planning to stay in the home longer. If you're likely to move in the coming years, schools can be important even if you don't currently have school-age children. Many future buyers will have good schools high on their shopping lists. Factor in your short- and long-term goals and plans when you're thinking about wants and needs.

- **Budget**

It's important to understand that different wants and needs come with different costs, all of which vary depending on the housing market you're in, the price range and more. Sellers want to recoup their investments in things granite counter tops, jetted tubs, three-car garages and more. Newer features and sought-after amenities are likely to drive up a seller's asking price. Keep your loan preapproval and your housing budget at the forefront.

- **Setting Expectations**

Prepare yourself at the outset for the likelihood that you won't get everything you want. The hope is you at least get everything you need. You may need to make some tough decisions when you start comparing one home to another, especially when you're considering making an offer.

It becomes more about compromise, trade-offs and finding the best possible property given your priorities. One home might lack an updated kitchen but have a better location. Another might have a great yard and a beautiful master bedroom but force you into a longer commute.

Having a solid, evolving grasp on your true wants and needs can help make sure you get the best possible property given your goals, your lifestyle and your budget.

Touring Homes

Found a home that meets all your initial criteria? It's time for a home tour. Touring a home takes you past the listing data and into the heart and soul of a property. Photos and video are helpful, but the best way to get a real sense of the house is to spend time there.

The typical homebuyer looks at about 10 homes over a dozen weeks, according to the National Association of Realtors. But everyone is different. Some people look at two houses, while others tour two dozen. There's no right or wrong approach.

Here are 10 tips to keep in mind when the time comes to start touring properties:

1) Give Yourself Time

Don't try to cram a dozen home tours into an afternoon. You don't want to feel rushed, especially when you land on a property you like. You also need to factor in the time it takes to get to each property. A good real estate agent can help you get the most from each tour.

2) Notes, Pictures & Measurements

Bring a notebook or print off our handy Home Tour checklist

before you go. Record your reactions and questions. But also ask your real estate agent if it's OK to take pictures inside and outside the home. There's a lot to see, and odds are you won't remember everything. Some buyers even like to sketch a simple floor plan before they leave, as it can be helpful when comparing properties later. Bring a tape measure, too. MLS listings will usually feature the dimensions of a home's rooms, but it never hurts to double check.

3) Consider Curb Appeal

Curb appeal is important to a lot of homebuyers. A recent study by the National Association of Realtors found that 49 percent of buying decisions are based on curb appeal. Take time to look past this initial "gut" reaction. Try to determine if you can improve a home's appearance with a few simple projects, or if a costlier fix would be in order. Maybe you can spruce up the front of the home with simple planting and maintenance. Don't discount a home with great location or other attractive features based solely on that first impression, especially if you could improve the curb appeal without spending a fortune.

4) Don't Sweat Simple Fixes

Don't let bad carpet, ugly wallpaper or outdated appliances and furniture chase you from a house that otherwise has a lot to offer. These aren't always cheap fixes or replacements, but it's obviously a lot easier to change carpet or appliances than a home's location or lot size.

5) You're Not Being "Nosy"

Open cabinets, doors and windows. Check out the closets and look under the rugs. It might feel like you're being "nosy," but consider it doing your due diligence. You want to make sure the home meets your needs. You also don't want any surprises, like a warped or stained floor hiding beneath that gorgeous rug. Bring a golf ball or a marble to check whether floors are level, too.

6) Keep Emotions in Check

Some sellers might just take a walk or hang out at the neighbor's during your home tour. Avoid "oohing and ahhing" about the home's features (or bad-mouthing them) if there's a chance the seller might hear. Wait until you're back in the car with your agent to talk about what you loved and what you didn't. The last thing you want is to compromise your negotiating position or offend the seller of your dream home.

7) Visit at Different Times

If you like a home enough to warrant a second showing, try to schedule it for a different time of day from the first. Get a feel for the traffic on a weekday morning and what that could mean for your commute. Are neighbors playing with their children outside or walking their dogs after work? Can you hear road noise or other sounds that maybe weren't there on your first visit?

8) Look for a Seller's Disclosure

Home sellers are required to disclose information about issues with their property. Rules and regulations about seller disclosures vary based on where you're buying. But these will typically document known problems with things like leaky roofs or basements, major systems and rehab work completed by the seller. Sellers aren't usually required to provide a disclosure until you're under contract. But in some markets sellers will leave a copy of their disclosure statement for you to peruse during a home tour. If you spot one while touring a home you like, review the disclosure in detail with your agent. Potential buyers can use this information along with a home inspection to really scrutinize the property and decide whether they want to move forward.

9) Look at Utility Costs

When shopping for a home, also consider a home's utility costs. The average monthly bill for electricity and natural gas is about $120, according to the WhiteFence Index, which calculates utility bill averages for 20 U.S. cities. One way to slash utility costs is to update a home's appliances. Modern appliances are generally more energy efficient than older ones and may pay for themselves in utility savings. Your real estate agent can obtain previous utility bills for any homes you are considering, which may help you to decide whether it's necessary to replace old appliances.

One way to finance some of your home's energy efficiency improvements is through a VA Energy Efficient Mortgage. This specialized financing option provides all the benefits of a VA loan, plus offers an additional allowance to improve a home's energy efficiency. Buyers who qualify can add up to $6,000 to their loan amount to make certain energy efficiency improvements. We'll take a closer look at EEMs a little later.

10) Remember Your Priorities

You've already spent time defining what you want in a home. Think about the handful of genuine must-haves and hold them close. You might see all kinds of cool, new features as you tour more and more homes. Keeping your true priorities top of mind will help you stay focused on what's most important.

It's also OK if those priorities shift as you look at more homes. Just be honest with yourself about needs versus wants.

Housing Hunting & Property Guidelines

We've talked about the acceptable and unacceptable uses of VA home loans. Condos, manufactured homes, modular housing and new construction may all be in play, depending on the lender and the specific situation. But there's a broad range of potential guidelines and requirements that could factor into your home search. Real estate agents can help better target your search by focusing on properties that are likely to meet the VA's appraisal guidelines and lender requirements. The VA appraisal is meant to help veterans and service members purchase homes that are safe, sanitary, structurally sound and appropriately valued. We'll take a closer look at the VA appraisal process in the next chapter.

There are broad criteria that a VA-backed home must be measured against, known as "Minimum Property Requirements," or

MPRs.

Some of these property requirements include:

- Mechanical systems must be safe and have reasonable future utility
- Heating must be adequate
- Roofing must be adequate
- Crawl spaces and basements must be dry
- Property must be free of termites, dry rot and fungus growth
- Lead-based paint must be remediated

VA-savvy agents can help you immediately identify homes that might prove problematic for the VA appraisal process or lenders. To be sure, property condition problems don't mean a home is automatically out of reach. But many property condition issues will need to be repaired or otherwise addressed before the loan can close, which means sellers or buyers may have to spend additional money upfront to keep the deal alive.

In addition to the VA's property requirements, lenders can have their own standards that homes need to meet. That means some properties may not ultimately be eligible for financing from a particular lender, even if they otherwise meet VA guidelines.

It can be frustrating (and expensive) to get under contract on a home, pay for a home inspection and even an appraisal only to find out the property falls short of VA or lender guidelines. At that point, you have to decide whether it's worth it—or even possible—to move forward.

Different lenders and different locales can mean varying property requirements. But here are a few immediate red flags that could signal problems ahead with a particular home:

- **Condo Approvals**

We talked about condos in Chapter 3, but it's worth repeating: Condo developments need to be approved by the VA. Your lender or a VA-savvy real estate agent can help you determine if a development is already on the approved list. You can also check the VA's searchable condo database. Don't despair if you fall in love with a condo that isn't in an approved development. Your lender can ask the VA to approve a development that isn't on the list, but understand that process can take months to complete and isn't guaranteed to succeed.

- **Unique Properties**

If you have your eye on the A-frame home down the street, you may want to reconsider. A VA appraiser will use recent comparable home sales, or "**comps**," to help determine the value of a home. In the case of unique properties, the appraiser may have trouble finding similar homes that have sold recently. Lenders aren't likely to consider financing a purchase without at least one good recent comparable sale. Similarly, while there's no acreage limit with VA loans, properties with a lot of land can sometimes prove problematic in terms of finding good comps. Talk with your lender immediately if you're interested in a property that's in any way out of the ordinary.

- **Income-Producing Properties**

Properties that have income-producing attributes may be a problem for some VA lenders. Defining what constitutes an income-producing property can get tricky, but things like a working farm, a outbuilding with a shop or even a horse barn can all be problematic. Lenders are usually concerned about financial liabilities and liens when there's business crossover with your residence. It may not matter if you have no intention of using the property to make money. The income-producing attributes may need to be removed in order for the loan to close.

- **Homes Listed "As-Is"**

As-is properties may come with a bargain price-tag, but beware—it's common for these types of listings to have serious structural issues or deferred maintenance that the seller doesn't want to deal with. If an inspection or an appraisal turns up problems, these sellers aren't likely to cover the cost of any needed repairs. You'd either have to pay for the repairs yourself to keep your loan alive, if that's even possible, or move on to the next house on your list.

- **Major Improvements**

If the seller did any rehab work or made improvements to the home, make sure they (or their contractor) obtained all necessary permits. Building codes can vary by community, and not all renovations and home improvements require a permit from the local municipality. But if the seller failed to get a permit for work that requires one, you may have a headache on your hands. Non-permitted improvements can spell trouble on your VA appraisal report, and obtaining permits retroactively can be time-consuming. Look for the proper paper trail following any big home improvement projects.

- **Foundation Problems**

Cracks or other foundation issues can seriously affect the structural integrity of the home. These can also be expensive repairs. Foundation problems would need to be repaired before a loan could close, and whether the seller will make the repairs is often the question. Paying for foundation work on a property you hope to purchase may not be a wise investment.

- **Heating or Cooling Problems**

Working heating and cooling systems will be required in most parts of the country. The VA and lenders want to see a permanent heat source, which means space heaters and similar sources will not alone suffice. Homes with permanently installed non-electric, non-vented fireplaces or space heaters may be eligible, provided the buyer signs a "hold harmless" agreement and the unit meets applicable codes and has an approved oxygen depletion sensor.

- **Roof Problems**

The roof will need to be in good shape and have sufficient remaining economic life. Just how many years that needs to be can vary depending on the lender. The VA doesn't specify a certain number.

- **Historic Properties**

If a home's remaining economic life falls short of VA requirements, your purchase could be flagged as a risky investment. This could be problematic during the loan process. Older homes sometimes fail to meet other requirements as well. Stacked stone foundations, inadequate heating and cooling systems, lead paint and improper insulation are just a few things to look out for if you're in the market for an older home.

- **Buying Foreclosures or Short Sales**

A foreclosure occurs when a financial institution takes back a home from a borrower who's unable or unwilling to pay. A short sale is when a bank allows homeowners to sell their home for less than what's owed. Buyers can be drawn to the prospect of substantial discounts reflected in distressed properties. But buyers can pay a price for that discount, often in frustration and delays. Purchasing a bank-owned home can take considerably longer than a traditional home purchase.

Another challenge to consider: Every potential VA property must go through the VA appraisal process. Many distressed properties haven't been properly maintained and may fall short of the VA's Minimum Property Requirements. Some sellers are willing to make repairs to bring a home up to VA standards, but banks may have other priorities. Banks usually want a quick, hassle-free sale, so they often prefer to sell properties "as is."

Don't set your sights on a fixer-upper in foreclosure. Even though banks want to sell quickly, many won't make or allow repairs to their foreclosures. You may have more luck if your less-than-perfect home is a short sale property, as individual homeowners may be more willing to make needed improvements. You can also pursue an FHA 203k loan, which allows qualified borrowers to include money for repair and rehabilitation work.

Also, keep your expectations low if you've fallen in love with a wreck of a home. You can ask a bank to make repairs or even see if they'll allow you to do so, but be prepared for them to say no. Always have a backup plan in case the sale falls through, and don't pursue foreclosures in poor condition if you're on a strict timeline. Also, understand that it can take longer to finalize the purchase of a distressed property, so your homebuying journey may take longer. Adjust your schedule and your expectations accordingly.

Occupancy Requirements

The VA also has occupancy requirements that help keep the program's focus on primary residences. Service members who secure a VA purchase loan have to certify that they intend to personally occupy the property as their primary residence.

VA borrowers usually have a 60-day window after completing the loan process to move into the house. Requirements can differ on VA refinance loans.

Some homebuyers find that two months isn't enough time. The VA does allow buyers in certain situations to go beyond that 60-day mark, although occupancy delayed more than a year is generally unacceptable.

Here are a few common situations and possible outcomes:

Active duty borrower: Your spouse can fulfill the occupancy requirement. Lenders will typically take your travel and living expenses into account when evaluating your finances. That means including those costs into your DTI ratio and residual income calculations.

Married civilian borrower working overseas: A spouse can often fulfill the occupancy requirement in these situations. Lenders will consider your travel and living expenses.

Single civilian working overseas: This can be more challenging and depends on a number of factors. You may need to show that you'll be home significant portions of the year and have ties to the area. Lenders will consider travel and living expenses and likely want to verify who will care for the home in your absence.

Married civilian working in one state but looking to buy in another: This can also be challenging. Borrowers may need to show that they'll be occupying the new home sometime in the near future, or that they can't live with their family for reasons beyond their control. Lenders will also consider your travel and living expenses.

Single civilian working in one state but looking to buy in another: This scenario won't generally be acceptable to the VA or lenders.

Every occupancy scenario is different, and requirements and policies can differ among lenders. If you think you might have difficulty occupying a home within 60 days of closing, let your loan officer know as soon as possible. Depending on your unique situation, there may be an exception or a workaround.

Housing Grants for Disabled Veterans

Veterans and service members with service-connected disabilities can have distinct needs when it comes to housing. That can prove a challenge during the house-hunting stage. The VA has two grant programs that can help veterans with certain permanent and total service-connected disabilities build or modify a home to best meet their needs.

One is the Specially Adapted Housing (SAH) grant, and the other is the Special Housing Adaptation (SHA) grant. Renovations and modifications can include accessible bathrooms, bedrooms and kitchens; specially sized doorways; garages and carports; retrofitted faucets and showerheads; ramps and banisters; and a host of other important changes.

The maximum dollar amount available for these grants is set by law but can change annually depending on construction costs and other factors. Veterans interested in exploring the SAH and SHA grants can apply online through the eBenefits portal (www.ebenefits.va.gov) or contact their nearest VA regional office (1-800-827-1000) for more information.

Making an Offer

There are books, pamphlets and web pages galore dedicated to teaching borrowers how to negotiate with sellers for their dream home. They're all a bit beyond the scope here, but there is one thing that we would stress in particular: Lean on your real estate agent for help.

Real estate agents craft offers and negotiate contracts every month. Your opinion and gut are important here, but carefully consider their input and suggestions. It's ultimately up to you to determine where that first offer begins.

Here are a few broad considerations to bear in mind:

- **Due Diligence Done?**

Make sure you've done your homework. Verify the school information, property boundary lines and more. Visit the home and the neighborhood at different times of day. Scour local news sources and talk with your real estate agent or local officials regarding any pending changes to or near the property. You don't want to find out after closing that a factory or a four-lane highway is going up nearby.

- **Seller Motivation**

See what your agent can learn about the seller's motivations. Are they looking to sell because of that incoming factory or four-lane highway? Or maybe they're taking a new job and are desperate to unload the property. Other homeowners may be in no hurry and focused on getting the best possible offer. Getting insight into the seller's mindset and motivation can help strengthen your negotiating position.

- **Take a Close Look at "Comps"**

Before making an offer, you'll want to compare the sales prices of similar homes. Your real estate agent will handle the number crunching and prepare a "Comparative Market Analysis" (CMA). The CMA compares and contrasts the characteristics and sales prices of similar homes. It's an educated estimate of the fair market value of your future home and a great tool for picking a starting point for negotiations. Also look at how long the property has been on the market and what the sellers paid for it originally.

- **Start Where it Makes Sense**

You've already determined how much you want to spend on a home. Protect your financial future by sticking to this figure. Keep in mind that a first offer is seldom accepted, so you'll want to leave some wiggle room between your initial offer and your total housing budget. Rely on your agent's guidance and make a first offer that makes sense. You don't want to overpay for the home, but you also don't want to start with a lowball offer that poisons the negotiating environment.

- **Include Earnest Money**

We mentioned earnest money as an upfront cost of homebuying back in Chapter 2. This is basically a good-faith deposit many would-be buyers include with their offer. Some agents suggest depositing a small percentage of the sales price, while others recommend a flat amount ranging from $500 to $2,000. VA protections ensure that buyers get this money back if the deal falls through because of a low appraised value. But other situations and outcomes could jeopardize your deposit. Talk with your real estate agent about how best to proceed.

- **Protect Yourself With Contingencies**

VA buyers are required to have an appraisal. But that doesn't give you the same insight and protection as a home inspection. Make your purchase contingent on the results of a home inspection. These can reveal all sorts of costly problems, and you can use the results of the inspection to renegotiate with the seller or even walk away from the deal. Veterans and military members who currently own a home may want to add a home sale contingency that makes the new purchase contingent upon their ability to sell their old home.

- **Sell Yourself**

Some buyers include a photo and a handwritten letter that talks about why they love the home and their plans for it. This is more common in hotter markets and multiple-offer situations. Telling your story and sharing your dreams for the home can help personalize your offer and ensure it stands out. That personal touch can help clients in a bidding war, especially if their offer isn't the most competitive.

A purchase offer will feature your stipulations and contingencies. This is your way of saying, "I want to buy this house, but only if X, Y and Z happen." Your agent will have a good handle on what contingencies and specific requests you should include.

Some of the most common stipulations and contingencies include:

Purchase price: You detail to the exact dollar what you'll pay for the home.

Finance terms: Even if you've gone through preapproval, state in your offer that your purchase is contingent upon obtaining a VA loan at a specific interest rate. If you are unable to get a loan for some reason, you'll be able to pull out of the contract and get back your earnest money.

Closing date: You'll spell out the day you would like to close on the loan and take possession of the home. It's tempting to push for a quick closing, but it's a good idea to allow a cushion for delays or other issues. The most important thing is to set a date that's realistic. Also, be on the lookout for contract provisions that allow the sellers to charge a daily fee for delays in closing. Remember, too, that when your contract "expires" or reaches the agreed-upon close date, the seller is not obligated to grant an extension.

Window to respond: Some purchase offers will require sellers to respond within a certain period of time, otherwise the offer is void. You don't want to be left hanging for days while other properties come on and off the market. This also helps avoid a scenario where a seller uses your offer as a bargaining chip.

Home inspection: Most buyers want to make the purchase contingent on the results of a home inspection. Don't make the mistake of skipping an inspection to save money. A professional home inspection can reveal all sorts of costly problems that you will be unable to detect.

Existing home sale: Veterans and military members who currently own a home may want to make their new purchase contingent upon their ability to sell their old home.

Earnest money protection: Homebuyers will typically include a clause that requires the return of their earnest money in the event the home inspection turns up problems, financing falls through or some other unforeseen issue beyond their control occurs. VA loans automatically protect a buyer's earnest money if they walk away from a deal because the appraised value comes in below the purchase price (it's called the VA Amendment to Contract).

Seller to pay closing costs: A seller will often agree to pay some or all of a buyer's closing costs. Closing costs are the costs and fees associated with originating and finalizing your loan. On a VA purchase, buyers can ask a seller to pay all of their mortgage-related closing costs and up to 4 percent of the purchase price in concessions, which can cover things like prepaid taxes and insurance, paying off a buyer's collections or judgments and more. We'll take a look at closing costs next.

Closing Costs

Every mortgage comes with closing costs and related expenses. For many homebuyers, closing costs are one of the most confusing parts of this entire journey.

In fact, "closing costs" is really a catchall term. There are all different kinds of costs and fees that can be part of finalizing this process. In the mortgage world, you might also hear these referred to as "settlement charges." Some of these costs represent the actual costs of doing a loan. Others involve expenses like homeowners insurance and property taxes. Some need to be paid before you get to the closing table, while others can wait until that happy day arrives.

Your closing costs will vary depending on a host of factors, from your lender and loan type to the location and more. With VA loans, this program actually limits what buyers can pay in closing costs. In fact, there are certain costs and fees that VA buyers aren't allowed to pay.

Who pays what in closing costs and concessions is always up for negotiation. It's important to understand that sellers aren't obliged to pay any costs on your behalf. But you can always request that the sellers pay a portion or all of the closing costs when you're making a formal offer on a home. Let's first take a look at the different kinds of loan-related costs you're likely to encounter.

Here's a rundown of some of the common loan-related closing costs:

- **Origination charge**

The VA allows lenders to charge up to 1 percent of the loan amount to cover origination, processing and underwriting costs. They can choose to either charge you a flat 1 percent origination fee, or pick and choose among a host of fees, so long as they add up to no more than 1 percent. There are also some fees VA buyers aren't allowed to pay no matter the situation. Lenders charging this flat fee aren't allowed to tack on other fees for things like document or underwriting fees; escrow fees; attorney fees for non-title work; postage fees; and more. A non-allowable fee can't be charged unless the borrower's city, county or state requires it. In addition, there are a handful of costs that a VA buyer cannot pay, regardless of whether the lender is charging that flat fee. Those include the cost of a termite inspection (in all but nine states); a lender's attorney fees; mortgage broker fees; or prepayment penalties.

- **Appraisal fee**

VA buyers are required to get an appraisal. We cover the VA appraisal process in more detail in Chapter 6. Appraisals typically run about $425. The VA sets the costs for appraisals, not the lender. This is a cost buyers will have to pay upfront.

- **Title charges**

Title insurance protects lenders and homebuyers if liens, legal defects or other title-related issues are discovered after closing. Lenders will usually require the purchase of lender's title insurance, which only protects their interest in the property. You should strongly consider paying the one-time fee for owner's title insurance to ensure you're covered as well. Prices for title insurance vary. Homebuyers can negotiate with home sellers about paying these costs and shop around for policies.

- **Discount points**

Buyers can pay "points" to lower their interest rate. A point is equal to 1 percent of the loan amount. You'll also hear this called a "permanent buydown," because you're paying money upfront to buy a lower interest rate. This isn't something many VA buyers do, but it's an option and a loan-related cost. We'll take a closer look at interest rates and discount points later in this chapter.

- **Credit report**

Some lenders may charge a fee for accessing your credit information. Generally, the VA says this cost shouldn't exceed $50.

- **Well, septic and termite inspection fees**

Buyers may need some or all of these depending on the property. VA buyers in all but nine states aren't allowed to pay the termite inspection fee, which in most cases is covered by the seller.

Now, here's a look at some of the common closing costs not directly related to obtaining a home loan:

- **Taxes and insurance**

This involves prepayment of your property taxes and homeowners insurance, which you might hear referred to in the context of an "escrow account." Your local municipality will levy property taxes on an annual basis. You'll also be responsible for paying for homeowners insurance. At least a portion of these annual bills will be due at closing.

- **Daily interest charges**

Your mortgage is paid in arrears, meaning your monthly payment actually covers the previous month you lived in the home. So if you close in mid-September, your first mortgage payment wouldn't typically be due until November 1. But lenders will collect prepaid interest on the loan between your closing date and the end of the month you close. Lenders calculate it as a per-day rate (yearly interest cost/365 days per year = one day of interest payment). That prepayment is due at the closing table.

- **Recording fees**

State and local governments charge a fee to record your deed and mortgage-related documents. Some of the details of your real estate transaction will become public records, accessible to anyone in your community and beyond.

- **Homeowners Association (HOA) fees**

There may be costs and fees associated with closing a loan on a property in a homeowners association.

- **Home Warranty fees**

There may be a fee involved with obtaining a home warranty on a property. These policies will often cover the cost of certain repairs during the first year you own the home.

- **Real estate commissions**

The listing agent and the buyer's agent will often split a predetermined commission that reflects a percentage of the home's sale price. Sellers typically cover this cost at closing.

One of the big benefits of VA loans is that sellers can pay all of your loan-related closing costs. Again, they're not required to pay any of them, so this will always be a product of negotiation between buyer and seller. In addition, you can ask the seller to pay up to 4 percent of the purchase price in "concessions," which can cover those non-loan-related costs and more. VA broadly defines seller concessions as "anything of value added to the transaction by the builder or seller for which the buyer pays nothing additional and which the seller is not customarily expected or required to pay or provide."

Some of the most common seller concessions include:

- Having a seller cover your prepaid taxes and insurance costs
- Having a seller provide credits for items left behind in the home, like a pool table or a riding lawn mower
- Having a seller pay off your collections, judgments or lease termination fees at closing

In some respects, as long as you stick to that 4 percent cap, the sky's the limit when it comes to asking for concessions.

VA buyers are also subject to the VA Funding Fee. This is a set fee applied to every purchase loan or refinance. The proceeds go directly to the VA and help cover losses on the loans that go into default. The fee changes slightly depending on the down payment amount, whether the borrower has a prior VA loan and the nature of the borrower's service. Surviving spouses and buyers who receive VA compensation for a service-connected disability are exempt from paying this fee.

Here's a breakdown of the VA Funding Fee for Regular Military:

Down payment	Funding Fee (1st use)	Funding Fee (2nd use)
None	2.15 percent	3.3 percent
5-10 percent	1.5 percent	1.5 percent
10 and up	1.25 percent	1.25 percent

The percentages shift slightly for members of the Reserves and the National Guard:

Down payment	Funding Fee (1st use)	Funding Fee (2nd use)
None	2.4 percent	3.3 percent
5-10 percent	1.75 percent	1.75 percent
10 and up	1.5 percent	1.5 percent

The funding fee is the only closing cost VA buyers can roll on top of their loan balance, and that's how most borrowers approach this fee. You could ask the seller to pay it, but doing so would count against the 4 percent concessions cap. The other potential approach would be to ask the seller to lower the purchase price by whatever the fee totals.

One of the early questions many borrowers have is: What are my closing costs? It's an important question for a lot of reasons. Many VA buyers want or need the seller to pay at least some of these costs, if not all of them. And that means asking for a specific percentage or dollar amount in your purchase offer.

Where things can get confusing is that lenders can only give you a rough estimate until you've zeroed in on a property. That's in part because they'll need the property address in order to estimate things like homeowners insurance, property taxes and more. Some lenders will provide a "fees worksheet" or some other document to help give you a broad idea of closing costs. Other times, a loan officer might provide a rough estimate based on other recent purchases in that community.

But you won't get an official estimate of your closing costs until a lender has a full application that includes information on your income, your credit and a specific property address. Once a lender has that application in hand, they're legally required to send you some key documents and disclosures within three business days. One of the most important is the Loan Estimate.

This is a relatively new document that came out of the banking and mortgage industry reforms following the housing crisis. Governmental and industry officials have worked diligently over the last few decades to prevent unscrupulous lenders from fleecing borrowers. Fees, costs and charges shouldn't be a mystery to consumers. But there's a sordid history of bait-and-switch tactics and under-the-table kickbacks that spring unexpected costs on homebuyers just before their deal gets done. Thankfully, those days are over, mostly because of new regulations and the updated disclosures.

There are always going to be costs and fees associated with your loan. Loan officers, loan processors, receptionists, executives and anyone else who works for a mortgage company expects to get paid. But homebuyers have a right to know, upfront, how much they're expected to pay and for what.

The new Loan Estimate replaced two longtime federal forms, the Good Faith Estimate and the initial Truth-in-Lending statement. The Loan Estimate offers a detailed picture of the loan's costs and fees along with some of its key features.

The Loan Estimate will include:

- A closer look at the loan amount, the interest rate and the monthly principal and interest payments of the loan
- Your projected monthly payments over the life of the loan
- A detailed breakdown of your estimated loan-related closing costs, such as origination charges, appraisal fees, title insurance and more
- A detailed breakdown of other estimated costs to close, such as prepaid taxes, homeowners insurance and interest charges
- A total estimate for how much cash you'll need to close, including the down payment amount

- Information about your borrowing costs, annual percentage rate (APR) and total interest percentage (TIP) that you can use to compare with other loan offers
- Information about appraisals, assumptions, late fees, loan servicing and more

Along with your Loan Estimate, the lender will identify what closing-related services you can shop for and include a list of companies you might consider. Some of these services can include things like title work, closing agents and homeowners insurance. Regarding the services for which you can shop, you're not required to use any of the companies identified by the lender.

The Loan Estimate is ultimately an estimate, and that means some of the projected costs can change. But there are limits on what charges can and cannot increase and by how much.

With the Loan Estimate, you'll have a good look at the estimated costs needed to get into your new home. That's critical information when you're making an offer and asking a seller to cover some or all of your closing costs. You need to know what to ask them for, right?

This is why it's so important for VA buyers to get preapproved and to talk with their lender before making an offer on a home. The sooner you and your real estate agent communicate with your lender about a specific property, the faster they can prepare a Loan Estimate. And that helps ensure you ask for the right amount of closing costs and concessions in your offer.

To be sure, every purchase situation is different. If you're in a hot real estate market or there are multiple offers on a property, you may not have time to wait for a Loan Estimate to be issued. Talk with your real estate agent and your lender about how best to proceed.

Sellers often realize they need to engage in some give-and-take in order to sell their property. But not all markets are competitive, and not all sellers are motivated.

Sellers aren't required to pay any of your closing costs. Even if the VA doesn't allow a buyer to pay for something, that doesn't automatically mean it's up to the seller. So what happens if the seller refuses to cover some or any of your closing costs?

Talk with your real estate agent and your lender about your options. You may be able to increase your purchase offer by the amount of your closing costs. For example, let's say you're buying at $150,000 and your closing costs are $5,000. You may be able to increase your offer to $155,000 and have the seller use those proceeds to cover your closing costs. They still net the same $150,000 in this example. One of the challenges with this approach is making sure the home appraises for the higher amount. Lenders will lend whichever is less between the purchase price and the property's appraised value. The other challenge is making sure you can afford the higher amount. You should also understand that this scenario means you're effectively paying these closing costs with interest over the life of the loan, because you're borrowing more money.

You also may be able to have the lender cover these costs. To do so, you'll usually have to take a higher interest rate. You may also be able to use gift funds from a family member or close relation.

Negotiating With Sellers

Once you've finalized your purchase offer, the details are presented to the seller in a contract. By signing off on the contract, you're legally committing to purchase the home, provided all the conditions are met.

But it's rare for an initial contract to be accepted. Usually your first offer is the starting point for negotiations with the seller. The items up for debate include price, costs to be covered by the seller, repairs to be completed and the closing date, among others.

Each offer can take one of three routes:

Acceptance: The seller agrees to each item presented in the contract, and the parties move ahead to loan processing, underwriting and closing.

Counteroffer: When sellers make a counteroffer, they're usually showing interest but looking to tweak the terms. A seller's counteroffer will suggest changes to the original offer, such as a higher price or quicker closing date. Once prepared, the counteroffer is sent back to the buyer's agent. Buyers have the option to accept the counteroffer, counter the counteroffer or simply walk away from the deal.

Rejection: A seller can reject your initial offer outright. Some sellers take this route when an offer is unnecessarily low or contains unrealistic terms. In this situation, buyers are free to make another offer to the seller or to move on to a new property.

The negotiation process continues until an agreement is made or until one party decides to walk away. If you're headed into the negotiation process, keep a level head. Real estate negotiations can be tough, even for seasoned real estate agents.

Maintain calm, and avoid making these mistakes during negotiations:

- **Failing to understand the seller's motivations**

See what your agent can learn about the owner's reasons for selling. It's common for owners to want to sell their homes as quickly as possible, but some may be especially anxious to do so. Perhaps the seller has already purchased another home and is struggling to pay both mortgages. Maybe the owner wants to complete the sale prior to a new school year. You may be able to use the seller's motivation to your advantage when negotiating.

- **Not having options**

Even if you fall in love with the first home you tour, it's in your best interest to continue looking at homes. You don't want to enter negotiations with the opinion that you simply "must" have a particular home. That philosophy could put you in a weaker position than your seller. Your emotions will probably be running high, but you can keep them in check with a backup plan. If negotiations fall through, you can either resort to your backup or resume your house hunt. Rest assured there's another home out there that's a great fit for you.

- **Trying to "win"**

During the heat of negotiations, it's easy to see the seller as "the bad guy." It's very common for a buyer to feel that defeating the seller is more important than getting a good contract in place. Don't turn negotiations into a battle of egos. Do your best to remember that you're making an investment, not preparing for a boxing match. A seller often has the same motivations that a buyer does, namely to get the best deal possible. Don't take it personally if the seller won't agree to all of your requests. If the home is within your budget, it meets your specifications and you're excited about being the new owner, you can probably let a few demands slide.

- **Failing to show that you're preapproved**

Don't forget to let your seller know that you are a qualified buyer. Many real estate contracts fall through because a buyer is unable to get financing. For this reason, sellers are often hesitant to work with a buyer who hasn't been preapproved. Make sure your agent notes your preapproval status in your initial offer. Sellers may be more willing to work with a buyer who's a safe bet to close.

Lean on your real estate agent for help when it comes to navigating the negotiating process. Try to be flexible without compromising your budget or your needs, and don't be afraid to ask for help.

Power of Attorney

Power of Attorney (POA) is a familiar concept for many VA buyers. This is a legal tool that allows you to designate someone who can enter into contracts on your behalf. Power of Attorney helps ensure that deployed service members and other veterans who can't be present to sign documents can still use their VA home loan benefit.

There are a couple different paths that the VA and lenders can take, and your unique circumstances will likely determine whether you need a General or a Specific POA.

General Power of Attorney is, well, general in nature. It gives your assigned agent the power to handle a bunch broad needs on your behalf, from filing taxes and making banking transactions to signing contracts.

There are two scenarios that allow VA buyers to use a General POA. The first is that buyer is able to sign the initial loan application and the purchase agreement. It doesn't matter if they're not able to sign other documents as the loan process moves forward. If they can sign these two early documents, you can use General POA.

The other scenario is the buyer isn't able to sign those initial documents, but they are able to sign all of the closing documents. This setup also allows buyers to use General POA. In either case, lenders may consider electronic signatures acceptable.

You'll need to use a Specific POA if the buyer is unable to meet the requirements for a General POA. Specific POA is also known as limited Power of Attorney. It's limited because the agent is only allowed to execute on a very specific issue, like, say, a VA home loan for one particular property address.

Lenders may have their own guidelines. At Veterans United, we need a Specific POA with details about the property, the price and some other important information.

In order to move forward with a VA purchase, your Specific POA must contain the following information:

- Purpose: Clearly expressed intent to obtain a loan to purchase a home
- Property Identification: Clear identification of the subject property for the transaction
- Price and Terms: Clearly outline the sales price (if applicable), total loan amount and any other relevant terms to the transaction

- Occupancy: Clearly identify the veteran's intent to occupy the property
- Entitlement: A lender may require clearly expressed intent to use all or a specified amount of entitlement

Regardless of the type of POA you use, lenders will need to verify that the military member or veteran is alive and, if on active duty, not missing in action. This "alive and well" statement can be a simple phone call or email to your loan officer on the day of closing or a formal letter from a supervisor.

Finalizing the Deal

As with any contract, there's no guarantee the seller will sign off on your proposed stipulations, but reasonable ones are always worth a shot. The most important thing is to ensure you're protected financially as much as possible.

That's why having an attorney look over the purchase agreement can be an important step. In general, attorneys play varying roles in the homebuying process, often depending on where you're purchasing. Some states require that attorneys examine and OK all mortgage papers before a transaction can be official. Others have no mandate and allow buyers and sellers to navigate the process themselves.

This is typically a cost borne by the veteran and not something you can roll into the cost of the loan or expect the seller to cover. Military buyers may not need to spend the extra cash when it's a straightforward, relatively no-nonsense purchase agreement. But if things start to get confusing or loaded with contingencies and clauses, it's certainly something to consider.

Once the purchase agreement is hammered out, agreed upon and signed, it's time to celebrate, albeit cautiously. Getting under contract doesn't mean you've bought yourself a house.

One thing a signed contract does mean, though, is that you can now lock in your interest rate. Lenders will quote you an interest rate when you begin the prequalification and preapproval process. But you can't set that rate in stone until you've signed a purchase agreement. Until then, you have a "floating" interest rate, meaning it can go up or down before closing.

Let's take a closer look at interest rates.

A Primer on Interest Rates

The interest rate on your home mortgage reflects a lot of things, not the least of which is simply the current cost of borrowing money.

It can be staggering for first-time buyers to stop and consider just how much they'll spend over the course of three decades. Depending on the rate, that $300,000 home can easily wind up costing more than twice that after 30 years of principal and interest payments. Such is the cost of borrowing a big pile of money.

For the first decade or so, the majority of a buyer's monthly mortgage payments are dedicated to paying down the interest. You don't start biting into the principal for years, which is why making an additional payment each month toward your principal can shave years and thousands of dollars off the life of your mortgage.

From Day One, the loan officer may be talking about the need to lock in at a certain interest rate. We'll talk about rate locks and how they work shortly. First, it's important to understand how interest rates are determined and what role loan officers play in issuing a final interest rate for borrowers.

One of the first things a loan officer will mention is that interest rates are constantly in flux. And that's certainly true. Interest rates change all the time based on a host of economic indicators and factors.

It's important to understand that the VA doesn't set interest rates. Lenders set their own rates, based in part on what's happening in the mortgage bond market. Rates can change multiple times in a single day, and two different lenders may quote you two very different rates.

But lenders don't just randomly pick rates each day. Nor do they cause them to change. Instead, the ebb and flow of rates depends on a few key things, including:

The Federal Reserve

The Fed, as it's called, is charged with managing the nation's monetary policy and trying to spur maximum economic growth while curbing inflation. The body sets the federal funds rate, which dictates the cost of short-term lending among banks. The Fed adjusts the rate depending on the health and vitality of the national economy. When this rate is low, mortgage interest rates are low.

The Secondary Mortgage Market

Lenders may sell some or all of their home loans to mortgage investors and government-sponsored enterprises in the secondary mortgage market, which we talked about earlier. These investors pool together a bunch of loans into mortgage-backed securities or sometimes simply tuck the loans away among their holdings. Securities are sold to Wall Street investment firms and others.

Supply and Demand

Invariably it's bond market investors who wind up shaping interest rates. The rate of return on their bond investments, also known as a yield, depends in large part on the state of the economy. If the economy is booming, that probably means the rate of return will be better down the road than at present. That, in turn, drives down demand for low-yield loans. And that, in turn, means lenders have to increase the rate of return to attract investors. They do that, of course, by passing on the cost to consumers. Run that whole scenario backward and that's how interest rates decline.

So, it's this swirling free market free-for-all that ultimately helps determine interest rates on a given day. Lenders set their rates based on what's happening in the bond market. In particular, rates for VA loans are tied to mortgage-backed securities guarantied by Ginnie Mae, a government-owned enterprise separate from Fannie Mae and Freddie Mac.

Mortgage lending is a competitive arena. Lenders employ folks who spend their days tracking bond prices and economic events that might influence pricing. It's here, in what's essentially the lender's rate department, that a rate sheet is compiled, sometimes more than once a day depending on what's happening in the markets.

With the start of the day, the rate department—you might hear it called the secondary department—will watch how Ginnie Mae bonds fare in the early going and adjust rates accordingly. They can shift rates again during the middle and at the end of each day depending on the market. Those rates are distributed to the lender's loan officers. In today's environment, many computerized loan programs showcase these rates on screen, giving the loan officer ready access to what's available.

Mortgage Industry Reforms

The conversation about interest rates and how borrowers encounter them looks a little different today than it did a few years ago.

The reason is that major changes continue to take root in the mortgage industry, the fruits of sweeping legislation passed in 2010. One change is a shift in the way mortgage brokers and loan officers are paid. Another big one is the creation of a new classification of mortgages, known as Qualified Mortgages, or QM, and a new regulatory body to oversee the industry (the Consumer Financial Protection Bureau).

Government regulators believe the changes will in part help consumers more accurately compare lenders and eliminate the practice of steering borrowers into less beneficial loans for the sake of higher commissions.

First, let's talk briefly about the new era of Qualified Mortgages.

This new class of mortgages is all about safety and affordability, two long-time hallmarks of the historic VA loan program.

Throughout the 2000s, some lenders made a ton of money providing home loans to people with poor credit and no realistic chance of repaying the loan. Those shaky loans played a major role in the financial crisis and ensuing collapse of the housing market.

In the aftermath, Congress sought a way to protect consumers and the economy at large. One of the results was the creation of the Qualified Mortgage. These loans are devoid of riskier features and meet a set of requirements aimed at ensuring the borrower can afford the loan they're getting. Mortgages that meet the QM requirement will also help shield lenders from claims that they put a borrower into a bad loan all but destined for default.

Qualified Mortgages, by definition, can't include any of the following:

- A period where the borrower pays only interest on the loan and nothing toward the principal, known as an interest-only loan
- Something known as "negative amortization," which occurs when your payment fails to cover all of the interest due, leading your principal balance to actually increase over time
- Balloon payments, where you're required to pay off the loan in one lump sum payment after a certain number of years
- Loan terms beyond 30 years

In addition, regulators laid out a set of eight credit and underwriting requirements that must be met in order for a loan to obtain Qualified Mortgage status. These requirements are the heart of what's called the Ability to Repay (ATR) rule. Most lenders have been using some or all of these requirements for a long time.

The Ability to Repay's eight financial metrics are:

- Current income or assets
- Current employment status

- Credit history
- Monthly mortgage payment
- Monthly payments on other mortgages
- Monthly payments for mortgage-related expenses, such as property taxes
- Current debt obligations, including things like child support or alimony
- Your monthly debt-to-income (DTI) ratio

These are common sense requirements that reputable lenders have employed for a long time. Veterans United has utilized these eight requirements for years, long before a legislative call to make them mandatory. Thoroughly documenting all eight of these is one of the pillars of a Qualified Mortgage, along with the absence of the risky features mentioned above.

There are a handful of other requirements in order for a loan to be considered QM. In most cases, costs and fees can't exceed 3 percent of the loan amount. There's also a maximum DTI ratio, but for most loans—including those backed by the Department of Veterans Affairs—this cap won't be part of the equation, at least anytime soon. Loans that already qualify for purchase or guaranty by a government entity (Fannie Mae, Freddie Mac, FHA, USDA, VA) are currently presumed to be Qualified Mortgages.

Given that background, the question is: What's it all mean for VA home loans and military borrowers?

Overall, there really shouldn't be much impact. This kind of safe, prudent underwriting has been part of the VA program for years, and it shows. VA loans have had the lowest foreclosure rate of any loan on the market for nearly all of the last six years. The financial requirements you need to meet for most VA lenders won't change, because they're already taking a long, hard look at all eight of the Ability to Repay requirements.

Borrowers will get some added protections. Many lenders that weren't already using these requirements will likely adopt the safer course. There will also be limits on the costs and fees associated with obtaining a mortgage.

And here's where we finally circle back to interest rates.

The wave of new regulations has also altered the compensation landscape for mortgage brokers and loan officers who want to originate Qualified Mortgages. In short, they can no longer be paid based on the costs and fees they charge, the interest rate or the loan's overall profitability.

The discussion can quickly become complicated. Let's start with a basic rundown of how borrowers secure rates and how brokers are paid under the old model.

Yield Spread and the Old Way of Doing Business

Borrowers qualify for a certain "par rate" at a given lender based on their unique financial and credit situation. You might also hear it called a base rate.

But borrowers aren't going to hear words like "par rate" or "base rate" from a prospective lender. Instead, they will get a rate quote that includes what is essentially a lender's mark-up.

As we talked about before, financial institutions may buy and sell loans on the secondary mortgage market. In that marketplace, mortgages with higher interest rates are worth more than those with lower rates.

The financial institution purchasing the loan actually compensates lenders that lock borrowers into interest rates above the par rate. That compensation, essentially a rebate, is known as Yield Spread Premium, or Yield Spread, and it's at the heart of some of these regulatory changes.

Let's stop for a second and look at a sample rate sheet, which should help illustrate the concept:

Rate	15 Day	30 Day
7.375	103.415	103.312
7.25	103.359	103.261
7.125	103.124	103.031
7	102.82	102.733
6.875	102.569	102.486
6.75	102.34	102.263
6.625	102.125	102.053
6.5	101.77	101.703
6.375	101.314	101.252
6.25	100.986	100.929
6.125	100.592	100.541
6	100.118	100.072
5.875	99.591	99.55
5.75	99.163	99.128
5.625	98.67	98.64
5.5	98.075	98.05
5.375	97.4	97.38
5.25	96.81	96.795

The 15-day and 30-day headings refer to rate locks, which we'll cover later in this chapter. Most rate locks involve 30- or 45-day terms, so we'll focus on the 30-day column. In this example, 6 percent is as close as we can get to a true par rate (100.072 at a 30-day rate lock).

Notice that for every interest rate above 6 percent, there's a corresponding (and higher) rate of compensation, or yield spread. As an example, let's use this rate sheet and say the borrower wants a $300,000 loan. A lender that quotes a rate of 6.125 percent stands to make 0.541 percent of the loan amount in yield spread. In dollars, that translates to $1,623 ($300,000 x 0.00541). At 6.5 percent, the yield spread jumps to 1.703, or $5,109 ($300,000 x 0.01703).

There's no hard and fast standard, but consumers could generally assume, at least under this old structure, that lenders are looking to make 2.0 to 2.5 percent in Yield Spread. On a $300,000 loan, that's about $6,000. The lender is free to quote the borrower any rate on the sheet, but the higher the rate, the greater the compensation.

Borrowers don't pay Yield Spread Premium per se. Financial institutions that sell home loans to your VA lender are responsible for paying that cost. But borrowers wind up paying more in the form of a higher rate. Taking a higher interest rate isn't necessarily a bad thing. Some borrowers may not have the cash on hand to cover up-front fees and costs associated with the loan closing. A borrower could elect to take a higher rate and have the lender use part of that yield spread rebate to pay those costs.

But what's to stop the loan officer from quoting every customer a 7.25 percent rate?

Nothing, at least in theory.

Mortgage lending is a hyper-competitive arena. Lenders and loan officers know that most borrowers are shopping around and comparing rates. Charging exorbitant rates to rack up huge yield spreads isn't much of a strategy for creating competitive advantage. Loan officers have to strike an appropriate balance between putting food on their tables and catering to the needs of choosy consumers.

And what about the rates below 6 percent?

Remember that the par rate is the breakeven point. Lenders *get paid* for a rate above par but *have to pay* for a rate below. Needless to say, lenders aren't in the habit of discounting mortgage loans or picking up the tab for a lower interest rate.

But that doesn't mean the borrower can't. We'll cover that shortly.

Changes to Broker Compensation and Rates

Under this type of compensation structure, loan officers would typically get a percentage of the total fees earned from the client and the Yield Spread. After the mortgage crisis, housing regulators decided it was time to sever the link between what borrowers pay and what loan officers make.

The new Qualified Mortgage regulations no longer allow loan originators to make Yield Spread Premium. There's no longer any direct financial incentive for them to lock borrowers into higher interest rates.

Today, it's increasingly common to see loan originators paid a base salary, with commissions possible depending on the size of the loan, their overall production and other factors. Lenders who sell their loans on the secondary market can still earn a rebate, but that money cannot trickle down to individual loan officers.

Understanding yield spread and loan originator compensation is important for service members on a couple different levels.

The first is that mortgage lending is a specialized, service-oriented business. It's easy for consumers to get riled up when they first learn about yield spread and the concept of compensation. Perhaps our natural inclination is to look at rebates like this as something illicit.

But loan officers and other key employees have to earn a living, and the longstanding method for compensating industry folks is through commissions. It isn't a novel concept in the world of business. These dedicated people navigate borrowers through the process of purchasing a home. They certainly deserve to be paid for it.

The second reason this is important: Yield Spread and this old compensation structure didn't just disappear. Loan officers originating loans that aren't classified as Qualified Mortgages can still utilize these rebates. QM loans are becoming the norm, but there will certainly be companies making non-QM loans to borrowers who need or want them.

So what does this all mean for interest rates?

Borrowers might be less likely to see wide variation moving forward. Lenders are going to quote you a rate based on a host of factors, which can include your credit score, a down payment if you're making one and their own in-house guidelines. But loan officers won't be looking to lock you into a higher rate to boost their own payday.

Negotiating a Rate

Now you're armed with a basic understanding of how rates and costs work. The question then becomes: What can I do with it?

You can't call up a lender and order a rate. It's not exactly a drive-through window. Veterans and service members should take the time to shop around and compare rates. While lenders aren't likely to give you the par rate, you can probably come up with a pretty good sense of it by gathering enough quotes. Feel free to push and prod when necessary. Remember that companies compete on rates and use that to your advantage.

Be specific when putting the question to mortgage folks. Instead of asking, "What are your rates today?" be more pointed: "What is the current rate on a 30-year fixed-rate VA loan with no buydown points?"

Look for any inch of leverage you can find. If you've got great credit, this is the time to trumpet your top-tier score. Does Lender X have a better rate or lower upfront fees? Be sure to point that out to

Lenders Y and Z. Some lenders are willing to come down and meet competitors on rates and fees—and even exceed them—in a tough market.

There's another option for folks who would rather avoid the phone calls, the homework and the potential haggling. Retail banks, credit unions and similar lending institutions tend to operate on a non-negotiable level. They may offer borrowers a flat, take-it-or-leave-it retail rate, which is typically higher than what you're able to get elsewhere. Also, remember that some banks and lenders do more VA loans than others. As we've talked about before, that experience and expertise can make a big difference.

The other important consideration with interest rates is they don't tell the whole story when it comes to financing. When you're comparison-shopping among different mortgage lenders, you shouldn't just look at the interest rate. You'll want to compare both the note rate and the annual percentage rate, or APR, as well. The APR considers your interest rate along with any other costs and fees associated with financing the purchase. In some cases, it can be a better representation of the overall costs of borrowing money. The APR will be disclosed in the Loan Estimate you receive from a lender.

Your interest rate and your APR aren't likely to be the same. Again, that's because the APR factors in the other costs and fees associated with the loan. When shopping around, focus on the big picture—the interest rate, the APR and closing cost estimates—to ensure you get a truly accurate comparison.

Discount Points

One element of the old order of business that isn't supposed to change is that borrowers can shell out money up front to purchase a lower interest rate. This is the concept of paying discount points, or a purchasing a permanent buydown. A discount point is 1 percent of the total loan amount. One point on a $300,000 loan is $3,000.

Lenders are allowed to apply standard fees to most mortgage loans. On a VA loan, the lender can charge an origination fee of 1 point plus up to two additional discount points (as long as the lender isn't earning Yield Spread).

For an example, let's return to the sample rate sheet. Let's say the lender gave you the option of a 6.25 percent rate with no points or a rate of 5.75 percent with 2 points. On a $300,000 mortgage, two discount points would cost the borrower $6,000. It's important to note this isn't a cost that can be rolled into the loan. You have to pay points up front. Or the seller can pay.

So are the points worth it? There's a relatively simple way to find out. On our example $300,000 loan, the monthly principal and interest payment at 6.25 percent is $1,847. At a 5.75 percent interest rate, the monthly principal and interest payment dips to $1,751. That's a difference of $96 per month, which is no small sum for many homebuyers, especially veterans with families.

Then again, $6,000 isn't exactly a small sum either. Here's a better way to gauge the investment: Divide the $6,000 in points by the $96 in monthly savings. That gives you 62.5, which is the number of months it will take you to "pay off" those points. So, in this example, it would take the veteran a little over five years to recoup that upfront investment.

Paying points isn't a common occurrence for many military homebuyers. VA borrowers typically come to the table without the kind of resources it takes to muster a big, one-time payment to buy down an interest rate. These are no-down payment loans that maximize buying power and help service members without significant financial resources become thriving homeowners. In many cases, coming up with the cash necessary to pay points is all but impossible.

Veterans who have cash reserves can certainly crunch the numbers and consider whether the upfront cost of paying points is worth the monthly savings over the life of the loan. Remember, too, that VA loans tend to have lower average interest rates than both conventional and FHA loans.

Temporary Buydown

Veterans may also be able to pay points to temporarily buy down their interest rate. The two most common temporary buydowns are the 3-2-1 buydown and the 2-1 buydown.

With a 3-2-1 buydown, the borrower's interest rate drops 3 percent below the note rate for the first year, 2 percent for the second year and 1 percent for the third year. The start of the fourth year marks the first year the borrower pays at the regular, full note rate.

Temporary buydowns can be a good option for borrowers on the edge. A lower initial interest rate means borrowers have more cash to pay down debt or take other steps to strengthen their financial position. That extra income can also allow borrowers with a higher debt-to-income ratio to qualify for a home they might not otherwise be able to land. Of course, temporary buydowns come with a cost. Here's a quick example of how to calculate it.

Let's assume you're considering a 2-1 buy down on a 30-year, $200,000 mortgage at 6.5 percent interest. Find an online mortgage calculator that gives you a full amortization breakdown for your loan. Brett Whissel maintains an excellent one at www.bretwhissel.net/cgi-bin/amortize. Plug in the numbers and add up how much interest you'll pay in the first year (at 4.5 percent), in the second year (at 5.5 percent) and in the third and remaining years (at 6.5 percent). It should look something like this:

Interest Rate	Interest Costs
4.5 percent	$8,934
5.5 percent	$10,932
6.5 percent	$12,934

After just a quick glance, you can already see that the lender is losing money by allowing you to buy down the rate for the first two years. A borrower with a regular fixed-rate mortgage at 6.5 percent would pay $25,718 during those first two years. Instead, with a temporary buydown the borrower is paying only $19,866 in interest ($8,934 + $10,932). Here's where the cost to the borrower comes in.

Looking at the numbers, the lender effectively loses out on $5,852 in interest because of the temporary buydown ($25,718-19,866). Lenders don't like to lose money. So they take that difference ($5,852) and divide it into the overall loan amount (which, in this case, is $200,000). That gives you 0.2926, which becomes 2.93 points that the borrower has to pay the lender to receive the buydown. On a $200,000 loan, that comes out to $5,840 that the borrower has to come up with to close the loan.

Borrowers without that kind of cash on hand can ask the lender to kick up the interest rate a bit and roll those costs into the life of the loan. Either way, it's not as if the borrower is getting a huge financial break with a buydown. They still pay. It's just a question of how and when.

Not every lender offers temporary buydowns, and they're not terribly common among military buyers. In fact, buyer-paid temporary buydowns are disappearing because of the new Qualified Mortgage regulations, which limit costs and fees.

Locking a Rate

Loan officers will talk a lot at the outset about locking into a great rate. But what exactly does that mean?

Well, it's not just an expression. A rate lock is a legal commitment that binds a borrower to a specific interest rate. Borrowers can typically lock their interest rate as soon as they sign a purchase agreement and up to five days before the loan closing. Rate locks are good for specific blocks of time. The most common lock periods are for 15 days, 30 days, 45 days and 60 days.

Getting locked into an interest rate is a serious step. It can also prove to be a savvy and wise decision if interest rates climb as your closing date nears.

There's no mathematical formula or chart to consult to help veterans determine when they should lock an interest rate. Just as rates can climb before a closing, they can also fall. Talk about a frustrating feeling.

This is another area where having a trusted lender is key. So is doing some homework on your own. Look at how rates have performed the previous few months. Dig around online and garner predictions and information from credible outlets about what rates are likely to do in the coming weeks and months.

You've ultimately got two choices: Lock or float. To float means you're going to hold off and watch rates as your closing nears. Some lenders will charge borrowers to lock in a rate, especially if it's for a lock term beyond 30 days. But not every lender charges a lock fee. It's a good question to ask your loan officer up front.

Borrowers who decide to float can count on a good loan officer keeping them abreast of rate news and predictions. Loan officers who sense that rates are on the verge of rising will usually contact their borrowers to let them know it might be time to lock. Other times, borrowers basically give their loan officer the freedom to lock a rate at his or her discretion, typically when rates appear headed for an increase.

No matter what, getting something in writing is crucial when it comes to rate locks. Conversations and oral commitments are about as useful as an umbrella in a hurricane. Once you decide on a rate, you should receive written confirmation that includes all the pertinent information you need: the rate, the dates and length of the lock, any fees and points and anything else that's relevant to your loan. Check the fine print with these rate commitments, too.

Borrowers can also purchase extensions on their rate locks if delays occurring during the closing process. Rate lock extensions usually come with a minimal cost depending on the duration.

Now, you might have to agree to a rate cap depending on the lender. Some borrowers would certainly argue that these are shady provisions by another name. But rate caps are relatively common tools that lenders use to insulate themselves. Basically, a rate cap gives the lender the right to give you a slightly higher interest rate if they rise before your closing.

New laws passed in 2010 require full disclosure to the borrower if the rate changes by more than an eighth of a point from the time of initial disclosure to closing.

You can also try to get an option added to your rate lock commitment that allows you to take advantage of a decrease in rates. Not all lenders allow these conditional commitments, and those that do tend to charge a premium for the service. And, in some cases, this option can backfire on a borrower if rates increase.

Any talk about rate locks inevitably leads to a single word: When?

Unfortunately, it doesn't come with a one-word answer. Obsessing over a rate lock can drive borrowers crazy. It's tough on loan officers, too.

Be an informed consumer. Stay in constant contact with your loan officer. Other than that, when to lock your rate depends on a host of factors that are often unique to the individual buyer. Look at your finances and crunch the numbers on an array of interest rates. You might decide it's worth floating if interest rates appear to be headed down (and you can afford a slightly higher payment if they don't).

Perhaps the best advice is simple common sense: Lock when you're completely comfortable with the rate environment and don't look back. Second guessing and obsessing isn't going to help anyone, and the days and weeks leading to a home closing can be stressful enough as it is. If something weird happens and rates take a huge nosedive, call your loan officer for a frank discussion. There's no guarantee they'll cut you a break, mainly because you're cutting into their commission.

One tactic that isn't recommended: Abandoning ship for another lender. It's a risky, last-minute gambit that could cost you that dream home. It would likely jeopardize your closing and any goodwill you established with the seller. Your credit score might also take a hit when a new lender pulls your credit.

Borrowers certainly do it from time to time if the rate drop is that dramatic. But it's an incredibly risky move that could delay, if not completely derail, your home purchase.

Borrower Spotlight: Jason Foster
Army Veteran Builds His Dream Home From 1,600 Miles Away

Colorado Springs, Colorado—Jason Foster served two tours in Iraq during his nearly 10 years in the Army. His time in the Middle East kept him away from friends and family for a combined 27 months.

Between his two deployments, Jason met his wife. He was stationed at Fort Carson when mutual friends introduced the pair. They connected instantly and eventually married in November 2004.

Jason and his new family were separated while he was deployed for his second tour in Iraq. But he returned home earlier than expected after getting injured. The family was living in Washington, D.C., when they received Jason's medical retirement papers. With those in hand, Jason and his wife started searching for a home for their growing family.

"We love the Midwest, and my wife has family there," Jason said.

It wasn't long until all signs pointed toward Colorado.

A job opened in Fort Carson, and Jason found information on the nursing program at the University of Colorado at Colorado Springs. Jason and his wife concentrated their online search efforts on finding a rental property in the Colorado Springs area.

Then the couple discovered an option they never considered before: building a home. A local builder explained that building the home they wanted would actually prove cheaper than renting. That's when Jason got in touch with local real estate agent Kris Korinek.

Jason presented Kris with quite the challenge. He and his family were going to have to remain in Washington, D.C., through the building and buying process.

Kris pointed Jason to Alice Schneider and the Colorado Springs branch of Veterans United Home Loans. Alice would not only help

Jason secure a VA loan, a benefit earned by his service, but she would also walk him through a long-distance loan.

"I agreed to work with Alice because of the way she greeted us, and she was able to work with us over long distance," Jason said. "She called every day to make sure everything was going OK on a personal level, since she knew we were stressed buying a home from Washington, D.C."

The distance wasn't the only thing between Jason's family and their new home. During his deployment, Jason had problems with one of his credit card companies. It was as if his home-building process hit a giant speed bump. Alice explained how credit works and gave Jason the information he needed to responsibly pay off his debt and boost his score.

"We got it paid off only because Alice helped us out," he said.

Despite the obstacles and long distance, the paperwork and process moved quickly.

"I've owned a house before, and I've never had any customer service like that," Jason said.

Jason and his family were finally able to start a new chapter in their lives. No more deployments. No more speed bumps. Just Colorado living from then on.

"I'm looking forward to settling down and having stability in our lives," Jason said.

MEET THE MILITARY ADVISORS TO VETERANS UNITED HOME LOANS

We're privileged to work alongside some of the nation's truly dynamic military leaders.

As the former senior enlisted leaders of the Armed Forces, these Veterans spent much of their careers preparing, leading and supporting those who serve—ensuring Soldiers, Marines, Sailors, Airmen, Coast Guardsmen, National Guardsmen and Reservists were ready and able to defend our freedoms.

Today, as employees of Veterans United, our military advisors travel the country to boost awareness of VA home loans and the key issues surrounding veteran and military homeownership.

It's truly an honor to call these inspiring leaders both colleagues and friends. Please take a few minutes and get to know some of the incredible veterans who stand alongside us.

Kenneth O. Preston, 13th Sergeant Major of the Army (Ret.)

"Education is critical when it comes to buying a home and making sure you're getting the most out of it. Veterans United has an unparalleled commitment to helping veterans, soldiers and their families truly understand the homebuying process and the benefits they've earned."

Bio: Ken served as the 13th Sergeant Major of the Army from January 15, 2004 to March 1, 2011. He retired as the longest-serving Sergeant Major of the Army.

As Sergeant Major of the Army, Preston served as the Army Chief of Staff's personal adviser on all soldier and family related matters, particularly areas affecting Soldier training and quality of life. He devoted the majority of his time in this position to traveling throughout the Army serving as a force provider for leaders at all levels of responsibility.

Ken is a native of Mount Savage, Md. He entered the Army on June 30, 1975, and attended Basic Training and Armor Advanced Individual Training at Fort Knox, Kentucky.

Throughout his 36-year career, he served in every enlisted leadership position from cavalry scout and tank commander to his final position as Sergeant Major of the Army. Other assignments he held as a Command Sergeant Major were with the 3rd Battalion, 8th Cavalry Regiment, 1st Cavalry Division; 3rd "Grey Wolf" Brigade, 1st Cavalry Division; 1st Armored Division in Bad Kreuznach, Germany; and V Corps in Heidelberg, Germany.

His most recent assignment prior to serving as the 13th Sergeant Major of the Army was as the Command Sergeant Major for Combined Joint Task Force 7 in Baghdad, Iraq.

His awards and decorations include the Distinguished Service Medal, the Legion of Merit with oak leaf cluster, the Bronze Star Medal, the Army Meritorious Service Medal with three oak leaf clusters, Joint Service Commendation Medal, Army Commendation Medal with three oak leaf clusters, the Army Achievement Medal with two oak leaf clusters, the Good Conduct Medal 11th award and the National Defense ribbon with bronze star.

He continues to support military service members and their families through his volunteer work serving on the Board of Directors for the United Services Organization (USO); Homes for Our Troops; and many other organizations.

Micheal P. Barrett, 17th Sergeant Major of the Marines Corps (Ret.)

"I love being with the employees at Veterans United. They are a passionate team that works hard every day to ensure service members and Veterans get the very best. The enthusiasm and dedication of every employee to help Veterans, service members and their families is very heartfelt. There is something special here."

Bio: A native of Youngstown, N.Y., Mike served in the Marine Corps for 33 years. He was appointed as the 17th Sergeant Major of the Marine Corps on June 9, 2011. In this position he was senior ranking enlisted member and personal advisor to the Commandant of the Marine Corps. He routinely testified before congressional committees on the training, quality of life, military compensation and the health and well-being representing over 200,000 active duty and reserve Marine Corps personnel and their families servicewide.

Mike enlisted at 17 and graduated from boot camp in 1981. He reported for duty at Twentynine Palms in California with the 1st Battalion, 4th Marines. Mike earned a Navy and Marine Corps Commendation Medal with "V" device for his service during the first Gulf War. He later served as a drill sergeant, a gunnery sergeant and chief instructor at the Scout Sniper Instructor School at Marine Corps Base Quantico.

He deployed to Al Anbar province, Iraq, in 2005 and 2007 with the 2nd Battalion 7th Marines, earning a Bronze Start with "V" device on each deployment. He spent much of the next two years assigned to Officer Candidates School at Quantico.

A graduate of the Army Ranger School, Mike was chosen as the Sergeant Major of the 1st Marine Division in June 2009. He deployed to Afghanistan less than a year later as I Marine Expeditionary Force/Regional Command Southwest Sergeant Major. Soon after, Mike became the Command Sergeant major for the NATO Regional

Command (Southwest) for Nimruz and Helmand Province, Afghanistan.

The Commandant of the Marine Corps, General James F. Amos, announced in April 2011 that Mike would succeed Carlton W. Kent as Sergeant Major of the Marine Corps. Mike's numerous military awards include the Distinguished Service Medal, the Legion of Merit, two Meritorious Service Medals, the Navy Marine Corps Commendation Medal with combat "V" and three gold stars, and the Presidential Service Badge.

Rick West, 12th Master Chief Petty Officer of the Navy (Ret.)

"As a military member for 32 years, we worked and we survived being part of a team. I saw that spirit of teamwork firsthand at Veterans United. I know the people at Veterans United translate that into the way they take care of every veteran and military member who comes to them for help."

Bio: Rick became the 12th Master Chief Petty Officer of the Navy on December 12, 2008, and retired from active duty in September 2012. Born in Rising Fawn, Georgia, Rick graduated from Northwest Georgia High School in 1981 and immediately entered the U.S. Navy.

Rick received recruit training and quartermaster training at Orlando, Florida, followed by Enlisted Submarine School at Groton, Connecticut. His first duty assignment was aboard USS Ethan Allen where he completed submarine qualifications. Other assignments include *USS Thomas Edison*, *USS Sea Devil*, Commander Naval Activities United Kingdom, *USS Tecumseh* and Commander, Submarine Force, U.S. Pacific Fleet (COMSUBPAC) Staff (TRE Team).

Rick was then assigned as Chief of the Boat aboard the San Diego-based fast attack submarine *USS Portsmouth* (SSN 707), where he completed two Western Pacific deployments and the crew earned two Battle Efficiency "E" awards.

Upon completion of a Command Master Chief (CMC) tour at Submarine Squadron (COMSUBRON) ELEVEN, he was selected as COMSUBPAC Force Master Chief, serving from January 2001 to 2004. During this time, Rick also attended the Senior Enlisted Academy in Newport, Rhode Island. Rick then reported as the Command Master Chief to *USS Preble* (DDG 88) homeported in San Diego, where he deployed to the Persian Gulf and qualified as Enlisted Surface Warfare Specialist.

Rick was selected during his tour on the *Preble* to serve as the Fleet Master Chief for Pacific Fleet (PACFLT) from February 2005 to June 2007. Following PACFLT, he served as the Fleet Master Chief for U.S. Fleet Forces Command from June 2007 to December 2008. He was the first senior enlisted leader to serve as the Fleet Master Chief for both Fleets.

Rick's personal awards include the Navy Distinguished Service Medal, Legion of Merit (two awards), Meritorious Service Medal (three awards), Navy Commendation Medal (four awards), Navy Achievement Medal (two awards), Enlisted Surface Warfare Insignia, Enlisted Submarine Insignia, and SSBN Deterrent Patrol Pin.

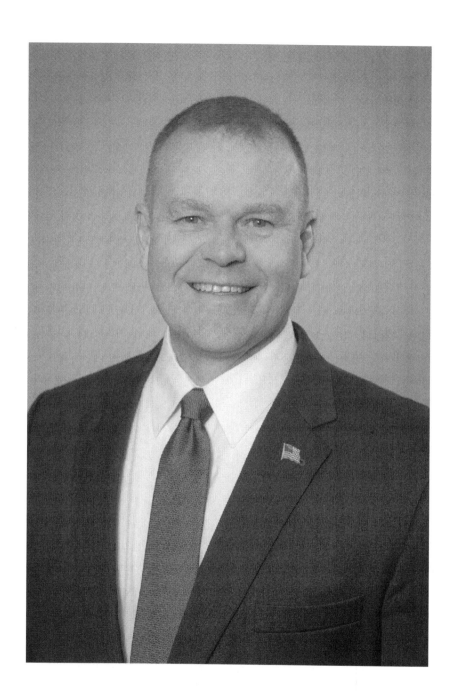

James A. Roy, 16th Chief Master Sergeant of the Air Force (Ret.)

"It's important to find an organization that can help educate you, not just sell you a product. One of the core values of Veterans United is to enhance lives. Their commitment to educating veterans, service members and military families is a clear and powerful example of how they live their values."

Bio: Jim is a native of Monroe, Michigan. His career spanned 30 years of distinguished military service, culminating in his appointment in June 2009 as the 16th Chief Master Sergeant of the Air Force. As the highest-ranking noncommissioned officer in the Air Force, he served as the personal adviser to the Chief of Staff and the Secretary of the Air Force on all issues regarding the readiness, welfare, morale, proper utilization and progress of the enlisted force.

Prior, Jim served in leadership positions at the squadron, group, wing, numbered air force and combatant command levels. He was Command Chief Master Sergeant at wings in Air Education and Training Command, Air Mobility Command, Air Combat Command and the 386th Air Expeditionary Wing in southwest Asia. He also served as the Command Chief Master Sergeant for U.S. Forces Japan and Fifth Air Force at Yokota Air Base, Japan.

Before being named Chief Master Sergeant of the Air Force, Jim last served as Senior Enlisted Leader and advisor to the U.S. Pacific Command Combatant Commander and staff at Camp H.M. Smith in Hawaii. Among his numerous awards and decorations are the Distinguished Service Medal, the Defense Superior Service Medal, the Meritorious Service Medal with silver oak leaf cluster and the Air Force Commendation Medal with two oak leaf clusters.

Jim earned a Master of Science in human resources management from Troy State College, a Bachelor of Science degree in engineering management with honors from Park College, and two associate of science degrees from the Community College of the Air Force in construction management and instructional technology.

Jim serves on Air Force Association (AFA) National, Executive Committee and National, Board of Directors; the Airman Memorial Museum Board of Directors; and Armed Forces Association (AFBA) Board of Directors. In the past, he has served on the Army, Air Force Exchange Service Board of Directors and the United States Armed Forces Commissary Board of Directors.

Charles "Skip" W. Bowen, 10th Master Chief Petty Officer of the Coast Guard (Ret.)

"The VA loan opens the door to homeownership for Veterans and their families. It's an amazing program, and the experts at Veterans United ensure you get the most from your hard-earned benefits. They genuinely care about military homebuyers, and they work hard every day to ensure Veterans and their families achieve the American Dream of homeownership."

Bio: Skip spent his early years on the southern coast of New Jersey before moving to Florida with his family. He enlisted in the Coast Guard in 1978 after graduating from high school. He became the 10th Master Chief Petty Officer of the Coast Guard on June 14, 2006.

Skip's first duty station was to the U.S. Coast Guard Cutter *Point Swift* in Clearwater, Florida. Over the next decade, he served at Coast Guard Station Marathon in the Florida Keys; Station Fort Pierce in Florida; aboard the U.S. Coast Guard Cutter *Farallon* based out of Miami; and at Station New Haven in Connecticut, where Skip was assigned as Officer in Charge following his advancement to Chief Petty Officer. He later served as Officer in Charge of the U.S. Coast Guard Cutter *Point Turner* in Newport, Rhode Island and the *Hammerhead*, based out of Woods Hole, Massachusetts. Skip then served as District Seven Command Master Chief from 1999 to 2001.

A year later, in 2002, Skip graduated with distinction from the Army Sergeants Major Academy. He served as class Vice President during his tenure – one of the few non-Army students to ever do so. Skip also received the "William G. Bainbridge Chair of Ethics Award" upon graduation. For the next two years, Skip served as Command Master Chief of Headquarters' Units, including a three-month stint as interim Master Chief Petty Officer of the Coast Guard.

In 2006, Commandant of the Coast Guard Admiral Thad Allen selected Skip to serve as Master Chief Petty Officer of the Coast Guard. Skip received numerous awards and decorations during his three decades of service, including the Coast Guard Distinguished Service Medal, four Meritorious Service Medals with "O" device, four Coast Guard Commendation Medals with "O" device, three Coast Guard Achievement Medals with "O" device, the Global War on Terrorism Service Medal and the Humanitarian Service Medal with service star.

Denise M. Jelinski-Hall, Air Force Chief Master Sgt. (Ret.) and 3rd Senior Enlisted Advisor to the Chief of the National Guard Bureau

"Veterans United is built around a set of core values. The integrity, camaraderie and dedication I see when I walk through the doors remind me of my time in the military. The men and women here are dedicated to helping you understand and navigate the homebuying process from start to finish."

Bio: Denise holds several remarkable distinctions in the history of our nation's Armed Forces. Her selection as Senior Enlisted Advisor to the Chief of the National Guard in February 2010 marks the highest position ever held by an enlisted female service member. She is also the first and only woman to serve as the Senior Enlisted Advisor to a member of the Joint Chiefs of Staff. Her tenure in that role capped an exemplary career spanning nearly three decades.

A native of Little Falls, Minnesota, Denise enlisted in the Air Force in November 1984 and completed basic training at Lackland Air Force Base in Texas. After finishing air traffic control training at Kessler Air Force Base in Mississippi, she was assigned to Offutt Air Force Base in Nebraska. Two years later, in April 1987, she transferred to the California Air National Guard through the Palace Chase Program. She relocated to Hawaii in 1990 and joined the 297th Air Traffic Control Flight at Barbers Point.

Denise later served as Combat Airspace Manager for the HQ 201st Combat Communications Group; Command Chief for the 154th Wing of the Hawaii Air National Guard; and Command Chief Master Sergeant for the Hawaii Air National Guard. Soon after, Denise was chosen as the state-level Senior Enlisted Leader for the Hawaii National Guard (Army and Air), becoming the first Air National Guard member (and the first and only woman) to do so.

Denise was the first enlisted member of the Hawaii National Guard to receive the state's highest honor, the Order of Distinguished Service. She was the third Chief Master Sergeant (and the first woman) to receive the Defense Superior Service Medal in the 67-year history of the Air Force and Air National Guard. And Denise is the first and only woman to be interviewed for the position of Chief Master Sergeant of the Air Force, a role for which she finished as runner-up to 17th CMSAF James A. Cody.

CHAPTER 6:
CLOSING ON YOUR VA HOME PURCHASE

At this point, you're entering the home stretch.

Once you've got a contract in hand, the first person you call—after friends and loved ones, perhaps—is your loan officer. At many mortgage companies, this is when your trusted LO would actually start to fade into the background. Consider it one of the ironies of the industry. Many companies turn their borrowers over to a loan processor once a purchase agreement is in place.

Processors have an important job. They're charged with shepherding your loan file through the remaining channels and bringing home your home loan.

Loan officers, meanwhile, typically go back to working the front lines, taking those initial calls and kick-starting the process for veterans.

That isn't a bad thing, and it's pretty much the mortgage industry's standard operating procedure. But we tend to do things a little differently.

We love our processors, but their focus is burrowing into the details and gaps in your loan file to prepare it for an underwriting review. Our loan officers and their teams stay connected to their customers from start to finish. The goal is to maintain that relationship from initial conversation to closing day. The LO is still fielding your late-night phone calls and early-morning emails. The LO is still chasing down answers and solving problems. It's a concerted, team effort. Veterans United borrowers aren't simply cast into the loan processing pen once they sign a contract.

Their loan officer is with them every step of the way.

The VA Appraisal Process

Once you're under contract to purchase a home, the real work starts for your lending team. One of the first steps for your lender is ordering a VA appraisal on the property.

The VA appraisal is an assessment of the property's value and condition by an independent VA appraiser. It's required for every VA purchase loan. But don't mistake the appraisal for a home inspection. These are two different things, and appraisals aren't as in-depth or detailed as a home inspection.

Unlike the appraisal, a home inspection isn't required when you're buying a home. But nearly all buyers choose to invest in one.

In fact, once they're under contract, many buyers start with a home inspection to get that in-depth look at the property and its potential (or existing) problems. If you're satisfied with the inspection and still want to move forward with the purchase, then you'll move on to having the lender order the VA appraisal. At that point, your loan team will send a request to the VA, and they'll assign one of their independent appraisers in your area.

Today, VA appraisals are ordered automatically and electronically through the Lender Appraisal Processing Program, also known as LAPP. This computerized system was created to modernize the appraisal process by allowing authorized lenders to directly order, receive and handle appraisals. LAPP isn't a perfect program, but it's another major signpost of the VA's commitment to streamlining and efficiency.

The purpose of the VA appraisal is two-fold. The first is to make sure the home is worth at least what you've offered to pay for it. The second is to make sure the property meets both VA and lender guidelines. We'll take a closer look at each.

The first purpose of the VA appraisal is to establish a "fair market value" for the property. A lender is going to finance whichever is less between the appraised value and the purchase price of the home. Defining "market value" can be a nebulous task, but it's generally considered the price two people are willing to settle on when neither is under any pressure to purchase or sell the property. You might also hear mortgage industry professionals refer to it as "appraised value" or sometimes "reasonable value."

There's a host of things that can change or play with a home's market value. The house's condition and architectural style can play a role. So do the number of bedrooms and the type of water and sewer system. What about the location and the school district?

No doubt.

Given that array of contributing factors, appraisers most often turn to comparable home sales to generate an idea of the property's market value. The appraiser will start by tracking down similar nearby properties that have sold recently. The VA recommends finding comparable sales, or "comps," from within the past six months and never more than the previous 12 months.

Obviously, the more similarities they have with the property being appraised the better. It's also important for appraisers to get the whole story behind each of those potentially comparable sales. Maybe the seller recently got divorced and was in a hurry to sell for cheap, or perhaps there was a crush of buyers and the winner wound up paying significantly above the asking price. Those are circumstances that shouldn't affect the market value of the property you hope to purchase.

In an ideal world, the appraiser would find three homes exactly like the one you're under contract to buy—the same number of bedrooms with the same architectural style and square footage all in the same neighborhood. But the real world is rarely that tidy.

What ultimately happens is that the appraiser makes adjustments and allowances to compensate for one comparable's smaller size or slightly less desirable location. VA appraisers must select what they believe are the three best comps and adjust the sales price of each for those recognized adjustments and differences. Appraisers have to issue detailed explanations if they rely on sales that strain compatibility with the other comps included in the report.

The VA appraisal also has to include other important items, like location maps, photographs of both the home in question and the comparables and perimeter sketches.

Depending on where you're buying, it can be tough to find good comps for unique properties like log cabins, A-frames and even homes on large acreage. Lenders will usually need at least one good recent comparable home sale in order to move forward on a loan.

In addition to the valuation aspect, the VA wants to ensure that homes are safe, structurally sound and free of health hazards. VA appraisers will look at the property's interior and exterior and assess the overall condition. They'll also recommend any obvious repairs needed to make the home meet the MPRs. Remember, this isn't a home inspection, and the VA doesn't guarantee the home is free of defects.

The MPRs cover basic issues that can affect the value of the property or its safety. These are mostly high-level concerns that present immediate or near-immediate problems for veterans and their families. Appraisers haven't devoted their lives to studying the art and science of wiring, plumbing and HVAC systems. This is more like a 100-foot view of the property, as opposed to the more detailed, at times microscopic view you get with a home inspection.

When it comes to a VA loan, appraisers are looking for potentially major issues that revolve around the three S's: safety, sanitation and structural integrity. Actually, let's make that four—the final "S" is salability. A home can be safe, sanitary and structurally sound but still prove problematic for appraisers if it isn't similar to any other comps or has other issues that could make it difficult to sell in the future.

Here's a look at some of the major MPR issues:

- **Residential properties only.** Only residential properties are eligible for VA financing. That means office buildings and storefronts are out of the question.
- **Property must have adequate living space.** The home must possess enough space for the basic functions of daily life. As long as your desired property has enough room for living, sleeping and cooking, you should be set.
- **Mechanical systems must be usable and safe.** Electrical and plumbing systems must be safe and have some usable life remaining. Minor electrical glitches are no major problem, but an entire home with old knob-and-tube wiring could pose some challenges.
- **Heating must be adequate.** The home's heating system must be safe and able to keep a home's temperature above 50 degrees Fahrenheit. Homes with permanently installed non-electric, non-vented fireplaces or space heaters may be eligible, provided the buyer signs a "hold harmless" agreement and the unit meets applicable codes and has an approved oxygen depletion sensor. Homes that use wood-burning stoves as a primary heating source must also have a conventional heating system that can maintain an adequate temperature.
- **Water availability.** The home must have a safe water supply, a water heater and a safe method of sewage disposal. Connection to a public water supply isn't required unless mandated by local codes or health authorities. Private wells will need to meet local or federal water quality standards. Septic systems won't typically need an inspection unless the appraiser notes a concern.
- **Roofing must be adequate.** The roof must be in good shape and provide "reasonable future utility." The VA doesn't specify exactly how long a roof needs to last, but lenders may have a hard number, such as three or five years. Missing shingles or gaping holes will present a problem.

- **Basements and crawl spaces must be problem-free.** Basements and crawl spaces must be dry, clear of debris and properly vented. Any excessive dampness or pooling of water must be corrected. Leaky basements can be a deal breaker for many VA house hunters. Foundation leaks are common among older homes and can be expensive to correct.
- **Property access.** All properties purchased with VA financing need to have safe access from the street. Homes need to have either private driveways or permanent easements to allow entry. Homes on shared or private roadways will often require legal agreements regarding use and maintenance.
- **No health/safety hazards.** Nuclear waste, asbestos and radon are huge red flags for VA appraisers. A property plagued with these kinds of hazards is unlikely to qualify for VA financing.
- **No defective construction.** Appraisers will assess the property for defective construction, poor workmanship, settlement problems, excessive dampness and decay. Minor problems can often be addressed prior to closing, but bigger problems could sideline your purchase indefinitely.
- **Termites.** A termite inspection may be required in your area. Properties with termites, fungus growth or dry rot must be treated and re-evaluated to garner VA approval. VA borrowers cannot pay for this inspection, but they are allowed to pay for the cost of repairs if a seller won't.
- **Lead-based paint.** Flaking paint in properties built before 1978 is assumed to involve lead paint. The problem area must be scraped and repainted, covered with drywall or totally removed.

This is by no means an exhaustive list. Properties may need to meet more localized requirements, too. Again, it's important to understand that the VA appraisal isn't the same thing as a home inspection. A home inspection is a more detailed and granular look at the property. Home inspections can uncover defects, problems and possible looming issues that appraisals might not. You're not required to get a home inspection, but we strongly encourage you to do so.

Veterans under contract to purchase an existing home can request an exemption from the Minimum Property Requirements. They have to do so in writing, along with their lender, and be able to show the property is habitable in terms of those three S's—safety, sanitation and structural soundness. In some cases, the "exemption" becomes more like an "extension," because lenders and the VA may ultimately want to see the problems fixed.

For example, one of our borrowers had a problematic appraisal because of flaking paint on exterior windows that, at minimum, needed to be scraped and primed. But this was during the dead of winter and four-foot snowdrifts made painting impossible. We secured an exemption after the borrower put some money into escrow—the requirement is 1.5 times the cost of the repair estimate—to pay for the repairs once spring arrived.

To be sure, every buyer's situation and needs are different. But there's a lot of mythmaking and uncertainty surrounding the VA appraisal process, especially the property requirements. These are ultimately in place to help safeguard veterans and their families.

The appraiser compiles the comparable sale and property condition information into a report that's uploaded to the VA's secure web portal within 10 business days on average, although it can be more or less depending on where the home is located and other factors. The appraisal report will have an estimated value for the property and list any repairs needed to bring it up to VA guidelines. Lenders don't have any control over the VA appraiser's timeline or their analysis.

Homebuyers are responsible for paying for the appraisal up front. Costs can vary by state, but the fee is typically about $425 for a single-family home. You can essentially seek a reimbursement for this as part of your closing costs negotiation with the seller.

Appraisers have an important job, but they don't actually have the final word on the property.

The VA requires every appraisal report to be reviewed by either a VA staff appraiser or a lender's Staff Appraisal Reviewer (SAR). Many lenders don't have their own SARs and must submit their appraisals directly to the VA for review. Veterans United employs about 100 Staff Appraisal Reviewers because of our focus on VA lending.

A lender's SAR is not an appraiser. The SAR's job is to review the appraiser's report to make sure the estimated value makes sense and that the property meets VA and lender guidelines. SARs can ask for clarification or corrections from the appraiser.

It's actually the lender's SAR who ultimately issues the final appraised value of the home, in what's known as the Notice of Value (NOV). Once the lender receives the appraisal report, the Staff Appraisal Reviewer is generally expected to issue the Notice of Value within five business days. This timeline can stretch beyond five days if the SAR needs to obtain additional information from the appraiser.

The Notice of Value will also list any issues that need to be addressed or verified before the loan can close. Common examples include:

- Any repairs needed to satisfy VA or lender requirements
- Termite inspection if one is required
- Proof that a condo is in a VA-approved development
- Proof that the property's water source meets requirements
- A copy of a private road agreement

Here's an example of the first two pages of a standard Notice of Value:

Exhibit 1—LAPP Lender's Notice of Value

LENDER'S NOTICE OF VALUE

[date of notice]   LENDER LOAN NO.:   VA CASE NO.:
                                                                      APPRAISAL REVIEWER:
[Mr. and/or Ms.] [purchaser's   PROPERTY ADDRESS:
name and current mailing address]

Dear [Mr. and/or Ms.]]:

The above property has been appraised by a fee appraiser assigned by the VA regional office in
[city and state]. On [   ], our VA-authorized appraisal reviewer personally reviewed the fee
appraiser's report and determined the property's estimated reasonable value to be $[
].   The maximum repayment period for a loan to purchase this property is [fee appraiser's
"economic life" estimate or 30, whichever is less] years.

**The VA appraisal was made to determine the reasonable value of the property for loan
purposes. It must not be considered a building inspection. Neither VA nor the lender
can guarantee that the home will be satisfactory to you in all respects or that all
equipment will operate properly. A thorough inspection of the property by you or a
reputable inspection firm may help minimize any problems that could arise after loan
closing. In an existing home, particular attention should be given to plumbing, heating,
electrical and roofing components.**

REMEMBER: VA GUARANTEES THE LOAN, NOT THE CONDITION OF THE PROPERTY.

THE CONDITIONS/REQUIREMENTS CHECKED BELOW APPLY TO THIS PROPERTY:

.... 1. **ENERGY CONSERVATION IMPROVEMENTS.** You may wish to contact the utility
company or a reputable firm for a home energy audit to identify needed energy efficiency
improvements to this previously occupied property. Lenders may increase the loan amount to allow
buyers to make energy efficiency improvements such as: Solar or conventional heating/cooling
systems, water heaters, insulation, weather-stripping/caulking and storm windows/doors. Other
energy-related improvements may also be considered. The mortgage may be increased by up to
$3,000 based solely on documented costs, or up to $6,000 provided the increase in monthly mortgage
payment does not exceed the likely reduction in monthly utility costs; or more than $6,000 subject to a
value determination by VA.

_____ 2. **WOOD-DESTROYING INSECT INFORMATION**

_____ a. **Inspection Report (Existing Construction).** The property must be inspected at no
cost to you by a qualified pest control operator using Form NPMA-33, or other form
acceptable to VA. Any reported infestation or structural damage affecting the value of
the property must be corrected to VA's satisfaction prior to loan settlement. You must
acknowledge receipt of a copy of the inspection report in the space provided on the
form.

_____ b. **Soil Treatment Guarantee (Proposed or Under Construction).** A properly
completed Form NPCA-99a is required. If the soil is treated with a termiticide, a
properly completed Form NPCA-99b is also required. The lender will provide you with
a copy.

_____3. **LIEN-SUPPORTED ASSESSMENT.** This property is located in a development with mandatory membership in a homeowners' association. The lender is responsible for ensuring that title meets VA requirements for such property and that homeowner association assessments are subordinate to the VA-guaranteed mortgage.

_____a. **Homeowner Association Fee.** Estimated fee of $[_____] per [   ].
_____b. **Other.** _____

_____4. **CONDOMINIUM REQUIREMENTS.** Evidence that VA requirements have been met for this condominium. There are may be additional information in "Other Conditions/Requirements" below.

_____5. **WATER/SEWAGE SYSTEM ACCEPTABILITY.** Evidence from the local health authority or other source authorized by VA that the individual _____ **water supply,** _____**sewage disposal** system(s) is/are acceptable.

_____6. **CONNECTION TO PUBLIC WATER/SEWER.** Evidence of connection to _____ **public water,** _____ **public sewer,** if available, and that all related costs have been paid in full.

_____7. **PRIVATE ROAD/COMMON-USE DRIVEWAY.** Evidence that use of the private road or common-use driveway is protected by a recorded permanent easement or recorded right-of-way from the property to a public road, and that a provision exists for its continued maintenance.

_____8. **FLOOD INSURANCE.** Since improvements on this property are located in a FEMA Special Flood Hazard Area, flood insurance is required.

_____9. **"AIRPORT" ACKNOWLEDGEMENT.** Your written acknowledgement that you are aware that this property is located near an airport and that aircraft noise may affect the livability, value and marketability of the property.

_____10. **REPAIRS.** The _____ **lender** _____ **fee appraiser** (_____[name]_____) _____ **fee compliance inspector** (_____[name]_____) is to certify that the following repairs have been satisfactorily completed. See the above second paragraph about your responsibility concerning the condition of the property.

_____
_____
_____I_____
_____

_____11. **LOCAL HOUSING/PLANNING AUTHORITY CODE REQUIREMENTS.** Evidence that local housing or planning authority code requirements, if any, have been met.

_____12. **"NOT INSPECTED" ACKNOWLEDGEMENT.** Your written Acknowledgement that, you are aware that since this new property was not inspected during construction by VA.
_____a. VA assistance with construction complaints will be limited to defects in equipment, material and workmanship reported during the one-year builder's warranty period.
_____b. VA will not intercede on your behalf in the processing of any construction complaints.

_____13. **TEN-YEAR INSURED PROTECTION PLAN.** Evidence of enrollment of this new property in a 10-year insured protection plan acceptable to the Department of Housing and Urban Development (HUD).

In a perfect world, the appraised value of the property matches or exceeds your purchase price, and no repairs are necessary to bring the home up to MPR standards. But that's the best of all possible worlds. You'll have some decisions to make if the appraised value falls short of the purchase price or if repairs are necessary.

A low appraised value can create serious problems for eager homebuyers. Your VA loan amount can't exceed the appraised value (plus allowable costs and fees). So you have a problem if the home you agreed to purchase for $200,000 only appraises for $150,000. An appraisal with a less drastic deficit often presents buyers with a few options.

Here's what you can do if your appraised value falls a bit short of your purchase price:

- **Ask the seller to lower the price.** You can ask the seller to lower the sales price given their home is worth less than what you offered to pay. Most sellers don't want to lose an enthusiastic buyer, so they're generally willing to make a modest price drop.

- **Seek a Reconsideration of Value.** The VA recognizes that appraisal values can be faulty, so buyers can seek what's known as a Reconsideration of Value. Your lender will need to document and submit up to three additional recent comparable home sales that weren't used in the original appraisal and that closed prior to the appraisal report's effective date, or evidence of errors in the original appraisal report.

- **Make up the difference in cash.** You can also choose to make up the difference between the appraised value and the loan value in cash. Be cautious before grabbing at this straw. Paying more for a home than it's worth may not be a wise investment.

- **Walk away from the deal.** As a prospective VA buyer, your VA Amendment to Contract contingency will allow you to walk away with your earnest money if the home doesn't appraise.

The appraisal may also require that certain repairs be made before your loan can move forward. Extensive damage or finicky sellers can be VA loan deal-breakers, so aim for homes in good condition.

There are a few ways to handle required repairs:

- **Ask the seller to complete repairs.** The first option is to ask the seller to make the necessary repairs. This should always be your first choice. They're under no obligation to do so, but they may be willing to spend the money if that's what it takes to sell their home.
- **See if you can make them.** If the seller refuses, the VA allows borrowers to pay for repairs, even related to MPR issues. Some lenders may not allow this or even know it's possible, and those who do can have their own policy for how it works. At Veterans United, we allow buyers to pay for any and all repairs, including some that can be completed after the loan closes. In these cases, the borrower would need to put money to pay for these repairs in an escrow account. This is known as an escrow holdback. You'll typically be required to put 1.5 times the cost of repairs into the escrow account. Common interior repairs that can be replaced after closing include torn carpet, installing handrails and replacing cracked tile. Bigger projects like major electrical work, plumbing repairs or foundation work would need to be addressed before the loan could close. Policies and requirements can vary by lender.
- **Walk away from the home purchase.** The VA appraisal might reveal some really serious concerns. The foundation may be collapsing. The plumbing may be in shambles. A home with these kinds of issues could take a fortune to repair. You'll be out the cost of the appraisal, but contract contingencies can help ensure you can walk away from the deal with your earnest money.

The VA appraisal process is one of the most important parts of your homebuying journey. Talk with your loan officer if you have any questions about what to expect.

Loan Processing & Underwriting

Ordering the VA appraisal is one of the first jobs of the loan processor. It's far from the last.

The processor will forward your contract to your insurance company, who in turn will get cranking on a policy for the home. Most lenders will recommend insurance companies and push borrowers to solicit multiple quotes. Rates for homeowners insurance can vary wildly depending on a number of factors. You may want to get at least three quotes from reputable companies.

The processor will do the same with a title company to ensure the property has proper title insurance.

Let's pause here for a closer look at title insurance, which we mentioned briefly in the last chapter. It's a foreign term for many first-time buyers. Homebuyers want to make sure they have a "clear title," meaning there aren't any liens or legal defects related to the property. Title insurance protects lenders and owners from title-related problems.

Once you're under contract on a home, a title company will conduct a search of public records looking for liens, easements, legal claims and other issues that could impact the property. Most of the time it's smooth sailing—either there are no problems or issues that arise are cleared up before closing. But title issues do occasionally slip through the cracks, which can be costly and devastating for homebuyers.

Say, for a rare but possible example, that a title transfer decades ago was predicated upon forged documents and someone claiming to be the "rightful owner" comes knocking on the door two weeks after you move in. This is where title insurance comes into play. There are two different types—policies for homebuyers (owner's title) and for lenders (lender's title).

Buyers can choose to pay a one-time fee at closing for owner's title insurance. This policy protects you and your heirs and requires the insurer to pay costs and claims associated with a qualified title issue. Lenders will usually require the purchase of lender's title insurance. This policy protects only the lender's financial interest in the property.

Like other forms of insurance, title insurance in many states comes with varying rates (there are a few where rates are set by the state Department of Insurance or a similar governmental agency). And there's no guarantee that the listing agent will recommend a title company with the best rates for military borrowers. Veterans should shop around or at least check with their lender to see what else is available.

At the same time, the loan processor will work to clear up any remaining documentation and paperwork needs related to your loan financing. Inspections need to be completed. Insurance policies must be drafted and signed. Veterans might need to gather up another year's worth of tax statements or have their bank balances verified.

It's hard to put a specific time frame on this, but generally you're looking at a week or two to nail down some of this financial information and take care of appraisals, inspections and the rest. Once the processor is confident that the loan package looks complete, it will make its way to arguably the most important person in the chain: the underwriter.

This step can seem a bit confusing and needless to first-time buyers, many of whom will quickly note their loan was already approved by the Automated Underwriting System. There's already a green light, right? Sort of.

A lot can change during the course of the purchasing process. Financial statements and credit reports can get stale. Prospective borrowers lose their jobs. Spouses file for divorce. Issues arise with the property. For these and countless other reasons, the initial verdict of an automated system can't possibly be the final word on a home loan. There's just too much potential for things to change.

That's why lenders like to turn to human beings as the process nears culmination. Some employ underwriters in-house, while others use outside firms. Either way, the underwriter is the person who makes the ultimate determination regarding your loan. And that's why an AUS approval isn't necessarily a green light.

Veterans must have their loan package approved by a real person. It's also important to remember that an AUS approval often comes with a list of conditions the borrower must meet. The underwriting office is the crucible for all those conditions.

For example, the veteran might have received AUS approval on the condition that two years worth of tax returns be supplied. In the best of all possible worlds, the veteran supplies those documents, the loan processor tosses them into the file and the underwriter gives the loan a big thumbs-up.

The underwriter is also there to ensure the loan follows VA guidelines and requirements. Most often, that's going to involve another hard look at the borrower's debt-to-income ratio and residual income figures. A lender's self-interest drives the process. Given that there's no down payment, the lender is on the hook for the entire amount if a loan defaults and the VA determines the company ignored or somehow skirted agency guidelines. In other words, the VA guaranty evaporates if a lender fails to follow the rules.

Needless to say, that's a scary thought for lenders who would otherwise be somewhat insulated against a borrower who goes belly up. In addition, lenders often need loan files to meet additional requirements in order to sell them on the secondary mortgage market. That means underwriters are charged with an important task, and it's one they don't take lightly.

Despite the hard work of loan processors, most loan files aren't slam dunks. Tax returns may be slow in coming from the IRS. Pay stubs can become outdated if shopping for a home takes longer than expected. The same can be true of credit reports.

But those aren't deal breakers. After reviewing your file, an underwriter will typically do one of three things.

One, they can issue a conditional approval of your loan. This usually means you'll need to provide additional documents, answer questions or correct errors in your file before being able to move forward.

Two, they can issue a clear to close, which means your loan file is clean and you're ready to close on your new home. It's rare for a loan file to get a CTC, as it's called, the first time it goes to an underwriter.

Three, an underwriter can deny your file outright. This is also a rare occurrence, and it's not likely to happen if you're working with a good loan officer who knows VA loans.

Every lender and every loan file is different. But, broadly speaking, a conditional approval is the most common outcome and traditionally the next step. Getting conditional approval for a loan is perfectly common. It's also commonly frustrating for veterans, who often wonder why they're being incessantly bombarded for thousands of pieces of information—or, at least that's how it can feel—so close to the end.

Veterans with conditional approval will be back on the phone with their loan team, working to supply whatever outstanding information and documentation is necessary to fulfill the underwriter's concerns. But know that having conditions on your file is routine.

Underwriting Conditions

Homebuyers rarely sail through the underwriting process without conditions. These are often simple issues that borrowers can quickly clear up, sometimes in the same day. Your loan officer might ask you to write a "letter of explanation" that addresses a specific question or problem. Lenders also rely on third parties to verify things like your tax returns or income documents.

Underwriters may request things like additional pay stubs or more tax returns before issuing final approval. There are hundreds of possible conditions. Again, every loan file is different.

Here are a few common questions underwriters will often consider:

- Has the borrower's income and employment situation changed? Lenders will conduct verification of employment (VOE) no more than 10 days before closing.
- Has the borrower made any large bank account deposits that need further documentation?
- Does the borrower have a "clear" CAIVRS? Anyone presently delinquent or in default on federal debt can't be considered a satisfactory credit risk. Underwriters will confirm that the borrower is in the clear or that there's a satisfactory repayment plan in place.
- Are there any judgment liens against the borrower's property? These would need to be repaid or otherwise satisfied before a loan could close. Unpaid debts or liens with the IRS that don't appear on your credit report can still show up on title work later in the loan process.
- If the borrower is currently a homeowner, have they been late on any mortgage payments in the last 12 months? Some lenders may allow up to one 30-day late payment in the last year, but others will require at least 12 consecutive months of on-time payments.

It's important to understand you're not being targeted or picked on if there are conditions on your loan file. The underwriter's job is to protect the lender. But lenders who don't actually make loans have a tough time staying in business. It's a balancing act.

If you're asked to provide additional documents, strive to get them back to your loan officer as soon as possible. Also, be sure you're sending exactly what the lender needs. Sending incomplete or illegible documents can delay the process. Talk with your loan officer if you have any questions about what's needed.

The faster you move, the faster your lending team moves toward resolving the conditions and getting you to closing day. Once the underwriter is satisfied with all of your paperwork, the lender issues a clear to close. The lender will send your loan documents and paperwork to the title company to prepare for your loan closing.

Reviewing Closing Paperwork

You and your real estate agent should review your closing paperwork shortly before your closing day. The Closing Disclosure is a final review of all loan fees and costs and must be made available to buyers at least three business days before closing.

This is a relatively new document that came out of the banking and mortgage industry reforms following the housing crisis. The new Closing Disclosure replaced two longtime federal forms, the final Truth-in-Lending statement and the HUD-1 settlement statement.

The Closing Disclosure will help you compare how costs and fees may have changed since you received your Loan Estimate during the preapproval stage. The Loan Estimate does a good job of approximating loan fees, but it isn't an exact representation of your final costs.

Along with your Loan Estimate, the lender will identify what closing-related services you can shop for and include a list of companies to consider. Some of these services can include things like title work, closing agents and homeowners insurance. Regarding the services for which you can shop, you're not required to use any of the companies identified by the lender.

Some of your closing costs and fees aren't allowed to change without an exception between when you receive the Loan Estimate and your closing day. Those set fees include:

- What lenders charge for their own services, such as an origination fee
- Costs charged by an affiliate of the lender
- Transfer taxes

- Any costs for which the lender doesn't allow you to shop for competing offers

Other charges that were estimated on the Loan Estimate can change in your Closing Disclosure. Perhaps your homeowners insurance bill increased. Government recording fees may have dropped. Property tax due dates can cause swings in closing cost estimates. Fee changes are also common if you shop around for and choose third-party services not suggested by your lender.

Some fees are allowed to increase up to 10 percent upon settlement unless there's an exception, including government recording charges and fees for third-party services where you're not paying the lender or an affiliate of the lender, but you shop around and ultimately choose a company from the list your lender provided.

There's also a third category of charges that can fluctuate without limit, including:

- Required services that you can shop for (if you do not use companies that your lender identifies)
- Title services and title insurance (if you do not use companies that your lender identifies)
- Initial deposit for your escrow account
- Prepaid interest charges
- Homeowners insurance charges

Since there are so many charges that can fluctuate, a Loan Estimate rarely hits all costs on the head. That's where the Closing Disclosure comes into play. Let's take a closer look at this important document.

The first page of the Closing Disclosure features the same headings and categories as the first page of the Loan Estimate. You'll be able to see how your estimated total monthly payment has changed from your Loan Estimate, if at all. You'll also see final tallies for your closing costs and the overall amount of cash needed to close.

Here's a snapshot of Page 1:

Closing Disclosure

This form is a statement of final loan terms and closing costs. Compare this document with your Loan Estimate.

Closing Information	Transaction Information	Loan Information
Date Issued	Borrower	Loan Term
Closing Date		Purpose
Disbursement Date		Product
Settlement Agent	Seller	
File #		Loan Type ☐ Conventional ☐ FHA ☐ VA ☐ _____
Property		
	Lender	Loan ID #
Sale Price		MIC #

Loan Terms

	Can this amount increase after closing?
Loan Amount	
Interest Rate	
Monthly Principal & Interest See Projected Payments below for your Estimated Total Monthly Payment	
	Does the loan have these features?
Prepayment Penalty	
Balloon Payment	

Projected Payments

Payment Calculation	
Principal & Interest	
Mortgage Insurance	
Estimated Escrow Amount can increase over time	
Estimated Total Monthly Payment	

Estimated Taxes, Insurance & Assessments Amount can increase over time See page 4 for details	This estimate includes ☐ Property Taxes ☐ Homeowner's Insurance ☐ Other: See Escrow Account on page 4 for details. You must pay for other property costs separately.	In escrow?

Costs at Closing

Closing Costs	Includes in Loan Costs + in Lender Credits. See page 2 for details.	in Other Costs –
Cash to Close	Includes Closing Costs. See Calculating Cash to Close on page 3 for details.	

The second page provides a full breakdown of all closing costs, including a look at which costs are paid at closing; which costs were paid before closing; which costs are paid by the buyer; and which ones are covered by the seller.

Here's a look at Page 2:

Closing Cost Details

Loan Costs	Borrower-Paid		Seller-Paid		Paid by Others
	At Closing	Before Closing	At Closing	Before Closing	
A. Origination Charges					
01 % of Loan Amount (Points)					
02					
03					
04					
05					
06					
07					
08					
B. Services Borrower Did Not Shop For					
01					
02					
03					
04					
05					
06					
07					
08					
09					
10					
C. Services Borrower Did Shop For					
01					
02					
03					
04					
05					
06					
07					
08					
D. TOTAL LOAN COSTS (Borrower-Paid)					
Loan Costs Subtotals (A + B + C)					

Other Costs					
E. Taxes and Other Government Fees					
01 Recording Fees Deed: Mortgage					
02					
F. Prepaids					
01 Homeowner's Insurance Premium (mo.)					
02 Mortgage Insurance Premium (mo.)					
03 Prepaid Interest (per day from to)					
04 Property Taxes (mo.)					
05					
G. Initial Escrow Payment at Closing					
01 Homeowner's Insurance per month for mo.					
02 Mortgage Insurance per month for mo.					
03 Property Taxes per month for mo.					
04					
05					
06					
07					
08 Aggregate Adjustment					
H. Other					
01					
02					
03					
04					
05					
06					
07					
08					
I. TOTAL OTHER COSTS (Borrower-Paid)					
Other Costs Subtotals (E + F + G + H)					
J. TOTAL CLOSING COSTS (Borrower-Paid)					
Closing Costs Subtotals (D + I)					
Lender Credits					

The third page contains a table comparing the final cash-to-close calculation to the initial numbers from your Loan Estimate. You'll also get a summary of the transaction from both the buyer's and the seller's perspectives, meaning you'll see your total cash needed to close as well as how much cash the seller stands to gain.

Here's a look at Page 3:

Calculating Cash to Close

Use this table to see what has changed from your Loan Estimate.

	Loan Estimate	Final	Did this change?
Total Closing Costs (J)			
Closing Costs Paid Before Closing			
Closing Costs Financed (Paid from your Loan Amount)			
Down Payment/Funds from Borrower			
Deposit			
Funds for Borrower			
Seller Credits			
Adjustments and Other Credits			
Cash to Close			

Summaries of Transactions

Use this table to see a summary of your transaction.

BORROWER'S TRANSACTION

K. Due from Borrower at Closing

01 Sale Price of Property
02 Sale Price of Any Personal Property Included in Sale
03 Closing Costs Paid at Closing (J)
04

Adjustments

05
06
07

Adjustments for Items Paid by Seller in Advance

08 City/Town Taxes   to
09 County Taxes   to
10 Assessments   to
11
12
13
14
15

L. Paid Already by or on Behalf of Borrower at Closing

01 Deposit
02 Loan Amount
03 Existing Loan(s) Assumed or Taken Subject to
04
05 Seller Credit

Other Credits

06
07

Adjustments

08
09
10
11

Adjustments for Items Unpaid by Seller

12 City/Town Taxes   to
13 County Taxes   to
14 Assessments   to
15
16
17

CALCULATION

Total Due from Borrower at Closing (K)
Total Paid Already by or on Behalf of Borrower at Closing (L)
Cash to Close ☐ From ☐ To Borrower

SELLER'S TRANSACTION

M. Due to Seller at Closing

01 Sale Price of Property
02 Sale Price of Any Personal Property Included in Sale
03
04
05
06
07
08

Adjustments for Items Paid by Seller in Advance

09 City/Town Taxes   to
10 County Taxes   to
11 Assessments   to
12
13
14
15
16

N. Due from Seller at Closing

01 Excess Deposit
02 Closing Costs Paid at Closing (J)
03 Existing Loan(s) Assumed or Taken Subject to
04 Payoff of First Mortgage Loan
05 Payoff of Second Mortgage Loan
06
07
08 Seller Credit
09
10
11
12
13

Adjustments for Items Unpaid by Seller

14 City/Town Taxes   to
15 County Taxes   to
16 Assessments   to
17
18
19

CALCULATION

Total Due to Seller at Closing (M)
Total Due from Seller at Closing (N)
Cash ☐ From ☐ To Seller

The fourth page provides additional information about the loan. You'll learn more about:

- Whether loan assumptions are permitted
- What kind of late payment deadline and fees come with the loan

- Whether your loan can accrue negative amortization, which happens when your monthly payments don't cover all of the interest due; recent mortgage industry changes have made this risky feature increasingly rare
- Whether your lender will accept partial mortgage payments
- How much you'll be escrowing for homeowners insurance and property taxes during the first year of the loan and what that costs on a monthly basis

Here's a closer look at Page 4:

Additional Information About This Loan

Assumption
If you sell or transfer this property to another person, your lender
- [ ] will allow, under certain conditions, this person to assume this loan on the original terms.
- [ ] will not allow assumption of this loan on the original terms.

Demand Feature
Your loan
- [ ] has a demand feature, which permits your lender to require early repayment of the loan. You should review your note for details.
- [ ] does not have a demand feature.

Late Payment
If your payment is more than ____ days late, your lender will charge a late fee of _____

Negative Amortization (Increase in Loan Amount)
Under your loan terms, you
- [ ] are scheduled to make monthly payments that do not pay all of the interest due that month. As a result, your loan amount will increase (negatively amortize), and your loan amount will likely become larger than your original loan amount. Increases in your loan amount lower the equity you have in this property.
- [ ] may have monthly payments that do not pay all of the interest due that month. If you do, your loan amount will increase (negatively amortize), and, as a result, your loan amount may become larger than your original loan amount. Increases in your loan amount lower the equity you have in this property.
- [ ] do not have a negative amortization feature.

Partial Payments
Your lender
- [ ] may accept payments that are less than the full amount due (partial payments) and apply them to your loan.
- [ ] may hold them in a separate account until you pay the rest of the payment, and then apply the full payment to your loan.
- [ ] does not accept any partial payments.
If this loan is sold, your new lender may have a different policy.

Security Interest
You are granting a security interest in _____
_____
_____

You may lose this property if you do not make your payments or satisfy other obligations for this loan.

Escrow Account
For now, your loan
- [ ] will have an escrow account (also called an "impound" or "trust" account) to pay the property costs listed below. Without an escrow account, you would pay them directly, possibly in one or two large payments a year. Your lender may be liable for penalties and interest for failing to make a payment.

Escrow		
Escrowed Property Costs over Year 1		Estimated total amount over year 1 for your escrowed property costs:
Non-Escrowed Property Costs over Year 1		Estimated total amount over year 1 for your non-escrowed property costs:
		You may have other property costs.
Initial Escrow Payment		A cushion for the escrow account you pay at closing. See Section G on page 2.
Monthly Escrow Payment		The amount included in your total monthly payment.

- [ ] will not have an escrow account because [ ] you declined it [ ] your lender does not offer one. You must directly pay your property costs, such as taxes and homeowner's insurance. Contact your lender to ask if your loan can have an escrow account.

No Escrow		
Estimated Property Costs over Year 1		Estimated total amount over year 1. You must pay these costs directly, possibly in one or two large payments a year.
Escrow Waiver Fee		

In the future,
Your property costs may change and, as a result, your escrow payment may change. You may be able to cancel your escrow account, but if you do, you must pay your property costs directly. If you fail to pay your property taxes, your state or local government may (1) impose fines and penalties or (2) place a tax lien on this property. If you fail to pay any of your property costs, your lender may (1) add the amounts to your loan balance, (2) add an escrow account to your loan, or (3) require you to pay for property insurance that the lender buys on your behalf, which likely would cost more and provide fewer benefits than what you could buy on your own.

The fifth page of the Closing Disclosure shows borrowers how much the loan will cost them over the entire term of the mortgage. You'll also see your final Annual Percentage Rate (APR), which is different from the loan's interest rate and reflects the total costs of borrowing, and the Total Interest Percentage (TIP), a figure that shows how much interest you'll pay over the life of the loan as a percentage of the loan amount.

You'll also find contact information for your lender, your real estate agent and other key stakeholders in your closing process.

Here's a look at Page 5:

Loan Calculations

Total of Payments. Total you will have paid after you make all payments of principal, interest, mortgage insurance, and loan costs, as scheduled.

Finance Charge. The dollar amount the loan will cost you.

Amount Financed. The loan amount available after paying your upfront finance charge.

Annual Percentage Rate (APR). Your costs over the loan term expressed as a rate. This is not your interest rate.

Total Interest Percentage (TIP). The total amount of interest that you will pay over the loan term as a percentage of your loan amount.

? Questions? If you have questions about the loan terms or costs on this form, use the contact information below. To get more information or make a complaint, contact the Consumer Financial Protection Bureau at **www.consumerfinance.gov/mortgage-closing**

Other Disclosures

Appraisal
If the property was appraised for your loan, your lender is required to give you a copy at no additional cost at least 3 days before closing. If you have not yet received it, please contact your lender at the information listed below.

Contract Details
See your note and security instrument for information about
- what happens if you fail to make your payments,
- what is a default on the loan,
- situations in which your lender can require early repayment of the loan, and
- the rules for making payments before they are due.

Liability after Foreclosure
If your lender forecloses on this property and the foreclosure does not cover the amount of unpaid balance on this loan,
☐ state law may protect you from liability for the unpaid balance. If you refinance or take on any additional debt on this property, you may lose this protection and have to pay any debt remaining even after foreclosure. You may want to consult a lawyer for more information.
☐ state law does not protect you from liability for the unpaid balance.

Refinance
Refinancing this loan will depend on your future financial situation, the property value, and market conditions. You may not be able to refinance this loan.

Tax Deductions
If you borrow more than this property is worth, the interest on the loan amount above this property's fair market value is not deductible from your federal income taxes. You should consult a tax advisor for more information.

Contact Information

	Lender	Mortgage Broker	Real Estate Broker (B)	Real Estate Broker (S)	Settlement Agent
Name					
Address					
NMLS ID					
License ID					
Contact					
Contact NMLS ID					
Contact License ID					
Email					
Phone					

Confirm Receipt

By signing, you are only confirming that you have received this form. You do not have to accept this loan because you have signed or received this form.

_____   _____   _____   _____
Applicant Signature   Date   Co-Applicant Signature   Date

CLOSING DISCLOSURE

It's also important to understand that big changes to your loan terms or last-minute changes to your contract could result in the need for an updated Closing Disclosure. Because the document must be disclosed to borrowers at least three business days before their closing, the need for an updated disclosure could delay your originally scheduled loan closing.

Talk with your loan officer and your real estate agent if you have any questions about your Closing Disclosure.

Closing Timeframe

You first start talking about a closing date before you're even under contract on a home. It's usually something the buyer will suggest in their offer, and the seller either agrees or the two of you settle on a different time frame.

The closing date in your contract isn't set in stone. Some of it depends on things beyond your control. For example, during the peak homebuying season, third-party items like title work, appraisals and inspections may take longer than usual. In other cases, it's about how quickly you can satisfy any conditions holding up your clear to close.

Broadly, there's a lingering misconception out there that VA purchase loans take forever to close. The reality is VA loans more than keep pace with the other loan types, including conventional loans. Most VA purchase loans close in 30 to 45 days, just like the average conventional or FHA purchase loan.

To be sure, every buyer's timeline is different. But using a VA loan doesn't put veterans and service members at a disadvantage regarding how long it takes to close.

Keeping Your Loan on Track

Getting to and through the underwriting process is an exciting journey. It's also one that prizes continuity and care. As you march toward finalizing your home loan, lenders will be watching carefully for any major changes that could knock a potential borrower out of contention for VA approval.

Let's look at this through a lender's eyes. A lot can change between preapproval and your closing date. Income can take a nosedive. Spouses can file for divorce. Potential borrowers can take on a mountain of new debt.

You have a lot of control when it comes to keeping your loan on track. Once you decide to start the homebuying process, safeguard your credit and finances. During the days ahead, protect your home purchase by steering clear of the following six pitfalls:

1) Major purchases: Don't make any big purchases right before buying a home. Lenders want to be assured that a buyer can continually make mortgage payments. Buyers who take on big debt like a car or new furniture might be stretching their budgets beyond a lender's requirements. Lenders will usually receive an alert from the credit bureaus if there's a credit inquiry on your report during the loan process. Taking on new credit before your loan closes can lead to delays or even derail the entire process. Keep your mortgage in good shape by saving those big purchases for the day after your loan funds.

2) Big career changes: Losing a job or embarking on a new career path is a big red flag for lenders. A mortgage lender wants to make sure your income is consistent and that the monthly payment is manageable. Any changes to your employment and income can jeopardize your loan. Jumping to a different field or starting your own business is often a deal-breaker. Even a promotion could be problematic if, say, some or all of your income switches to a commission basis. Lenders will confirm your employment situation on or just before your closing day.

3) Credit problems or inquiries: Try to avoid hard credit inquiries and credit slip-ups while you're waiting for your loan to close. Don't miss payments, and try to avoid applying for new credit before finalizing your mortgage. Hard inquiries could hurt your credit score and even knock you below a lender's qualifying score benchmark. Some lenders may receive an alert from the credit bureaus if borrowers get a hard credit inquiry during the loan process. When in doubt about how to handle credit during this interim period, check with your loan officer. Lenders have a wealth of experience in this area and can provide solid guidance to keep your mortgage on track.

4) Moving money around: All transfers of money between your accounts will need to have a paper trail. Moving money around before your loan closes can lead to underwriting delays. Any deposit totaling more than 50 percent of your total gross monthly salary is typically considered a large deposit and will need a paper trail. This excludes direct deposits, paychecks, retirement, Social Security income, disability income or any other documented income.

5) Maintain reserves: Keep reserves in your bank account during the entire loan transaction. If you submit your original loan application with $1,000 in the bank, lenders will want to see at least $1,000 in liquid funds all the way to closing. A large drop in your bank balance can cause problems during the processing and underwriting of your file.

6) Keep documents: Please don't pack or put away any documentation. Until your financing is approved, your loan application should be considered a work in progress. With this in mind, your loan team will review your file continuously to ensure it's ready for underwriting and that all documents are accurate and up to date.

When in doubt, check with your loan officer. Some borrowers assume that loan preapproval is pretty much the same thing as formal approval. But that's definitely not the case. Your loan profile must remain the same (or improve) during the processing and underwriting of your loan. A small change to credit or bank balances can affect your loan approval. When in doubt or when it comes to credit or your bank accounts, talk with your loan officer before taking an action.

Closing Day & Beyond

This marks the end of the homebuying process and the start of your new life as a homeowner. The homebuying journey comes to a close with a flourish of signatures. It's time to celebrate achieving the dream of homeownership!

Your purchase contract should stipulate your right to a final walk-through within 24 hours of closing. Your real estate agent may or may not accompany you to this last pre-purchase visit. Take a close look and make sure that all repairs have been completed; all included appliances and fixtures are present; and that all unwanted items have been removed by the previous owner. Alert your real estate agent immediately if you detect any problems.

After a careful review of the Closing Disclosure, your agent and lender will let you know if you need to bring payment to the closing table. Closing agents usually require either a certified or cashier's check or a verified wire transfer as the only suitable forms of payment. You can't just write a personal check or bring cash. If your seller has already agreed to pay closing costs, you may not have to bring any money to close.

A representative of the title company usually runs the closing meeting. Give yourself at least an hour to be safe. Some closings may take more time, and some take less. The closing agent explains all paperwork and gets the necessary signatures.

Your real estate agent will usually attend the meeting, too. It's extremely comforting to have a knowledgeable and familiar advocate by your side in case any problems or questions arise. The sellers and their real estate agent may also be present. A seller might also choose to complete the necessary paperwork in advance.

When it comes to paperwork, get ready to feel like a celebrity. Your signature plays a pivotal role during the closing process, and is required on numerous documents, including:

- **Closing Disclosure:** The Closing Disclosure is the final review of all loan fees and costs we mentioned earlier. This must be made available to buyers at least three business days before closing.

- **Promissory note:** This is basically a legal IOU. The promissory note details the lending agreement between you and the lender, including the loan amount, the interest rate and the number of years in your mortgage term.

- **Mortgage or deed of trust:** You'll either sign a mortgage note or a deed of trust, depending on where you're purchasing. These basically do the same thing—pledge the property as security for the loan. This allows the lender to take back the property if you stop repaying the loan.

- **Warranty deed:** The deed transfers legal title of the property to the new owners.

- **VA Form 26-1820 (Report and Certification of Loan Disbursement):** This document helps confirm that the lender is closing a loan that meets VA guidelines and regulations. VA buyers will also certify their intent to occupy the property as their primary residence.

- **IRS Form 4506-T (Request for Transcript of Tax Return):** You've likely already signed this form once during the loan preapproval process. But it's become common for lenders to double check your income and tax information, including individual tax returns, W-2 wage and tax statements and more.

- **Initial Escrow Account Disclosure:** This statement estimates how much you'll contribute to your escrow account during the first year of your mortgage. VA buyers typically escrow money each month to cover their annual property tax and homeowners insurance bills. Your mortgage servicer is responsible for making sure these get paid.

- **Borrower's Certification & Authorization:** This is a common form for home loans and certifies that the information you're providing is accurate. This form also authorizes the release of credit, tax, employment and income records to the VA or to lenders that may purchase the mortgage on the secondary market.
- **Affidavit of Occupancy:** This is another common form during loan closings. VA buyers must certify their intent to occupy the property as their primary residence, typically within 60 days of closing.

During the loan closing, you'll finalize the title for the property. There's a number of ways to hold title, and it's not a throwaway decision. Divorce, death, lawsuits and more can all lead to title-related implications.

Common ways to title a property include:

- **Joint tenancy:** Two or more people holding title jointly, with equal interest in the property. This is common for spouses and couples. Joint tenancy features a right of survivorship, which basically means the ownership of the home transfers fully to the remaining tenant.
- **Tenancy in common:** Unlike joint tenancy, one tenant in this setup can own a larger share of the property than others. There's also no right of survivorship.
- **Sole ownership:** This is when just one person holds title, even if there are multiple parties involved with the home loan.

If you have questions about how to title your property, talk with your loan officer, a financial professional, an attorney or all of the above well before closing day. Every buyer's situation is different, and some title scenarios may be more beneficial than others.

Your lawful ownership of the property is enshrined in what's known as a deed. It's a legal document that attests to a transfer of homeownership—the home is changing hands from the seller's to yours.

After your loan closing a title company employee will usually take your deed to your county's administrative offices, where it will be formally recorded. The recording fee is typically part of your closing costs.

At this point, your home purchase is a matter of public record. Some of the information associated with the transaction will be accessible to anyone in your community and beyond.

Servicing Your Loan

When it comes time to make your first mortgage payment, you may not be sending the money to the same company that financed your home purchase. That might sound odd, but it's completely normal.

Some mortgage lenders will make a loan and then go on to service it, meaning they collect the monthly payments, handle the escrow accounts for your property taxes and homeowners insurance and more. But lenders can also sell the servicing rights for the loans they make.

That means another company is now responsible for collecting those payments, forwarding on your principal and interest portions and even initiating foreclosure proceedings. It's important to understand that the rate and terms of your loan won't change if this happens.

Buyers will encounter and sign a "Servicing Disclosure Statement" as part of their loan process paperwork. This document outlines your lender's servicing policy. Basically, you'll learn one of three things: The lender will not service your loan; the lender will service your loan; or the lender may decide to sell your loan servicing at some point after the loan closes.

Lenders are required to notify you at least 15 days before your loan servicing is transferred to another company. These disclosures must include:

- The effective date of the transfer
- The name, address and phone number for an employee or a department at both the current lender and the new servicer who buyers can contact with questions
- The date the original lender will stop accepting payments and the new servicer will start
- Written acknowledgment that the transfer of servicing rights doesn't affect any other terms or conditions of the loan

During a 60-day period beginning with the effective date of your servicing transfer, your new mortgage servicer can't charge any late fees or penalties if you accidentally send your payment to the wrong place.

Please don't take it personally if your lender winds up selling your loan servicing. Some lenders don't service any of their loans. Others service some and sell others. It's a purely financial decision.

This is another way for VA lenders to generate revenue, which in turn, helps them make more home loans to veterans, service members and military families.

Keeping Healthy Habits

Many prospective buyers exercise heaps of caution on the road to homeownership. Purchases are delayed. Payments are made on time, if not early. Credit scores are closely monitored.

Don't let those good habits evaporate after closing day. As a new homeowner, you have even more to lose from poor fiscal management. The effects of foreclosure can be devastating, both emotionally and financially. It's a harrowing event that homeowners should strive to avoid.

Spend slowly, and schedule your big expenses over time. A big, empty house can easily stir new homeowners into a shopping frenzy. New TVs, furniture or appliances are exciting purchases and can seem essential at first. But then the bills start rolling in. On top of a new mortgage payment, you have new furniture, top-of-the-line kitchen appliances and fresh carpet to pay for each month. Don't make all improvements the day after closing on a new home. Give yourself a few weeks to figure out the essential improvements, and space your expenditures adequately.

If you've been living with family or renting a condo where utilities are included, your first batch of utility bills can send you into shock. Now add in a water bill, trash service, cable fees and more. Before purchasing a home, you should have received an estimate of average utility bills for the location. Make sure your budget can safely cover those expenses, and give yourself some time to adjust to your new bills before making big purchases.

It's also important to build reserves. Try to maintain anywhere from three to six months' worth of living expenses at all times. Challenges both minor and monstrous in scale can occur. Plumbing problems can result in a small DIY fix or a weeklong project for a professional contractor. Your employer could cut back on hours or, even worse, your job. When facing any sort of financial challenge, it's extremely reassuring to have a safety net. These reserves are not designed to fund your dream vacation or a rainy day splurge. Reserves are only to be used in case of emergency. That kind of diligence can be tough to maintain. If you're faced with a crisis, you won't regret your dedication to an emergency fund.

Keeping mortgage payments current is one of the simplest ways to maintain the health of your mortgage. Late mortgage payments can rack up huge penalties and send your credit score tumbling. An even scarier realization is the fact that late mortgage payments can trigger foreclosure. Mortgage servicers can send a first notice or even file for foreclosure once your mortgage is more than 120 days delinquent. Avoid the headache and heartbreak of foreclosure by always making your mortgage payments on time. Contact your mortgage lender or servicer immediately if you're having trouble making your payments.

You should also be on the lookout for shady refinance offers. Now that you've closed on your home, your real estate transaction is a matter of public record. This means other mortgage companies can and often will access your information and send you refinance and credit offers.

Some may be reputable advertisements from legitimate companies. But many others won't be. These shady offers may even feature imitation insignias and fake logos meant to look like official correspondence from the VA or other government agencies.

You'll often see rock-bottom interest rates and terms that promise significant savings. No matter how tempting these offers seem, please remember: If it looks too good to be true, it probably is.

Lenders who aggressively (and sometimes illegally) solicit adjustable rate mortgages and other too-good-to-be-true refinance offers don't have your best interests at heart. Some hide or obscure the relatively short time you get to enjoy that low interest rate before it can skyrocket and send your payments soaring.

Other offers may include steep closing costs and fees that lenders stuff into your overall loan balance. Low introductory interest rates help mask the fact that your mortgage balance has ballooned to cover their costs. You could even wind up owing more than your home is worth after one of these shady refinance loans.

Here are some things to keep in mind:

- Be wary of mortgage and credit offers that seem to imply a government affiliation by using official-looking logos, insignias and titles. The VA and other governmental agencies don't make home loans or advertise them.
- Be wary of incredibly low interest rates. Always check the

fine print, as these rates tend to last only a short time before increasing, sometimes significantly. Also, these rates don't usually reflect the Annual Percentage Rate (APR) on the loan, which can be a better reflection of the total cost of borrowing.

- Be wary of anything that sounds like a guarantee. Loan preapproval is not the same thing as loan approval.

The best thing to do when you receive an offer like this is simply throw it away. Better yet, you can opt out of receiving them entirely. Visit the Federal Trade Commission's website to learn more about managing prescreened credit and insurance offers.

In addition, you can always call your loan officer with questions about a refinance offer you've received. They can help you separate fact from fiction and determine whether a refinance might be in your best financial interest.

What to Do if You Run Into Mortgage Trouble

No one expects to lose a job, go through a divorce or face a medical problem. But financial difficulties can find all of us at some time or another.

For whatever the reason, failing to stay current on your mortgage payments can take a significant toll on your credit and finances. Foreclosure can crush your credit score and have a serious long-term impact on your financial profile. Research from credit scoring firm FICO shows a foreclosure could knock anywhere from 85 to 160 points from your credit score.

The actions you take at this stage of the game can have a dramatic impact on your credit and your mortgage.

Contact your lender or servicer immediately if you find yourself struggling to keep up with the payments on your VA loan. This is who's ultimately going to determine what happens to your home. Contrary to common belief, most lenders don't want to foreclosure on homeowners. It's a costly and time-consuming process. Lenders and servicers may be willing to set up a repayment plan, or give you extra time to make the payment or even modify the terms of your loan, typically by adding what you owe to the balance and basically starting fresh.

You can also reach out to your VA Regional Loan Center for help. While the VA doesn't make home loans, they have the authority to intervene on your behalf with your lender or servicer. In fact, the VA gets notified anytime a borrower gets more than 60 days past due on their loan. But you don't have to wait that long to ask the VA for help.

The VA's foreclosure avoidance specialists can advocate on your behalf and encourage your lender or servicer to offer an alternative to foreclosure. Their efforts have helped more than 460,000 homeowners avoid foreclosure in the last six years alone. You can contact the VA's foreclosure avoidance team at 877-827-3702.

Last, active duty homeowners may have protections in place through the Servicemembers Civil Relief Act (SCRA). This legislation protects active duty service members from a host of civil and financial penalties. There are protections that govern how and when lenders can initiate foreclosure proceedings, interest rate caps and more. Check with a military legal assistance office for more information.

So, to sum up, if you're having a hard time making your mortgage payment, speak up as soon as possible. Talk with your lender, talk with the VA and work toward a solution that makes the most sense given your unique financial situation. Foreclosure doesn't automatically mean you'll never have another VA loan. But it can certainly make it more challenging.

Borrower spotlight: John Clark
Hawaiian Homecoming for Naval Commander

Pearl Harbor, Hawaii—Career has always come first for Naval Commander John H. Clark III.

The son and grandson of General Motors workers, John sought a life beyond the factory towns of Michigan. He enlisted at 18 was eventually selected to attend the Navy's officer selection and training school in California.

His expertise in contracting and logistics took him from Guam and South Texas to Iraq and Washington, D.C. But what stuck with him amid all the military moves was the month he spent in Hawaii early in his career.

A midshipman tour aboard the USS Sam Houston introduced him to the island and its rich culture and genuine people. Hawaii was always there, in the back of his mind, as he and his family jumped from assignment to assignment.

Over the years, he tried unsuccessfully to secure an assignment there. Finally, as he was nearing the end of his stint with the Navy's Strategic Systems Programs in Washington, John got the good news: He was being reassigned to the Fleet and Industrial Supply Center at Pearl Harbor.

Elated, John and his wife, Delia, decided they were tired of renting and had little desire to return to base housing. The couple wanted to buy their own home in Hawaii, one of the nation's costliest real estate markets.

As first-time buyers, they scoured online listings from 5,500 miles away. John spoke with friends and colleagues in Hawaii and found a trusted real estate agent. He also knew he was eligible for a VA loan but didn't know a lot about the process or details.

Hearing of his interest in VA financing, John's agent pointed him to the team at Veterans United Home Loans of Hawaii.

John, who had scores of questions, wasted little time in calling and found the context and expertise he needed.

"[He] was down to earth, he was not high pressure," John said. "This was someone who was going to walk me through the VA process."

John's loan officer did just that, explaining the program's key benefits and what John and his wife were likely to encounter at each step. As their moving date came closer, Delia hopped online and found a great house fresh to the market. The couple jumped at the listing and put down an offer. The seller accepted, and the Clarks made a nearly $700,000 purchase from thousands of miles away.

They finally had a place to call home.

"As with most things in life, it's all about relationships," John said. "My family and I were so blessed."

This story does not represent an endorsement of Veterans United Home Loans by the Department of Defense, the Department of the Navy or any other governmental agency.

CHAPTER 7:
REUSING YOUR VA LOAN BENEFITS

The VA loan program isn't a one-time benefit. Once you earn this, it's yours for life.

Veterans who use a VA loan to purchase a home can absolutely seek another, either to refinance their current mortgage or buy again. What many buyers and other stakeholders may not know is that it's even possible to have more than one VA loan at the same time.

Even veterans who've lost a VA loan to foreclosure can look to purchase again using this long-cherished benefit program.

So why is there so much confusion and misunderstanding out there about reusing the VA loan program?

A lot has to do with the technical nature of VA loan entitlement, which is the actual dollar amount the VA promises to repay in the event a borrower defaults. Entitlement can be a confusing subject even for people who work in the mortgage industry.

The bottom line is VA buyers can use this program over and over again. Let's take a closer look.

Selling Your Home & Buying Again

Veterans and service members who want to sell their current home and purchase a new primary residence using a VA loan have a pretty simple path. Understanding VA loan entitlement is a key part of the process.

As you'll remember, the VA backs a portion of every loan, which is reflected in a dollar amount called "entitlement." Your amount of entitlement in part determines how much you could potentially borrow before having to factor in a down payment.

As long as you sell the home and pay off the loan in full, you can have your full entitlement restored and available for another purchase. Restoration of entitlement involves a little bit of paperwork, but it's a simple process that can be done quickly. Swiftness can be especially important for buyers planning to sell their old home and close on a new one at or around the same time.

Every borrower's situation is different. But it's possible to close on your home sale, get your entitlement restored and close on your new purchase all in the same day. Having at least a few days' worth of cushion is always preferable.

Otherwise, if you're not able to fully restore your entitlement before moving forward with the next purchase, you may find yourself with limited $0 down buying power and a few restrictions. You'll see why in the next section.

Keeping Your Home & Buying Again

VA borrowers can look to retain their current home and purchase another using their remaining, or second-tier, entitlement.

One of the most common circumstances is when an active military member has to PCS to a new duty station. Sometimes it's tough to sell their current home. Other borrowers like the idea of using the home as a rental property. While you can't purchase a home with this as your intent, it's possible to buy with a VA loan, live in the property for a while and then rent it out to others upon relocating.

There are a few major considerations in situations like this. Entitlement is a big one. When you retain a property rather than sell it, whatever VA loan entitlement you used stays tied up in that home. You can't touch it. But you may be able to purchase again—possibly with $0 down—using another VA home loan.

Let's look at an example. We'll say you purchased a home a few years ago for $200,000. Because the VA typically guarantees a quarter of the loan amount, you would have utilized $50,000 ($200,000 x 25 percent) of your VA loan entitlement. Now, you're moving to take a new job. You want to hold onto and rent out your current home and buy a $300,000 home in a regular cost county. As a refresher, the loan limit in a regular cost county is currently $453,100, which means the full entitlement would be $113,275 ($453,100 x 25 percent).

Here's how the math breaks down:

$113,275 full entitlement - $50,000 in current entitlement = $63,275 remaining entitlement

$63,275 remaining entitlement x 4 = $253,100

That $253,100 figure represents how much you could look to borrow before having to factor in a down payment. You could certainly aim for a bigger loan, but buyers who purchase above where their entitlement caps out must put down 25 percent of the difference between their cap and the purchase price.

For this example $300,000 purchase, you would need to come up with $11,725 for a down payment because of your incomplete VA loan entitlement.

Here's what the math looks like:

$300,000 purchase price − 253,100 entitlement cap = $46,900 difference

$46,900 x 25 percent = $11,275

That could still wind up being a great deal compared to conventional and FHA financing, which require minimum 5 percent and 3.5 percent down payments, respectively. Our example $11,275 down payment on a $300,000 loan represents a 3.75 percent down payment. You'd also wind up paying for mortgage insurance with FHA and conventional loans.

If you're purchasing in one of the VA's high-cost counties, you'll have more entitlement at your disposal. Here's where things can start to get a little complicated.

Remember, the $113,275 in total entitlement reflects a loan limit of $453,100, which is standard for most of the country. But high-cost counties can have loan limits well in excess of that. That means more $0 down buying power.

Let's say the limit where you want to buy again is $625,500. The full entitlement for a qualified borrower in this county would be $156,375 (625,000 x 25 percent).

Continuing our previous example, let's say you have $50,000 in entitlement tied up in an existing property. Buying in this high-cost county means you have $106,375 in remaining entitlement ($156,375 − 50,000). And that means qualified buyers could borrow up to $425,500 ($106,375 x 4) in this high-cost county before having to worry about a down payment.

Remember, the additional entitlement only applies when you're buying in a high-cost county. If you're moving from a high-cost county to a regular cost county, then you would be using the $113,275 max as your starting point.

Purchasing again using your second-tier entitlement also comes with a unique caveat: You can't have a loan amount below $144,001. VA borrowers can count their VA Funding Fee toward that total, but not any qualified energy efficiency improvements. Keep in mind you may also have to factor a down payment into that equation. You'll still need to borrow at least $144,001 to make a second-tier purchase work.

Buyers who have some of their basic entitlement remaining may be able to utilize that and avoid the minimum loan amount. You can ask a loan officer to go over your Certificate of Eligibility with you in more detail.

One of the potential challenges of having two VA loans at the same time is being able to afford two mortgage payments. Borrowers who plan to rent out their old home may be able to use that pending income to basically cancel out the old mortgage payment.

It's important to understand that lenders typically treat this as an "offset" and not as effective income. If the mortgage payment on your old house is $1,000 per month and you're charging $1,500 per month in rent, lenders will only count that initial $1,000. Lenders won't typically count rental income as effective income until you can document it on two years' worth of tax returns. Different lenders can have different policies on this.

Veterans United will typically allow a 100 percent offset as long as you have a renter locked into a lease and can document their security deposit. The renter can't be a family member.

It's also important to remember this program is focused on helping veterans and service members purchase primary residences. You'll need to satisfy the VA's occupancy requirements and buy a home you'll live in as your primary residence. Generally, that means living in the new home within 60 days of closing.

There's also a unique, one-off way to retain a home and buy again. The VA gives borrowers a one-time opportunity to fully restore their entitlement without selling or otherwise disposing of their home. This benefit essentially allows veterans to retain an investment property or a second home and purchase again using the full reach of their entitlement. The catch is the original VA loan would need to be paid in full. You can't take advantage of this one-time restoration if you're still making mortgage payments on the property.

Buying After a VA Foreclosure

Despite the no-down payment benefit, VA loans have emerged as a model of stability and safety. They continue to have an incredibly low foreclosure rate, due in large part to the VA's common-sense requirements and commitment to helping veterans keep their homes. But default does happen.

Foreclosure, short sale or deed-in-lieu of foreclosure can all take a toll on your credit score. Plus, whatever VA loan entitlement you used on the foreclosure is effectively lost. The only way to get it back is to repay the amount in full, which isn't something most people can or want to do.

But VA borrowers who lose a home to foreclosure or one of its offshoots can absolutely look to purchase again using the VA loan program. You'll typically need to wait two years from a foreclosure in order to pursue another VA loan. Some lenders, like Veterans United, won't have any kind of waiting period following a VA short sale in most cases.

You'll also need to rely on whatever VA loan entitlement you have remaining. For the purposes of estimating your $0 down buying power, you'd treat the entitlement lost to default the same as if you were retaining a home. All the requirements and caveats from the previous section would apply, from the minimum loan amount to the additional entitlement in high-cost counties.

You can see why so many people get confused about entitlement and VA foreclosures. But this is actually an incredible opportunity for veterans who have gone through hard times. Second-tier entitlement allowed Tom Lindgren and his family to become homeowners again.

A disabled Vietnam veteran, Tom struggled to keep a regular job upon his return from Cambodia in 1971. Credit and financial issues mounted over time, and he eventually filed for bankruptcy protection. The bank foreclosed on his home, which he had purchased with a VA loan.

Years later, with his bankruptcy in the rear view, Tom and his wife fell in love with a house near their northern Utah rental. They started working with a local mortgage company and were told the process would be simple, streamlined and on budget.

The results were anything but. The Lindgrens were approved for an FHA loan, provided they put down $25,000. Since they couldn't cover that sizable down payment, they would have to use a state program that would essentially loan them the down payment, creating a second mortgage.

All told, with two mortgages and other related costs, they were staring at a monthly payment around $1,800, far beyond what they could afford. Devastated, the couple started looking online for a way to utilize Tom's VA benefit. They found Veterans United, talked with a loan officer and a new phrase entered the couple's vocabulary—second-tier entitlement.

Back home, a local mortgage company tried to discourage the Lindgrens from using a VA loan. Tom's old broker said he had never heard of second-tier entitlement and told the couple they would wind up homeless because of the VA's bureaucracy. Undeterred, the Lindgrens plowed ahead and pursued a VA loan with us.

They closed on their new home without the need for a down payment, a second mortgage or mortgage insurance. Their monthly housing payment came out to about $1,300.

Tom was a homeowner once more.

"It was just an answer to a prayer," Tom said. "It's the most comforting, the most exciting thing that I can say has ever really happened to us. I felt there was empathy, compassion, even, and concern for our well being."

When it comes to foreclosure, every buyer's situation is different. But it's important to understand you can bounce back. Simply having a foreclosure in your past—even one on a VA-backed loan—doesn't automatically mean a VA loan is out of the question.

VA Refinance Options

Military borrowers have access to what's arguably the most powerful home purchasing program on the market. So it certainly stands to reason that the same would hold true when it comes to a refinance loan.

There are two major VA refinance options, an Interest Rate Reduction Refinance Loan, also known as an IRRRL or a VA

Streamline, and a VA Cash-Out Refinance. We'll look at each one separately. First, though, let's talk about refinancing in general.

Much like the "When should I lock my rate?" dilemma, the question of "When should I refinance?" is one of those lingering issues that can haunt homeowners. And, of course, there's no formula or simple way to answer the question. Refinancing every couple of years just to refinance probably isn't the smartest tactic. It's important that veterans and military borrowers *know why* they want to refinance. The most obvious and likely reason is that interest rates have dropped and you want to save some money on that monthly mortgage payment.

But there may be other considerations. Maybe you've worked hard to improve your credit profile and your score has finally climbed, meaning you're eligible for a better rate. Or perhaps you got a promotion or took a new job and the monthly household income is higher, making it possible to convert that 30-year mortgage into a 15-year one. Maybe—and we hope not—the converse is true and you need to adjust to a smaller income level.

Or maybe you need to make home improvements or pay off revolving debts and can capitalize on the equity built up in your home. Or you're tired of worrying about your ARM and want to refinance into a fixed-rate mortgage.

There are scores of potential reasons why a veteran should consider refinancing a mortgage. Offering up "Because someone told me I should" isn't typically the best answer. A VA refinance will almost always result in lower monthly payments (there are a few exceptions we'll look at later in the chapter). But they also come with a price. Borrowers may have to pay closing costs every time they refinance. Part of deciding when to refinance is determining whether those added costs are worth the investment.

It's also important to note that veterans and military borrowers with conventional loans can refinance into a VA loan. This, as you'll soon see, is a pretty incredible opportunity.

VA Streamline

The "Streamline" moniker isn't just a clever marketing ploy. The VA Streamline is a no-frills, low-impact refinance loan that features almost none of the hassle and paperwork that accompanies a conventional refinance. You'll also hear this called an IRRRL, which stands for "Interest Rate Reduction Refinance Loan." Mortgage professionals tend to pronounce it like "Earl."

Streamline refinance loans typically require little paperwork and often require little-to-no costs out of pocket. Streamline borrowers can roll closing costs into their overall loan amount. In some cases, VA Streamline borrowers won't need an appraisal or even to meet a credit score benchmark. Requirements will vary depending on the lender and your specific situation.

When it comes to occupancy, previous occupancy is all that's required for a VA Streamline, meaning you can look to refinance a mortgaged property you no longer live in. That's a great option for borrowers renting out a home at a previous duty station, for example.

You may need to have been paying on your current loan for at least six months before pursuing a VA Streamline. Homeowners who have made a late payment on their loan at any point in the last 12 months may run into problems. You may also need to meet certain seasoning requirements, meaning you've had the loan for a minimum number of days and have made a minimum number of payments. Policies and requirements can vary by lender.

Homeowners seeking a VA Streamline will have to again pay the VA Funding Fee. The good news is it's just half a percent (0.5 percent) of the loan amount. Surviving spouses and veterans and service members who receive compensation for a service-connected disability don't pay this fee.

The VA Streamline exists to get veterans into a lower-rate mortgage with lower monthly costs. In fact, that's one of the loan's primary requirements. Unless the borrower is refinancing an adjustable-rate mortgage, the Streamline has to lower the interest rate. Veterans can also add up to $6,000 in energy efficiency improvements.

In addition, Streamline refinance loans need to meet a "net tangible benefit" test that helps show the new loan is in the veteran's best financial interest. Talk with a trusted VA lender for more information on how this test works.

The VA requires veterans to go through the credit and underwriting process if the refinance is going to increase their monthly PITI payment by 20 percent or more. In those cases, there's an onus on the lender to satisfy the VA's concern about whether the veteran can afford this new, higher payment.

You can certainly start with your original lender, but by no means are you bound to them. Veterans can and should hunt for the best deal possible, on both interest rates and costs and fees. At times, that might mean a VA loan isn't the best option for a refinance. The main reason is the VA Funding Fee, which isn't a part of the conventional financing picture. Veterans with equity in their homes and some cash on hand may opt to avoid the VA Funding Fee and seek out a conventional refinance.

A capable VA loan specialist will help borrowers do the math and compare a VA refinance to a conventional refinance loan. VA Streamlines are available only to existing VA borrowers. But veterans with conventional mortgages can refinance into a VA loan. They can even take out cash while doing so. We'll look at that option next.

VA Cash-Out Refinance

The VA Streamline is inherently flexible, but there's one major thing you can't do with it: Get cash back. No worries, though. There's a loan for that.

The VA's Cash-Out refinance loan allows qualified veterans— with VA or non-VA loans—to refinance to a lower rate and extract cash from their home's equity. Essentially, you're getting a new mortgage at a value higher than what you owe and taking the difference in a cash lump.

Remember that two things are happening in the background: Your interest rate is likely lower but your loan amount is higher. That means a flux in monthly mortgage payments.

Borrowers have traditionally used Cash-Out refinance loans to pay off high-interest debts or make home improvements. But there aren't concrete constraints on how you spend the money. The VA and the lender are mostly concerned with making sure you can afford the new mortgage payment. Unlike on a Streamline, the VA mandates that borrowers pursuing a Cash-Out refinance loan submit to the standard credit and underwriting process. The loan processing for a Cash-Out is similar to a VA purchase loan, from the income verification and debt-to-income ratio calculation to a home appraisal.

Today, qualified veterans can seek a Cash-Out refinance for up to 100 percent of the home's appraised value, plus the VA Funding Fee and any costs from energy-efficiency improvements. Veterans who want a Cash-Out refinance pay a higher VA Funding Fee than their Streamline counterparts. The current fee for a first-use refinance is 2.15 percent of the loan amount for regular military and 2.4 percent for Reserves and National Guard members. The fee jumps to 3.3 percent for both demographics for each subsequent refinance.

Veterans with non-VA loans aren't required to take out any cash in these cases—this is just the path you'll take to get a conventional or FHA loan into the VA loan program. Unlike the Streamline refinance, a Cash-Out refinance does come with the VA's standard occupancy requirements.

A Cash-Out refinance shouldn't be confused with a home equity loan, which is a second loan that runs alongside your current mortgage. A refinance loan replaces that existing mortgage instead of complementing it. Depending on rates, a home equity loan could be a better option for some veterans. These come with minimal, if any, closing costs but tend to have higher rates than what you'll find with a VA Cash-Out refinance. The key is to keep a close eye on rates and shop comparatively.

Streamline v. Cash-Out Refinance

To help give borrowers a more high-level view of the two refinancing options, the VA maintains a helpful comparison table. Here's a shorter version of it that includes key features for prospective borrowers.

Remember that what the VA mandates and what VA-approved lenders will require can be two different things, especially when it comes to credit, underwriting and appraisals:

Feature	IRRRL	Cash-Out
Purpose	To refinance an existing VA loan at a lower interest rate	To pay off lien(s) of any type - can also provide cash to borrower
Interest Rate	Rate must be lower than on existing VA loan (unless existing loan is an ARM)	Any negotiated rate
Monthly Payment	Payment must be lower than that on an existing VA loan (unless the ARM is being refinanced, a term is shortened, or energy efficiency improvements are being included)	No requirement
Discount Points	Reasonable points can be paid - only two of these points can be included in the loan amount	Reasonable points can be paid from loan proceeds
Maximu	Existing VA loan balance, plus allowable fees and	100 percent of the reasonable value of the

m Loan	charges, plus up to two discount points, plus the cost of any energy efficiency improvements, plus the VA Funding Fee	property indicated on the NOV, plus the cost of any energy efficiency improvements, plus the VA Funding Fee
Entitlement	Veteran reuses the entitlement used on the existing VA loan; the IRRRL does not impact the amount of entitlement the veteran has in use	Must have sufficient available entitlement; if existing VA loan on the same property is being refinanced, entitlement can be restored for the refinance
Fees in the Loan	All allowable fees and charges, including up to two discount points, may be included in the loan	Allowable fees and charges and points may be paid from the loan proceeds
Cash to Borrower	Not permitted	Borrower can receive cash for any purposes acceptable to the lender
Appraisal	No appraisal is required	Appraisal is required
Credit Underwriting	No underwriting is required except in certain cases	Full credit information and underwriting are always required
Occupancy	Veteran or spouse of an active duty service member must show prior occupancy	Veteran or spouse of an active duty service member must intend to occupy

Some borrowers who go into the process thinking Streamline ultimately decide they would rather opt for a Cash-Out Refinance. Each has its own benefits and drawbacks. There also isn't any sort of rule that veterans have to get a VA refinance. In fact, a conventional refinance loan may be attractive to borrowers who have cultivated a decent chunk of equity.

Remember, though, that credit, income and underwriting standards will likely be more stringent with a conventional loan than a VA refinance. Pursuing a refinance means veterans again have to consider that most frustrating of questions: When should I lock my rate? The rules of the road aren't much different when it comes to a refinance. But one of the luxuries of a refinance loan is that there's no real deadline or pressure to push forward. You can watch rates for weeks before deciding to jumpstart the process. At the same time, good loan officers are going to be doing the same thing for their past clients.

Borrower spotlight: Matthew Tammen

Navy Veteran, Mountaineer Uses VA Refinance to Scale His Dream

Bremerton, Washington — 26,906 feet.

That's as tall as 178 Statues of Liberty stacked on top of each other, more than 5 miles up where the minus 30 degree air is too thin to breathe.

That's the height of Cho Oyu, the world's sixth-tallest mountain. A few thousand feet shorter than nearby Mount Everest, the peak rises above the Nepal-Tibet border, daring even the most experienced climbers to reach its summit.

Scaling the mountain takes an incredible combination of patience, physical endurance and training. Leave it to a Navy veteran to overcome all obstacles and make it to the top.

Matthew Tammen began his career in the U.S. Navy in 1979, graduated from the Naval Academy four years later and served 20 years as a submarine officer. He retired as a Lieutenant Commander, and settled down with his wife, Jennifer, and their three kids in Puget Sound, Wash.

They later purchased their dream home, which overlooks Mount Rainier. The family loves the outdoors, and the proximity to the beauty of nature was critical for them.

"We love the mountains and sea," Jennifer said. They take trips to the mountain for skiing and hiking, and enjoy taking their kayaks out on Puget Sound.

Matthew loves the outdoors, too, but takes a more adventurous angle. An avid climber, he has summited mountains like Mount Aconcogua in Argentina and Denali in Alaska.

But looking at Mount Rainier every day kept nagging at Matthew, reminding him of the dream climb he still hadn't made. That challenge was Cho Oyu.

The strength and determination he gained from the military could take him to the top, but his finances could barely get him to the foot of the mountain.

That's when Veterans United Home Loans threw Matthew a rope.

Climbing one of the world's tallest peaks takes tenacity and money. Hiring guides, buying gear and traveling to some of the most remote places on earth can set mountaineers back tens of thousands of dollars.

With kids and a mortgage, the financial burden for the Tammens would be too much to bear. But their house was ripe for a refinancing, and a lower interest rate could save them a mountain of money.

As Matthew and Jennifer shopped for lenders, they felt stranded and alone. The Tammens couldn't obtain a refinance because the value of their house had fallen because of the recession.

"In my opinion, they just didn't try very hard to help us," Jennifer said.

But Veterans United Home Loans stepped in to work with them when other lenders wouldn't. With the help of Veterans United, the Tammens were able to refinance their mortgage and save a significant chunk of change.

"Our mortgage payment went down by $1,000 per month," Jennifer said.

The price tag for Matthew's expedition was set at $25,000. Pocketing an extra $1,000 per month thanks to the refinance, Matthew would have to wait two years to make the attempt to summit. He trained four hours per day for 14 months to build the physical stamina to summit.

No stranger to tough challenges, Matthew persevered. He and his team flew into Kathmandu, Nepal, and then crossed into Tibet to begin a six-week trip. After struggling up the 8,200 meters for weeks, they finally reached the summit.

After two years of hard work, he reached his goal. On a cold October morning, Matthew saw the sun rise from the summit of Cho Oyu. Just 12 miles away, Mount Everest glowed in the morning light.

Matthew accomplished his goal, and the whole family came out on top by getting a better deal on their dream home.

"When you refinance, you may not think about big mountains and life-long dreams, but you should," Jennifer said. "He couldn't have made it without Veterans United."

CHAPTER 8:
THE FUTURE OF VA LOANS

Purchasing a home purchase today isn't the same as it was a decade ago. The collapse of the housing market in the wake of the subprime mortgage meltdown has created a more restrictive and cautious lending environment.

That's a good thing in many respects, although talking about lessons learned provides little comfort to veterans who are now on the edge. Securing a home loan today is generally more difficult, with lenders looking for greater certainty that an applicant can and will handle the financial burden. The days of so-called no-documentation loans, which allowed borrowers to secure a home loan with scant evidence of their ability to pay for it, are gone. Regulations that took effect in early 2014 have added further layers of protection to the process.

Still, one of the lingering questions is whether these new, cautious underwriting standards will become the new normal. It's difficult to imagine otherwise. Lenders might start to loosen up a bit in the coming years, but in most cases a more conservative approach to lending will likely continue to define the industry and govern the path to homeownership in the United States.

What does that mean for VA loans?

Veterans nationwide have already felt the effects. Despite the low foreclosure rate of VA loans, lenders across the country have tightened credit and underwriting standards. Today, veterans with a credit score below 620 have relatively few financing options. That's why building a solid credit profile is only going to become more important in the months and years ahead.

More than ever before, military members and veterans have to keep close watch of their credit profiles, debt-to-income levels and discretionary spending. That can add new layers of stress during deployments, permanent changes of station and other challenging phases that civilian borrowers don't have to contend with. Increasingly, discipline and responsible financial decisions are going to serve as the keys to landing a home loan.

The VA loan itself is stronger than ever. Not only does it remain a refuge for military borrowers, but the VA Loan Guaranty program also continues to provide qualified borrowers with better rates and greater buying power than any loan program out there. Veterans with a 620 FICO score may be able to snare rates on a 30-year fixed loan that are just a hair above the national average. Good luck getting that kind of deal on a conventional loan.

Today, VA loans are absolutely booming. The huge gains in volume we mentioned in Chapter 1 come as lenders have tightened their lending requirements and as interest rates have hit rock bottom. There's no telling how long this combination will last, but the tougher standards are likely here to stay.

The history of the VA Loan Guaranty program is marked in many ways by evolutionary change. That course has led to today's more streamlined VA loan process, which complements existing technology rather than fighting against it. The VA Loan Guaranty program has been a constant in the lives of military members and their families since 1944. The agency has helped level the playing field for those who have served our country, making homeownership more accessible and more affordable.

That isn't going to change. But mortgage laws, lender regulations and underwriting expectations all do. That's why veterans and service members with any interest in homeownership— not to mention those who already own homes—need to make sure they understand the process and what's available to them.

The mortgage industry has always been one that rewards informed, educated consumers, and that's even truer today. Whether you're in the market for your first home or looking to refinance an existing mortgage, do as much homework as possible. Ask questions, demand honest, thoughtful answers and don't be afraid to get a second or third opinion. Veterans who come to the process with a solid knowledge base have an immediate leg up on other buyers.

At some point, though, you're ultimately entrusting the process to someone on the other side. And that can be a scary proposition, especially for first-time buyers. Telling the world you're a prospective homebuyer can be like tossing chum in a shark tank. Mortgage folks will emerge from the shadows with last-minute deals, special financing and an array of other potential offers that might sound a little too good to be true.

The best advice is to go with your gut. Sometimes your gut might simply point you to the lowest cost, which certainly isn't a terrible strategy.

Perhaps think of it this way: VA loans were created to honor and reward the hard work and sacrifices of our nation's veterans.

Gravitate to the loan officers, mortgage companies and real estate agents who genuinely embrace that spirit.

ACKNOWLEDGEMENTS

I am indebted to the entire team at Veterans United for helping make this book possible.

I want to thank our executive leadership for their relentless support, especially co-founders Brant and Brock Bukowsky; Chief Executive Officer Nate Long; Chief Marketing Officer Kris Farmer; and Chief Client Officer Gardell Powell.

Mr. Powell, in particular, deserves special thanks. Gardell graciously responded to every question, every clarification and every lengthy email, offering his expertise and insight from the planning stages through a final read. His commitment to this project was integral and invaluable.

A host of other Veterans United colleagues made significant contributions, including John Meyer, Zane Corn, Winsor Cooper III, John Lyman, Chris Lunn, Jake Vehige, Sid Winters, Kurt Krieger, Tim Tallis, Scott Schaefer, Pam Swan, Lisa O'Bannon, Lauren Okruch and Jon Galloway.

Mortgage industry sages Peter G. Miller and Justin McHood provided encouragement along the way. And William White at the Department of Veterans Affairs patiently fulfilled data requests.

I would also like to thank the Veterans United borrowers who made time to share their stories. We have the privilege of helping some amazing people capitalize on benefits earned through service and sacrifice. They are the kind of people who relish the opportunity to help those who will one day be in their shoes.

Last, I would like to thank my family, my friends and, most especially, my wife, Michela.

GLOSSARY

Adjustable-rate mortgage (ARM): These are mortgages where the interest rates can fluctuate based on what's happening in the greater economic landscape. Most ARMs allow for an annual rate change based on the one-year Treasury bill index.

Annual Percentage Rate (APR): This rate reflects the total cost of borrowing money, including the interest rate and other costs built into the loan amount. The interest rate and the APR are typically different, and veterans should look at both when comparing VA lenders. Two loans can have similar interest rates, but the one with a higher APR will cost more.

Automated Underwriting System (AUS): This computer system utilized by select VA-approved lenders allows for an automatic approval on a borrower's loan application. Loan officers can tweak loan amounts in the AUS to help secure approval.

Basic Allowance for Housing: A service member's BAH can be included as monthly income. Housing allowances can help defray or entirely cover monthly mortgage payments.

Buyer's agent: This is the real estate agent who represents the homebuyer.

Cash-Out Refinance: This refinance loan allows veterans to refinance to a lower interest rate and tap into their equity. Borrowers may be able to get a Cash-Out Refinance for up to 100 percent of the home's appraised value, plus the VA Funding Fee and any costs from energy-efficiency improvements.

Certificate of Eligibility: This is a formal VA document that delineates what entitlement a prospective borrower has available. It is the only acceptable method to document entitlement.

Clear to close: This means that all loan conditions have been met to the underwriter's satisfaction and the borrower is ready to formally close on the home purchase.

Closing costs: These are charges and fees associated with finalizing a loan. The VA limits what veterans can pay in closing costs to a 1 percent lender origination fee, reasonable discount points and other reasonable and standard fees and charges. Sellers can pay all of a VA buyer's mortgage-related closing costs and up to 4 percent in concessions.

Closing Disclosure: This is a final review of all loan fees and costs and must be made available to buyers at least three business days before closing.

Comparable sales: They're better known as "comps." These are recently sold properties that are similar in size, location and other key facets to a home being purchased.

Compensating factors: These are strengths on a loan application that can help offset lender concerns about a borrower's credit or financial weaknesses. Low debt, great credit history and liquidity are all examples. Compensating factors must go above and beyond what would be considered a normal program requirement.

Conditional approval: A loan with conditional approval will be issued as long as the veteran meets the requirements and stipulations—the conditions—spelled out by the underwriter.

Conforming loan limit: Fannie Mae and Freddie Mac can only purchase mortgages below what's known as the conforming loan limit. This limit, which is subject to change, is currently $453,100.

Construction-to-Permanent Refinance Loan: This allows qualified borrowers to refinance a construction loan into a VA loan.

Conventional loan: These loans feature no government guaranties and typically adhere to the standards and requirements of government-sponsored enterprises Fannie Mae and Freddie Mac.

DD-214: This is an official VA document that explains a veteran's discharge information. Lenders will look for the Member 4 copy of your DD-214. Reservists and National Guard members, who don't have a single discharge certificate like the DD-214, should procure their latest annual retirement points summary along with evidence of their honorable service.

Debt-to-income ratio (DTI ratio): This is the ratio of your total monthly debt payments to your gross monthly income. The VA wants to see a DTI ratio at or below 41 percent, but it's possible to have a higher one and still secure financing. DTI caps can vary by lender.

Deed-in-lieu of foreclosure: An alternative to straightforward foreclosure. The borrower basically returns the house to the bank. A deed-in-lieu will negatively affect your credit score and usually trigger a required waiting period before you can close on another home loan.

Discount points: A point is equal to 1 percent of the loan amount. Borrowers can pay points to buy down their interest rate. Paying points is relatively infrequent among most VA borrowers.

Earnest money: Borrowers put this into an escrow account when the time comes to purchase a home. These good faith funds can be put toward closing costs or a down payment or refunded to the borrower. The amount depends on several factors, including geography and the property.

Energy Efficient Mortgage (EEM): This specialized mortgage allows veterans to make energy-efficient improvements to a home they're purchasing or refinancing. Veterans can typically add up to $6,000 to the loan amount provided they can verify the cost of improvements or prove the efficiencies will result in savings.

Entitlement: The VA uses the word to mean the amount of money it will guaranty on a given loan. In most parts of the country, the primary entitlement is $36,000, with a secondary entitlement of $68,250. Buyers in high-cost counties can have additional entitlement available.

FICO score: FICO stands for Fair Isaac Corp., a California-based company that created the first-ever credit score. FICO scores run from 300 to 850.

Fixed-rate mortgage: Interest rates cannot fluctuate on a fixed-rate mortgage. The most common fixed-rate terms are 15 years and 30 years.

Float: Borrowers can either float or lock when it comes to an interest rate. Float is the default setting until a purchase agreement is in place.

Foreclosure: This basically means the lender takes back its house because you failed to keep up with mortgage payments. There are restrictions on foreclosures against service members through the Servicemembers Civil Relief Act.

Government-sponsored enterprises (GSEs): These are federal financial services corporations, with Fannie Mae and Freddie Mac being the most familiar. Fannie Mae securitizes mortgages in the secondary market. Freddie Mac purchases, pools and sells mortgages to investors.

Homeowners insurance: Lenders require borrowers to secure a home insurance policy to cover at least the value of their mortgage. Homeowners insurance isn't included in the mortgage.

Hybrid adjustable-rate mortgage (ARM): Borrowers with a hybrid ARM have a fixed interest rate for a set number of years before the rate can fluctuate.

Interest Rate Reduction Refinance Loan (IRRRL): This is also known as a VA Streamline. This is a no-frills refinance designed to get veterans into a lower-rate mortgage. Borrowers cannot take cash out with an IRRRL.

Lender Appraisal Processing Program (LAPP): This computer system allows authorized lenders to directly order and process VA appraisals, which are conducted by independent VA-approved appraisers.

Lighthouse Program: This special wing of Veterans United Home Loans works with veterans to better understand their credit and finances and develop a personalized plan to get on the path to loan prequalification.

Loan Estimate: This document estimates the costs and fees associated with closing on your home loan. Lenders are required to provide one within three business days of taking a full loan application.

Loan processor: This person pulls together outstanding documents and information once a borrower has signed a purchase contact. Their job is to piece together loan applications for an underwriter.

Loan-to-value adjustment: A mark-up on conventional loan rates based on a borrower's credit score and down payment.

Lock fee: Some lenders charge borrowers for rate locks, depending on the time period, the rate and other factors. Veterans should ask lenders about lock fees when comparison shopping.

Listing agent: This is the real estate agent representing a home seller.

Manual underwriting: This occurs when a borrower cannot get AUS approval. Underwriters evaluate the loan file manually and make a determination without the computer automation. Veterans who can't secure AUS approval tend to face tougher lending requirements.

Minimum Property Requirements: These are basic health and safety conditions that a property must meet to satisfy the VA. They're also the conditions that make the home sellable. The VA in most cases requires homes to be "move-in ready."

Multiple Listing Service (MLS): Real estate databases and software that allow agents and brokers to look at transactions, home listings and a suite of other information tools.

Negative amortization: This is essentially unpaid interest that gets added to the loan balance. This makes a loan ineligible for Qualified Mortgage status.

Negative compensating factor: Compensating factors are strengths on a loan application that can help borrowers secure a loan. Negative compensating factors can do the opposite. Bankruptcies, foreclosures, late payments can all be considered negative compensating factors.

Note rate: This is your interest rate.

Notice of Value (NOV): This is the culmination of the VA appraisal and details the appraised value of the subject property. Ultimately, it's up to a lender's staff appraisal reviewer or a VA reviewer to issue the final notice of value.

Origination fee: The VA allows lenders to charge borrowers a flat fee of up to 1 percent of the loan amount to cover in-house costs and services.

Permanent buydown: Veterans can pay reasonable discount points to buy down their interest rate. A discount point is 1 percent of the loan amount. Borrowers have to pay this cost up front.

PITI: The acronym stands for Principal, Interest, Taxes and Insurance. These are the four pillars of a veteran's monthly mortgage payment. You might sometimes see an "A" on the end, which typically represents any dues for a homeowners association.

Power of Attorney: A surrogate with Power of Attorney can sign contracts and other documents on behalf of an absent service member. Veterans and service members may utilize a General or a Specific POA depending on their situation.

Preapproval: This is a more serious step than prequalification. Real estate agents and sellers put significant stock into loan preapproval. But this is not a guarantee from a lender or any kind of binding document for the borrower.

Prequalification: This introductory step involves an unverified, cursory discussion about a borrower's finances. Prequalification helps veterans get a sense of what they can afford but it means little to sellers and real estate agents, who are looking for preapproval letters.

Prime: This essentially means borrowers or loans at or above an accepted credit standard, typically around 620. Some loans and borrowers beneath that are considered greater risks and classified as subprime.

Private mortgage insurance (PMI): On most mortgages, borrowers who can't put down 20 percent of the loan amount are required to pay for private mortgage insurance. PMI protects lenders against borrowers who default and also helps borrowers who can't muster a large down payment. There is no PMI on a VA loan.

Rate lock: A binding commitment that locks a borrower to a specific interest rate. Borrowers can typically lock their interest rate as soon as they sign a purchase agreement and up to five days before the loan closing. Rate locks are good for specific blocks of time. The most common lock periods are for 15 days, 30 days, 45 days and 60 days.

Rate cap: Some lenders include a rate cap with their rate locks. These caps give lenders the ability to give borrowers a slightly higher interest rate if rates rise considerably before closing.

Reserves: This is cash set aside to cover costs and expenses. Having additional money set aside can help strengthen a loan application.

Retail rate: This is a flat, non-negotiable mortgage rate sometimes offered by banks, credit unions and other lending institutions.

Residual income: This is a lending standard unique to VA loans. Residual income is the amount of money a borrower retains each month after covering all major monthly debts and obligations. Veterans must hit a minimum level of residual income (depending on geography and family size) in order to satisfy VA requirements.

Seller concessions: Sellers can pay a range of costs and charges for VA borrowers, including closing costs, property taxes, the VA Funding Fee and other items. But the VA caps seller concessions at 4 percent of the loan amount.

Staff Appraisal Reviewer (SAR): A lender's staff appraisal reviewer, or SAR, examines a property's independent VA appraisal and issues the final Notice of Value.

Seasoning period: Foreclosure, bankruptcy or other negative financial events can trigger a required waiting period before you can close on a home loan. Seasoning periods can vary depending on the type of loan you're wanting, the lender and more.

Second-tier entitlement: This additional entitlement ($68,250 in most places) helps boost the VA guaranty on qualified loans. Borrowers can secure a loan solely with their second-tier entitlement, as long as the loan amount is at least $144,001.

Secondary mortgage market: Lenders sell mortgages, often packaged into mortgage-backed securities, in this marketplace. Private investors and government-sponsored enterprises buy loans in the secondary market. Proceeds help fuel the lending industry. Lenders may have requirements beyond what the VA wants to see in order to sell their loans on the secondary market.

Short sale: An alternative to straightforward foreclosure. This is when the bank agrees to let you sell your home for less than the balance owed. A short sale will negatively affect your credit score. Some lenders have no required waiting period following a short sale in some cases.

Special Adapted Housing (SAH): This VA program provides grants for veterans with service-connected disabilities to retrofit properties to meet their needs. There's a separate grant program called the Special Housing Adaptation (SHA) grant.

Streamline: A VA Streamline is another name for the Interest Rate Reduction Refinance Loan (IRRRL).

Subprime: This essentially means borrowers or loans below an accepted credit standard, typically around 620. Subprime borrowers carry greater risks and now have trouble securing financing.

Temporary buydown: Borrowers can pay discount points to buy down their rate for a limited time instead of permanently. On a 3-2-1 buydown, the borrower's interest rate drops 3 percent below the note rate for the first year, 2 percent for the second year and 1 percent for the third year. The start of the fourth year marks the first year the borrower pays at the regular, full note rate. These are disappearing because of new mortgage regulations.

Title insurance: This is mandatory insurance that protects borrowers, sellers and lenders against previous ownership claims on a property. Title insurance is a one-time cost that must be paid at closing. Buyers can shop around for the best price. Lender's title insurance is required. Owner's title insurance is optional but strongly encouraged.

Underwriter: These trained experts review a borrower's loan file and give an ultimate thumbs-up or down. They act as the lender's gatekeeper.

Uniform Residential Loan Application: This is the five-page loan application for almost all home mortgages.

Verification of Employment: This is an important document that lenders send to a veteran's employer(s). The VOE, as it's known, helps lenders verify employment, tenure, salary and any bonuses or raises.

Yield Spread Premium: Wholesale lenders pay this rebate to lenders for higher-rate loans.

Index

I

Wells, 145, 172, 234
Wind mitigation inspection, 141
Windows, 83
Workers compensation, income from, 122
World War II allies, eligibility for service members, 66

Y
Yield Spread
    and compensation of lender, 189–193
    and compensation of mortgage loan brokers, 186, 192–193
    and interest rates, 185, 189–193, 195
    and points, 195
    and Qualified Mortgages, 193

Made in the USA
Lexington, KY
28 December 2018